'2006'

Sincerely,

Mary McCaslin

R.S.Prussia
& more

SCHLEGELMILCH PORCELAIN
featuring
COBALT

Identification
& Values

Mary J. McCaslin

COLLECTOR BOOKS
A Division of Schroeder Publishing Co., Inc.

On the Cover

Front Cover:
Epergne (only one known): Epergne Horn, 11¾"h. and bowl, 10¾"d. Values undetermined.
Bowl: Melon Eaters, cobalt/gold/green, 11"d. x 3½"h., RSP (rm). $4,500.00 – 5,200.00.
Bowl: Snowbird with Madame LeBrun medallions, cobalt, 10½"d., RSP (rm). $6,000.00 – 7,500.00.
Chocolate set: Carnation mold, cobalt, gold handle and trim, 11¾"h., RSP (rm). $15,000.00 – 20,000.00.

Back cover:
Center bowl: Carnation mold, floral, gold/light blue trim, satin finish, 15"d., RSP (rm). $4,500.00 – 4,800.00.
Tankard: Summer season, very ornate, footed, 16"h., RSP (rm). $10,000.00 – 15,000.00.
Center bowl: Snowbird, five scenic medallions, icicle mold, 15"d., RSP (rm). $15,000.00 – 18,000.00.

Cover design: Beth Summers
Book design: Holly C. Long

Collector Books
P.O. Box 3009
Paducah, KY 42002-3009

www.collectorbooks.com

Copyright © 2006 Mary J. McCaslin

The current values in this book should be used only as a guide. They are not intended to set prices, which vary from one section of the country to another. Auction prices as well as dealer prices vary greatly and are affected by condition and demand. Neither the author nor the publisher assumes responsibility for any losses which might be incurred as a result of consulting this guide.

Searching for a Publisher?

We are always looking for people knowledgeable within their fields. If you feel there is a real need for a book on your collectible subject and have a large comprehensive collection, contact Collector Books.

Contents

Dedication

I would like to dedicate this book to my family, of whom I am so proud! They have encouraged me throughout my whole experience of writing books. Their patience and understanding have been greatly appreciated, and I hope they are pleased with my accomplishment.

Our four sons, daughter-in-laws, and grandchildren. Top row: Dave, Bob, Dan, Mike, Katie. Middle row: Jessie, Beverly, Peggy, Trina, Stephanie. Bottom row: Brad (twin), Madison, Alanna, Ryan (twin). This was a gift from our children for our 50th wedding anniversary (2000). Little Emma came along in 2004.

Grandchildren are a joy!

Katie

Stephanie

Jessica

Stephanie & Derrick

"The Twins"

Brad & Ryan

Madison

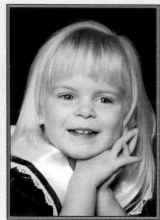
Alanna

Emma

Alanna, Madison, and Emma

Acknowledgments

First of all, I thank God for His presence and guidance throughout this endeavor.

My husband, Bob, was always there to take me wherever and whenever I had to go on photo shoots and research trips. With his cooperation and help, and my family's and friends' encouragement, it has truly been a wonderful experience.

Bob and I started collecting R.S. Prussia in 1970. Several years later, I decided to write a book on this subject. There were numerous books being published on the subject at that time, so I decided to wait awhile. In the meantime, I authored two other books on Royal Bayreuth, another German porcelain from the same time period as R.S. Prussia. That factory is located about 60 miles south of Suhl, Germany.

The authors of previous books have done a fine job of contributing information on R.S. Prussia. The few books that were written before World War II mostly showed examples from catalog advertisements. It was hard to obtain information before and during WWII because Suhl was located in East Germany, behind the "Iron Curtain." Therefore, data could only be gathered from family members (if possible) or maybe an old employee of a factory, and could not be verified as true. In many cases, dates, marks, and other facts were questionable. After the Berlin Wall came down in East Germany (known as the GDR), people were reunited with their families. This was the end of the Cold War. What a wonderful time in history! It was finally possible to research things that had long been a mystery. Many myths and references about the Schlegelmilch factories and families could now be corrected. Because I had corresponded with several citizens of Suhl before the Wall came down, we were very anxious to visit Germany and meet these people, hoping to learn more about the production of R.S. Prussia.

To all of the people that have shared their wonderful collections with me, be it one piece or many, I would like to give my sincere THANKS! Without your help and trust, I could not have written this book. Traveling to their many homes and photographing their beautiful pieces has been a real joy. The trust of those that allowed me to borrow their pieces to photograph and return them is greatly appreciated. If your piece or pieces are not seen in this book, it is not for lack of appreciation, but only because I did not have the item to photograph or the space. There is no doubt that many pieces are still in collections that I did not reach. I talked to many people whose names may not appear on the list below, but I thank them also for their input and thoughts. I enjoyed the research that took us to Germany several times to find a very limited amount of information. I also appreciate the German people that we came in contact with who were happy to share their knowledge. They were all gracious hosts and eager to answer my many questions. It has truly been worth it all to have "collected" so many lasting and life-long friendships with a common interest…R.S. Prussia.

I would like to give a special "Thank You" to previous authors concerning R.S. Prussia – Clifford Schlegelmilch, C. Chumley Hayden, Eileen Barlock, Don Sorenson, George Terrell, Mary Frank Gaston, Lee Marple, and Ron Capers. Their books have served as excellent guides to help the novice and the advanced collector in their search for Schlegelmilch porcelain.

Thanks to Mr. Mark Stuart, who was kind enough to transcribe research material from German to English.

The expertise of photographer and publisher Dave Richardson of Marietta, Ohio; Ken Jinde of Canada; David Mullins of Ohio; Ron Fawcett of Ohio; David McCaslin of Indiana; and Assid Corban of New Zealand is displayed in many of the beautiful photos in this book. Many thanks also to all who contributed their own photos.

These are some of the people that made our visits to Germany a pleasure and a success. To them I extend my fullest appreciation:

Herr Martin Kummer, Lord Mayor of Suhl;

Herr Dr. Gerhard Soppa of Galkenburg, Poland and Essen, Germany, since 1945, historian of Schlegelmilch porcelain;

Frau Elenore Richter of Suhl, historian and researcher;

Frau Christa Anshutz, city guide of Suhl. We enjoyed her hospitality on two separate occasions. She did not speak English and we spoke no German. She was such a good and gracious hostess (and a good cook too!), and we were able to communicate very well.

Frau Elizabeth Kramer, director of Waffenmuseum in Suhl;

Dr. Reiner Schlegelmilch, Bad Langensalza, Germany;

Joseph and Maria Kutz, Tillowitz, Poland. We enjoyed their hospitality for three days while we were in Poland.

A word of gratitude to the memory of Ron Fawcett, who was our dear friend for many years and an avid collector of R.S. Prussia. We are grateful for his many contributions to the hobby we all love. Knowing him was a pleasure and a privilege.

The personnel of Collector Books were so very helpful in the publishing of this book. I appreciate all those that had a part in making this book a credit to the antique world. It has been a pleasure to work with Billy Schroeder, publisher; Gail Ashburn, editor; Amy Sullivan, assistant editor; Beth Summers, cover designer; and Holly Long, book designer.

My gratitude and heartfelt appreciation go to:
Ed and Helen Bailey, Missouri
Jack Bailey, Missouri
Hank and Joyce Barbee, Illinois
Eileen Barlock, Ohio
Dale Bowser, Ohio
Rose Ellen Byer, Nebraska
Ron and Noreen Capers, Maryland
Assid and Miriam Corban, New Zealand
Kathy Cowgill, Missouri
Terry and Mary Frances Coy, Kentucky
Ron and Jane Fawcett, Ohio
Mary Frank Gaston, Texas
Mary Greeson, Illinois
John and Lavaun Headlee, Illinois
Marvin and Laura Heard, Minnesota
Cindy and Jim Helping, Ohio
Pat and Paul Holsinger, Ohio
David and Marlene Howard, Ohio
John and Peggy Imboden, Ohio

Ken and Louise Jinde, Canada
Dr. Joe and Wanda Faye Krick, Tennessee
Terry and Ed Lockhart, New Mexico
Sally and Doug Lucas, Arizona
Lee and Carol Marple, California
Lucille and Tom Mathis, Indiana
Clarence and Ida Meyers, Kansas
Gene and Marlene Miller, Indiana
Ken and Teressa Newcomer, Pennsylvania
Harold and Joeleen Passow, Iowa
C.L. and Lavonne Riley, Kansas
Dr. James and Janet Shetlar, Michigan
Ed and Inez Smith, Ohio
Neal and Barbara Smith, Tennessee
Inez Spaulding, Wyoming
Phyllis Srp, Ohio
Terry and Jane Stork, Texas
Woody Auction Co., Kansas
Wroda Auction Co., Ohio
Robert Yaklin, Michigan

To all the members of the International R.S. Prussia Club, and those that have given very informative programs at our various conventions, I certainly appreciate you sharing your knowledge and experiences with us.

Mary J. McCaslin
6887 Black Oak Ct. E.
Avon, Indiana 46123-8013
e-mail: maryjack@indy.rr.com

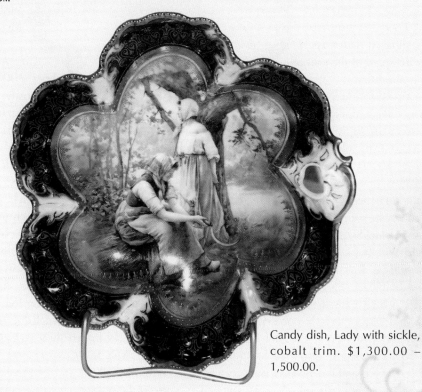

Candy dish, Lady with sickle, cobalt trim. $1,300.00 – 1,500.00.

7

Introduction

I have wanted to write an R.S. Prussia book for many years. It started out to be a book on just cobalt but I decided to include other beautiful collections. You may see duplications in the different collections, although the patterns or decals may be the same. I found some to be different in their trim or colors, or unique in some way. I hope you will enjoy seeing them as much as I did getting the photographs. My research took us to many places and gave us the privilege of viewing many wonderful collections. This is not a history book, although it involves a short summary of information gathered during our quest to find out more about R.S. Prussia. I hope that you will enjoy it.

Between 1990 and 2002, my husband Bob and I visited Germany, home of the beautiful R.S. Prussia porcelain, several times. The trips gave us experiences and opportunities to research Royal Bayreuth also; that factory is located in Tettau, Germany, a small village about 60 miles south of Suhl. In previous years, it had been reported that there were about 400 or more small factories in homes, barns, garages, or other small buildings nestled in the beautiful region of Thuringia. The production of porcelain was its main industry, as this area is rich in the materials that are needed to produce it.

Our first trip (1990) was the year after the Wall came down in Berlin, Germany. What an experience! We had never been to Europe. We arrived in Frankfort, Germany, rented a car, and took off for three weeks with Suhl as our destination. I had corresponded with people that lived behind the "Iron Curtain" (where Suhl is located), so we did have a destination in mind. Thank goodness their road signs depicted pictures showing directions. I won't even comment on the speed of the cars on their highway system, the autobahn.

Entering East Germany (known as the GDR during the Cold War) was like stepping back in history about 60 years. Passing the empty guard towers and military check points was like viewing the old 15-minute newsreels seen in movie theaters in the 1940s. (I remember them well).

Although the Wall was down in Berlin, the barbed wire fences that encircled the GDR were still visible in the countryside throughout the southern part of East Germany. We saw drab, unpainted homes and buildings, which had been that way since the end of World War II (1945). Six months later we returned, and the same villages were making efforts to paint and repair their homes and buildings. Plus, a lot of much needed road repair had begun, which caused several detours. Even though the countryside and villages were in poor condition, the small, fenced-in yards showcased bright, colorful flowers and well attended gardens. Every window displayed beautiful lace curtains with window boxes containing flowers in many vivid colors. We experienced a whole new atmosphere as we saw residents out sweeping the frontage of their homes and streets. Each time that we returned over the months and years that followed, there was noticeable progress in the rebuilding and restoration of their beautiful country. East Germany was returning to a better place to live with the help of the citizens of West Germany. As we traveled throughout Germany, we enjoyed the hospitality of the German people, staying in their immaculate "bread and breakfast" pensions. And what a breakfast they served! We met and made many new friends.

Seeing Suhl for the first time in 1990 was a real surprise, as I had always envisioned it as a small village. Instead, it is a city of about 60,000 residents. Through correspondence, I had arranged to meet Frau Elizabeth Kramer, who at that time was the wife of the director of the Waffenmuseum, a very well-known small arms museum in Suhl. Through the many changes that took place after the Communistic regime, she later became the director of the museum. The extraction and smelting of iron ore had been common in the mountains around the city of Suhl for centuries. Iron ore is ideal for the production of quality gun barrels. This created a very prosperous business for the city of Suhl. Both World War I and World War II had very important impacts on Suhl's economy. After 1945, the industry's development was controlled by the political and economic situation in this Soviet-controlled part of Germany. Today, the city's displays of guns make wonderful exhibits in the Waffenmuseum of Suhl and the Historical Museum of Dresden.

Frau Kramer escorted us to the City Armory, where we were shown about 200 pieces of Schlegelmilch porcelain (mostly Erdmann Schlegelmilch factory pieces). The items were behind locked doors and in locked cabinets. These pieces had been hidden from public view for many years. We were told that these pieces would be given to the city museum, which would provide a special section for the Schlegelmilch porcelain.

We were welcomed to Suhl by the Lord Mayor Martin Kummer and invited to have lunch with him in the local hotel dining room. He and other city officials were surprised that American collectors were interested in the Schlegelmilch factories of long ago. After meeting with the city officials and telling them of our interest and reason for being there, they told us that they would later sponsor an exhibition for the porcelain in the local Suhl-heinricks Museum, scheduled to open in November of 1992. Citizens of Suhl loaned their treasured pieces to be displayed to the public. With much preparation, this was to be a gala event and continue until the end of February 1993. We were not able to attend the opening, but did go in February of 1993. The citizens of Suhl were proud to show their pieces that came from the Reinhold Schlegelmilch factory (R.S.), the Erdmann Schlegelmilch factory (E.S.), the Carl Schlegelmilch factory (C.S.), and the Oscar Schlegelmilch factory (O.S.). Of course, the prices soon went up in the local antique shops.

Hearing of the new interest in these porcelain factories, other people were eager to share their knowledge of this porcelain. One fine lady, Frau Eleonore Richter, a local Suhl historian, invited us into her home to view her pieces that she had collected through the years. She offered to sell me her beautiful, large oval floral (RS) picture frame. I carried it on my lap the entire trip back to the United States. It still hangs on my wall and is pictured on page 28. Of course, we were always served tea and scones (great bakers in Germany)!

The buildings that had been the Reinhold and Erdmann Schlegelmilch factories were pointed out to us. The first time that we saw them, they still bore the gray, weathered slate exterior. Each time that we returned to Suhl, they showed the progress of being refurbished. Different companies and shop owners purchased them, and they became apartment buildings. Photos in this book show the dramatic changes.

We then located the villa that had been the home of Arnold Schlegelmilch (son of Reinhold). It is a large home located across the street from the railway station in Suhl. It had been converted into a kindergarten which remains there today. After getting permission to enter, it was a pleasant experience to walk through the halls and rooms in which the Schlegelmilch family had resided. There were small children running and laughing on the beautiful stairway, wondering who and why we were invading their school and speaking a funny language.

The Erdmann Schlegelmilch (E.S.) Porcelain Factory was also in Suhl and founded by Leonhard, Carl August, and Friedrich Wilhelm Schlegelmilch. They were sons of Erdmann, who died in 1844. They named their factory after their father. The production of the factory was first intended for export trade, consisting largely of table china and decorative accessories. The factory closed its doors in 1937.

The Oscar Schlegelmilch (O.S.) Porcelain Factory was founded in 1892 by Erdmann's grandson, Oscar. It was located in Langewiesen and closed its doors in 1972.

The Carl Schlegelmilch (C.S.) Porcelain Factory was founded in 1883 by Erdmann's grandson, Carl. It was located in Mabendorf, which is a few miles from Suhl. Being a very small business, it closed its doors in 1918.

History tells us that in 1869 Reinhold Schlegelmilch purchased a forge in Suhl with the purpose of establishing a porcelain factory. It developed into the largest in the area. After his death on February 19, 1906, the production began to slow down. Arnold, son of Reinhold and head of the Suhl factory, had to shut it down in 1917. He decided to move to Tillowitz in Upper Silesia (now Poland), where his brother, Erhard, had founded the Schlegelmilch Tillowitz Porcelain Factory.

In 1889, Erhard (son of Reinhold), went to Tillowitz where he leased the Graf Frankenberg'sche Porcelain Factory. He managed this factory for a short period of time, but soon left and started construction on a new factory (1894). Because this factory was financed by Erhard's father, Reinhold, it kept Reinhold's name. The Tililowitz Factory was considered a branch of the main factory in Suhl. Because the labor, raw materials, and production were much cheaper than in Suhl, the Tillowitz Factory soon became more important. World War I hastened this process, and by 1917 the Suhl factory was closed by Arnold, and the Suhl operation was then transferred to Tillowitz.

After Reinhold's death in 1906, Erhard and Arnold were the co-owners of these factories. After production was started in the new factory, it was impossible for the Graf Frankenberg'sche Porcelain Factory to compete, so Erhard bought it out in 1905. The buildings were converted into apartments for his workers. The new factory was very successful as it had been in Suhl. The U.S.A. was a big part of its export trade which was the factory's mainstay. World Wars I and II and the 1930s Great Depression were contributing factors to the rise and later decline of the factory.

This part of Germany was given to Poland after WWII (1945). The factory was not destroyed, but according to information from the present factory officials, its machines were dismantled by the Russians and moved elsewhere. At that time, the factory came under Polish administration and is still in operation. In the early 1950s, Poland reestablished the factory and the production of fine, translucent porcelain was replaced with a heavier product called "Porcelit" for the production of dinnerware and novelty pieces.

The Schlegelmilch family, being very wealthy, contributed much to the community by building places to help the new workers and the citizens of Tillowitz. After Erhard built the new factory in 1894, he also built a school, a sports center, a church (Evangelical Lutheran, as the people of Tillowitz were Catholic), and a row of houses in which his workers lived. This was done to entice the best workers and craftsmen to move from Suhl to work in the Tillowitz factory. This was a big decision for these people at that time in history. (I have included a letter from a family that made this transition on page 22). This small village presently has a population of more than 1,500 residents.

In 1992, Bob and I joined a fellow collector (Ron Capers) in Suhl, Germany, and motored to Tillowitz (now called Tillowice, Poland). We were invited to stay with a family, Josef and Maria Kutz, in Falkenberg, which is about three miles from Tillowice. They were friends of Herr Soppa, our friend from Essen, Germany, that was so helpful in sharing his knowledge of Schlegelmilch porcelain. We enjoyed their hospitality for three exciting days. A director of the new Porcelit factory escorted us through the "old" factory from which many of our pieces had been produced. To our surprise, the old buildings were still standing, and we observed the kilns that fired our old pieces were still being used to heat the molds for the new Porcelit factory that was built in the late 1970s and located immediately north of the old R.S.T. factory. We heard various stories about this old building. Some said it was almost totally destroyed in March of 1945, and some said that it was slightly damaged at that time. Area information now holds true that the factory escaped with only minor battle scars, but it was in fact dismantled and stripped of all usable machinery by the Russians. After Polish occupation in 1945 and 1946, this factory was re-equipped by the Polish government and geared for re-entry into the porcelain products market. Because of the fact that some of the raw materials that were needed to produce porcelain were not available, this factory went into the production of Porcelit (a glazed ceramic ware), in either 1946 or 1949. The new factory, built under Polish Communist authority, was a major supplier of ceramic tableware to Eastern Bloc countries from the 1970s through 1989. It now has a workforce of over 1,000 people seeking trade with over 25 of the larger countries in the world. There are representatives of this factory in Canada and the U.S.A., using the mark with the "PT" in the wreath as their factory mark. We were told later that a company had purchased the old buildings and dismantled the old kilns, ending the presence of an era gone by.

At that time, the factory officials said that all old molds were destroyed, as they were not the kind used in their Porcelit production. While we were there, they were burning some of their old Porcelit molds that were no longer "up to quality standards."

We then entered the new (PT) factory. The showroom did not display any red mark or R.S. Germany items. We only saw pieces marked "R.S.T." and "R.S.T.Epos." There were no portrait, scenic, or animal pieces. There were about 30 pieces said to be the only examples that remained at the factory site after it went under Polish management. A representative of the factory explained the procedure of producing the Porcelit and showed us the various rooms in which this occurred.

We were given directions to locate the villas of Erhard and Arnold Schlegelmilch. The home of Erhard is now owned by the state and used as a hospital for children with respiratory problems. From the outside of the spacious home, we could see a beautiful stained glass window that covered a complete stairwell. After gaining permission, we entered the "old" home, which opened into the "Grand Hallway." Not only did we see the beau-

tiful stained glass window that stretched to the ceiling of the second floor, but also to our amazement, there was the now-famous white porcelain chandelier hanging in the stairwell. There was no doubt that it was made for this spot. It was pictured in German books and guessed to have been made in the early 1920s, a true museum piece made of all white porcelain. From references by Herr Soppa, who lived in this area until World War II and now resides in Germany, the following information was obtained. The Schlegelmilch Factory's mold maker, Wilhelm Kahlert, designed the chandelier. It was based on a design by Frey, a Berlin sculptor. The porcelain links, which encased the cord and held the magnificent piece, was estimated to be 12 to 15 feet. Herr Frey was also credited with the design of the stained glass window and the relief work on the walls of the Grand Hallway. Because of the great success of this chandelier, Erhard and Arnold made Herr Kahlert their chief mold maker and chief of production for white porcelain. Kohlert held this position until he was forced to flee Tillowitz in January 1945. (Collector's Encyclopedia of R.S. Prussia, Third Series, by Mary Frank Gaston)

We then visited the Evangelical Lutheran church that the Schlegelmilchs had built for their workers. It had been restored and was now used by the Catholic Church, which was nearby. The state still owned the small cemetery that was located at the rear of the church building. It was all grown up with trees and underbrush. The gravestones, if there were any, were not readily visible. We started poking around in the underbrush, and to our great surprise, we found a large stone cross. It was approximately six feet in height, lying flat on the ground. It had evidently been pushed over or had fallen over due to years of neglect. It was inscribed "FAMILE SCHLEGELMILCH." Below this monument there were six individual gravesites. These were for the sons and grandsons of Reinhold Schlegelmilch. They were as follows: Erhard Schlegelmilch (born March 16, 1866, died July 11, 1934); Walter Schlegelmilch (born November 24, 1889, died March 9, 1920); Werner Schlegelmilch (born April 23, 1905, died November 18, 1913); Arnold Schlegelmilch (born February 10, 1868, died June 2, 1934). There were empty gravesites, probably for sons Herbert and Lothar Schlegelmilch (born September 5, 1904, died November 6, 1940). The layout of the gravesites indicates that Erhard had two sons (Walter and Werner). This would also indicate that Arnold had two sons (Herbert and Lothar). The two brothers, Erhard and Arnold, died within a month of each other in 1934.

Tillowitz city officials gave us permission to hire local people to restore the gravestones to their rightful positions and clean the area. It was reported later that they continued with the care of the site. This was done in the name of The International R.S. Prussia Collectors Club of America. The club members were proud to do this in memory of the Schlegelmilch family and the porcelain that so many collectors have and enjoy.

Pricing

This price guide reflects a range of market values that are based on the research of pieces found in mint condition. Color, size, mold type, category, type of finish, decoration, shop prices, auction sales, and private sales are all factors taken into consideration when pricing. Location of the piece can also be a factor. Prices are subject to rapid change according to the economy. I am sure that some pieces have been purchased or offered well over and some below the range given. However, I have made my best effort to give a realistic range for each piece. I hope that you will take this into consideration and enjoy your hunt for this special porcelain.

This book and price guide are intended to be a guidepost. The author and publisher will not guarantee any of the listed prices. No responsibility or liability will be incurred from this price guide as a basis of a sales transaction or from any clerical or typographical errors that might be present in this book.

The Baileys and Their Epergne

The late Helen and Ed Bailey of Kirksville, Missouri, were the proud owners of this beautiful epergne. It is the only one known to exist at this time. I am very grateful to Kathy Cowgill and Jack Bailey (daughter and son of Helen and Ed) for allowing me to photograph it for this book. Helen and Ed were dear friends and I know they would be proud that others now have the opportunity to see the piece. Helen had amassed several other pieces of R.S. Prussia with the same pattern, which are also displayed in various parts of this book.

Helen started collecting R.S. Prussia in the early 1970s, and Ed supported her passion by being her travel companion on many searches and attending the R.S. Prussia conventions.

The epergne was purchased in England, and with a lot of inspection and scrubbing, the markings on the silver were traced to a silversmith in England. Several of the porcelain factories in Germany used the expertise of the English silversmiths for their products. Being the only one found at this time, some have suggested a theory that it may have been a custom ordered piece by someone of significant wealth. Who knows?

Helen displayed the epergne at the 1987 R.S. Prussia convention in St. Louis, Missouri. This is the only time it has been displayed. At one time, Helen was a member of the board of directors of the International Association of RSP Collectors, Inc. She and Ed are missed and remembered by many friends. The epergne is now owned by their son, Jack Bailey.

Epergne, 11¾"h. Value undetermined.
Bowl, 10¾"d. Value undetermined.

Helen and Ed Bailey.

Categories and Themes
of R.S., E.S., O.S., and C.S. porcelain

Schelgelmilch porcelain falls into different categories and themes, which are either hand-painted or transfer designs. Gold or other enamels were often applied to a transfer piece. There is a wide range of pieces to choose from, including various sizes of bowls, plates, pitchers, vases, sugars, creamers, chocolate sets, tea sets, ewers, baskets, shaving mugs, mustard pots, dresser sets, trays, berry sets, and many other whimsical pieces. Most pieces are floral with patterns of various species of flowers, roses being the most frequently used. Patterns include portraits, scenic, colonial people, birds, animals, and other scenes. A decal or transfer is used for the décor. The background and trim are many delicate shapes and tints, usually finished with a gold trim. The edges may be reticulated or scalloped with delicate and ornate handles on vases or pitchers. Sometimes a fluted or beaded edge is added to enhance beauty. Two of the favorites are the carnation and the Iris molds.

Portrait pieces are very collectible. The "Four Seasons" pieces depict a young girl in an outdoor setting, denoting one of the four seasons. The Spring season girl is holding a sprig of white flowers and the background scene portrays early spring. The Summer girl holds a red flower above her head and a wheat field is seen in the background. The Fall or Autumn girl has a beautiful yellow rose at her neckline and a scarf partially covering her hair. Colorful autumn leaves are seen and the wind is blowing her hair and veil. The Winter girl is wearing a white gown and headband, has her arms crossed over her chest, and a sprig of holly is in the foreground. Snowflakes are falling, giving it a winter atmosphere. A few of these molds are bowls, plates, toothpick holders, mustard pots, chocolate sets, tea sets, cups, saucers, cracker jars, sugar, creamers, salt and pepper shakers, dresser trays, pin trays, hatpin holders, open-handled pieces, bun trays, and berry sets.

Madame LeBrun Portraits are both beautiful and very collectible. She is a well-known French artist. Her work can be identified with her portraits of beautiful women, including her self portrait with her child, Julie. A few of her well-known subjects were Madame Recamier and Countess Potocka. These were found on chocolate sets, tea sets, bowls, plates, vases, cracker jars, pin trays, celery/relishes, bun trays, cup/saucers, and other pieces.

The Melon Boys are paintings by Spanish artist Bartolome Esteban Murillo (1617 – 1682), often referred to as the "Spanish Raphael." He is famous for his portraits of young boys. The Melon Boys series consists of dice players, melon eaters, grape eaters, and beggar boys. You will see examples of dice players and melon eaters in this book. Bob and I viewed these masterpieces in the Louvre Museum in Paris, France. Some R.S. pieces are very elaborate with ornate decorations in high relief, jeweled with semi-precious stones and a lot of gold. This popular décor is found on many molds including bowls, plates, vases, chocolate sets, tea sets, tankards and pitchers, sugars/creamers, open-handled dishes, ewers, mugs, mustard pots, toothpick holders, table sets, pin trays, cracker jars, dresser trays, hatpin holders, covered pieces, hair receivers, berry sets, ferneries, and others.

Bird scenes depict many different birds in farm scenes, often with pine trees in the background. There are swans, chickens, ducks, pheasants, turkeys, bluebirds, snipes, golden pheasants, and Chinese pheasants. Those that are seen in a group, such as turkeys, ducks, and chickens, are known as Barnyard scenes. Black swans, ducks, geese, and crowned cranes are very treasured pieces. Brilliant colored, exotic parrots, birds of paradise, and hummingbirds are found in this category. They are found on bowls, plates, chocolate sets, tea sets, open-handled pieces, mugs, tankards, ewers, sugars/creamers, pitchers, toothpick holders, relishes, vases, dresser trays, hatpin holders, mustard pots, ferneries, mugs, cracker jars, berry sets, and others.

Animal scenes are very rare. These transfers or decals are usually found on a background of light green or brown shadowed leaves. The four jungle animals are the Giraffe, Gazelle, Lion, and Tiger. Only one authentic giraffe piece has surfaced. This is a tankard that completes the set of four. The gazelle has been found on vases, bowls, and plates, but on only one tankard. The Lion is found on tankards, plates, bowls, vases, chocolate sets, and mugs. The Tiger is also included in the set of tankards, but can also be found on vases, bowls, plates, sugars, creamers, chocolate sets, mugs, and baskets.

Scenic pieces include the Mill, Steeple (Castle), Cottage, Sheepherders, Man on the Mountain, and others. They may show people working in fields or herding animals, with houses or farm buildings in the background. There are many various woodland scenes, colonial period pieces, and lake scenes. There are two different versions of a Schooner (ship with two or more masts), a wrecked ship, and sailing ships. They all come in many molds such as vases, bowls, plates, toothpick holders, hatpin holders, chocolate sets, tea sets, tankards, pitchers, cups, saucers, cracker jars, sugars, creamers, dresser trays, pin trays, mustard pots, mugs, ferneries, and berry sets.

Deer and Stag are found on bowls, plates, vases, berry sets, and other pieces. English artist Sir Edwin Landseer's painting, Monarch of the Glen, is the basis for these pieces.

Admiral Perry Commemorative Pieces depict different scenes which include a man or men, an igloo, sled dogs, animal hides, the American flag, and a polar bear. "Midst snow and ice" is written in script, usually near the rim. It is a rare pattern to find in any mold. A lemonade pitcher, hatpin holder, open-handled relish, celery bowls, serving bowls (one with an underplate), and a mustard pot are among the limited pieces.

Snowbird pieces display a winter scene with snowbirds near a pond. On small molds, such as a mustard pot, the snowbirds are absent. Plates, bowls, berry sets, cake sets, mustard pots, creamers, sugars, and rare tankards with this design are desired in any collection.

Picture Frames are found in various sizes. The décor is usually floral, and birds are sometimes included.

Fruit scenes are made up of a combination of colorful pears, grapes, apples, and oranges. Bowls, plates, creamers, sugars, chocolate sets, pitchers, trays, tea sets, and ferneries are a few of the items available.

Courting scenes with people in colonial attire, and Figural scenes are seen on many choice pieces. Diana the huntress, Lady Feeding Chickens, Lady with Dog, Lady with a Fan, Lady Watering Flowers, Cupids, or Lady sitting on a rock add beauty to any collection.

Floral items are probably the most common, but may be the most beautiful, with their large variety of flowers, both cultured and wild. There are so many different patterns from which to choose. Vivid colors trimmed in gold are found on bowls, plates, open-handled pieces, mustard pots, shaving mugs, chocolate sets, tea sets, demitasse sets, ferneries, cracker jars, baskets, dresser sets, covered pieces, ewers, tankards, pitchers, and celery bowls.

Religious statues marked with R.S. Tillowitz and a religious symbol, other statues, an owl nightlight, and other novelty pieces are items to treasure.

Finishes

Finishes are a very distinctive part of R.S. Prussia. There are various textures.

Satin is usually a white glaze that has the sheen of satin material.

Matte is a dull finish, not shiny.

Glossy finish will have a shiny and slick appearance.

Tiffany finish is usually a glaze with a combination of red, green, and brown that gives the appearance of Tiffany Art Glass.

Tapestry is a very elegant finish used on borders, medallions, cups and saucers, or parts of an object. An band of an inch or two of tapestry blended with the floral decoration is often applied to a bowl or plate.

Stippling is beading in a design and is found in different colors besides gold.

Gold is the finishing touch used for most pieces. It highlights and enhances a border, handles, feet, or the base of an object, and is used on many stenciled designs.

Iridescent glaze has different colors, which appear to change if the light around the piece changes. Some may call this pearlized.

Watered Silk finish is usually applied to satin pieces and resembles a spot of water that is smudged on silk or satin.

Blanks are undecorated pieces that were sold and exported to other places or countries. They were then decorated by others for various uses. These pieces were seldom marked so that the new owner could use his own mark or logo. Pickard Studio was one company who bought pieces and applied its decorations and names.

Abbreviations and Definitions

Madame or Mme. - a married woman, a title of respect.

Mademoiselle or Mlle. - an unmarried woman or girl.

Countess - a wife or widow of a count.

Herr - mister

C.S. or CS - Carl Schlegelmilch

E.S. or ES - Erdmann Schlegelmilch

O.S. or OS - Oscar Schlegelmilch

R.S., RS, R.S.P., or RSP - Reinhold Schlegelmilch porcelain

RSG - R.S. Germany

RST - Reinhold Schlegelmich porcelain, Tillowitz factory

P.T. - Porcelitu Tulowice

d. - diameter

h. - height

l. - length

w. - width

ftd. - footed

lg. - large

sm. - small

unmk. - unmarked

pensions - German bed/breakfast inns

Handarbeit - hand-painted

rm - red mark

steeple - steeple mark

Marks

An embossed mark on a piece of R.S. Prussia does not necessarily identify it as being a Schlegelmilch product. The same mark may be on a porcelain piece made by another company. Marks are found in several forms (a bar, a circle, or a star) and are used to protect the piece of porcelain from cracking during drying and firing. A circle may be found on bowls, a bar on relishes, celeries, or oval pieces, and a star on others.

Distributor and importer marks or logos are also found on pieces with the Schlegelmilch mark, sometimes on pieces imported from other factories. Some that you might see are G. Sommers & Co. of St. Paul, Minnesota; Mitchell Woodbury Co. of Boston, Massachusetts; Biurley & Tyrell Co. of Chicago, Illinois; and C.E. Wheelock Co. of Peoria, Illinois.

"Royal" on a marking does not mean it was made for royalty or by royalty. The word "Royal" brings prestige to the piece.

Steeple mark, red.

Steeple mark, dark green (also found in black and gold).

RSP, red.

RSP, green.

RSG , RSP, and Tillowitz (script).

RSP (red) in embossed circle.

RSP, Royal Vienna.

RS Suhl, beehive.

E.S.

Suhl, green.

Prov. Sxe, E.S. Germany.

RSG, Reinhold Schlegelmilch, Tillowitz (script), Germany (block).

15

RSG.

RSG.

RSG, handpainted (script).

Hand-painted R.S. Germany (script).

Blue RS Tillowitz, Silesia, Germany, hand painted.

RS Silesia.

Triple mark – RS Poland, RS Poland Made in (German Poland), hand painted (script).

E.S. in script, monogram.

ES (brown) bird, Suhl.

E.S. bird, Suhla (Suhl), Germany.

Prov. Sxe, E.S. Thuringia.

Steeple mark.

RSP, embossed mark.

RSP, BT Co., Germany.

RSP, Dresden, double mark.

RSG, BT Co., Germany.

RSG, wing mark.

Red crown VIERSA mark.

O.S., St. Kilian,
Langewiessen, Thuringia.

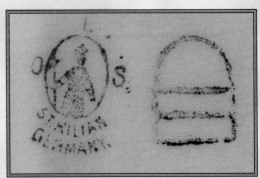
O.S., beehive.

Confusing Marks on R.S. Prussia

These photos will help identify typical NEW, FAKE, and FORGED R.S. Prussia MARKS. Most NEW MARKS exhibit several of the common problems shown below. But remember, marks are only one clue to authenticity. Also compare decoration and blank shape (mold).

New (fake)   Old (authentic)

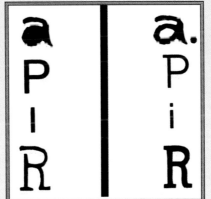

Center of "a" filled in, no period.

Top does not extend to left.

"I" not dotted.

Top of "R" not closed, thickness of letter varies from thick to thin.

Typical fake mark appearing on reproductions from mid- to late 1980s. Note how "R" and "S" vary from thick to thin. The top of the letter "P" does not extend to the right.

Typical fake mark appearing on reproductions from about 1990 to present. Poorly formed "R" and "S"; Prussia is missing.

Authentic RS Prussia mark used ca. 1870 – 1917. Generally all authentic marks have a dot above the letter "i" and a period after the letter "a, " and the letters "R" and "S" are a uniform weight and thickness.

Courtesy of Mark Chervenka, *Antique Collector's Reproduction News* and repronews.com.

Friedrich II

The mark "Friedrich II" is rarely, if ever, seen in the United States, and originated from the Reinhold Schlegelmilch Factory. This fine porcelain was apparently produced to mark the 200th anniversary of the birth of King Friedrich the Great of Prussia, a much loved king who lived from 1712 to 1786. British Commonwealth countries, such as New Zealand and Australia, are the main places where this mark has been found to date.

Pieces range from plain to elaborate — gold hand painting, scenic and allegorical decorations, and elegant cobalt pieces. It is believed that they came from the R.S. Suhl Factory, as similar pieces can carry the R.S. Suhl mark. The Friedrich II mark has also been found double-marked with other R.S. Prussia marks, including the R.S. Prussia red mark.

The Friedrich II mark is also combined with other marks on the porcelain such as:
a) Friedrich II green mark may be doubled marked with RS Germany green mark.
b) Friedrich II green mark may be double marked with the RS Prussia red mark.
c) Friedrich II in gold may be double marked with the RS Germany mark.

After seeing the quantity of Poland China in New Zealand, the conclusion is that England (not the United States) was the major outlet for this line. It has been reported that the R.S. factory sent pieces to London to have silver rims applied to the tops of many decorative vases, and metal work added to complete the assembly of the rare epergne and biscuit jars. From there, they were distributed to the British Empire (now the British Commonwealth) countries of New Zealand, Australia, and Canada. More have filtered into the United States in recent years due to the trading between these countries, the Internet, and the knowledge and beauty of this mark.

R.S. Poland
Made in (German) Poland
R.S. Poland – Poland China

R.S. Poland has been a controversial subject for many years. Research over the last few years has now firmly established that the R.S. Poland mark was produced simultaneously with the R.S. Prussia red mark (with star), using the same molds, and in many cases exactly the same decorations with their hand-painted embellishments.

Miriam and Assid Corban (former mayors of Henderson and Waitakere City, Auckland, New Zealand) have collected and studied Poland China, found in both New Zealand and Australia, for many years. They have researched origins of pieces and production dates, and have always shared their important ongoing studies in articles for the newsletters of the International Association of R.S. Prussia Collectors, Inc., and by presenting programs at the R.S. Prussia annual conventions. In their 1999 convention program, the Corbans' very convincing slide show revealed that the Poland mark was definitely produced before World War I.

When we visited New Zealand and Australia in 1996, we found that dealers and collectors always referred to Schlegelmilch porcelain as "Poland China," which is the predominant mark found in both countries.

There are two Poland China marks. The first and earliest mark carries the words "Poland China" above the laurel wreath, which contains the "RS" letters. Below the wreath are the words "Made in (German) Poland." Porcelain carrying this mark cannot be distinguished from objects with the R.S. Prussia red mark, made well before 1914.

A later mark, "Poland China" within the wreath, but without the "Made in (German) Poland," is post World War I. It is usually easily recognized on simpler molds. Pieces with Art Deco influence have different decorations with no hand-painted highlights, and are useable, everyday porcelain.

The timeframe of production established by the Corbans' research and confirmed by the further research of Lee and Carol Marple should leave no doubt that "R.S. Poland Made in (German) Poland" porcelain was produced by the Reinhold Schlegelmilch factory around the same time as the "R.S. Prussia" red mark.

Points of Interest

1. Meissen porcelain, also called Dresden porcelain, German hard-paste, or true porcelain, was produced at the Meissen factory, near Dresden in Saxony (now Germany), from 1710 until the present. It was the first successfully produced true porcelain in Europe and dominated the style of European porcelain manufactured until about 1756. The secret of true porcelain was kept quiet for many years. The knowledge was soon carried to other parts of Germany and other countries by workers who moved from one area to another. At one time there were estimated to be over 400 small factories in the Suhl area. These were sometimes located in homes, garages, or small buildings.

2. The Cage was painted by Francois Boucher (1703 – 1770), who was noted for landscapes, portraits, and mythological themes. This painting portrays a romantic theme with a boy and a girl with a cage in the foreground.

3. "The Stag" pieces are based on the painting Monarch of the Glen, painted by Sir Edwin Landseer.

4. According to mythology, Diana the huntress was a goddess of Olympia. She is pictured with a bow and a quiver of arrows, in a reclining position. Pieces with this decoration were based on the paintings of the French portrait painter, Nattier (1685 – 1766).

5. Flora, a mythological Italian goddess of flowers, was painted by Nattier. On R.S. Prussia pieces, she is known as the "Reclining Lady," holding a floral garland.

6. Madame Recamier (Jeannee Francoise Juliette Adelaide Bernard, 1777 – 1849), was based on the painting by the French portrait painter, Baron Francois Pascal Simon Gerard (1710 – 1837).

7. Admiral Perry Commemorative Pieces depicting Perry's expedition to the North Pole, are inscribed "Midst snow and ice," and are taken from the paintings of Sir Edward Landseer.

8. Allegorical scenes tell stories in which people and things have a hidden or symbolic meaning. An allegory is used for teaching or explaining ideas and moral principles. A few of the scenes on R.S. Prussia pieces are a Lady with a cherub, Lady in a swing, Lady with a bird and wreath, and a winged lady with a torch.

9. Madame LeBrun — Her maiden name is usually identified with her work. Marie Louise Elizabeth Vigee-LeBrun (1755 – 1842) is well known for her portraits of beautiful women of her era before the outbreak of the French Revolution. She, herself, was among the most beautiful women and painted several self-portraits. It is reported that she was the favorite portrait painter of Queen Marie Antoinette and her court. Born in Paris, France, Mme. LeBrun made drawing and art her preoccupation as a child and throughout all of her adult life. She taught herself, as she had no formal training. Painting was her passion as well as her profession. Having to support her family at an early age (her father died when she was 13 years old), she was able to make her living by painting portraits and soon had a large following. At the age of 20, she married a painter that was also an art dealer, Jean Baptiste Pierre LeBrun. Their child, Julie, at the age of seven, appears in her famous self-portrait in her mother's arms. At the age of 24, Madame LeBrun was called to Versailles and commissioned to paint a portrait of the Queen. This established her as a portraitist and started a lifelong friendship with the Queen.

The portrait of Madame Mole-Raymond, an actress of the Comedie Francaise, is considered to be a masterpiece and one of LeBrun's most popular works. It is called "The Lady with the Muff" on the many molds of R.S. Prussia, and is also seen on Royal Bayreuth as "The Muff Lady." These and other of her famous works are displayed on the walls of the Louvre Museum in Paris.

Peace Bringing Plenty is another one of LeBrun's works housed in the Louvre. Plenty (lady with the light blonde hair) was a model of Paris, Mademoiselle Lucie Hall, and Peace (lady with the dark hair) was her sister, Mademoiselle Adele. Madame LeBrun was made a member of the French Academy of Painting, and this portrait was exhibited in the academy's salon.

Polish Countess Anna Potocka was another of LeBrun's subjects and is portrayed with long reddish brown curls and a ribbon in her hair.

Italian Countess Catherine Litta's portrait portrays her looking over her shoulder.

Queen Louise, Josephine, and Napoleon are seen on a few R.S. Prussia pieces.

10. We and other collectors have found that R.S. Prussia is known in Europe as "Schlegelmilch Porcelain."

11. The R.S. Prussia mark (wreath and star) was not patented in the United States. Therefore, any company could have used the R.S. mark in this country.

12. Gibson Girls portraits were very popular. I will try to identify them by the color of their hats: yellow hat, Gretta; blue hat with dark blue ribbon, and facing right, Mary; red hat, Evelyn; light blue hat, facing forward, Gina; ecru hat with pink ribbon, Sally; dark blue hat, looking forward, Emma.

13. The Schlegelmilch name is a very common name in the Suhl area. It means, "churning milk."

14. It has been well documented that Reinhold and Erdmann Schlegelmilch were not brothers. In 1869, Reinhold established his first factory in Suhl, and then later his sons, Erhard and Arnold, moved to Tillowitz (now Poland), or Upper Silesia. Reinhold died in 1906. The sons of Erdmann Schlegelmilch named their factory after their father, who had died in 1844.

15. We visited the Eisfeld Museum, located in the village of Eisfeld, just a few miles south of Suhl. A showcase of RSP is proudly displayed for visitors to admire. This museum also exhibits important documents concerning the factories.

16. Oberschlesche Museum in Ratingen-hosel, near the city of Essen, Germany, is where we met Herr Soppa and viewed his outstanding collection of Prussia on display.

17. Hatpin holders are often thought to be sugar shakers. Shakers have holes in the bottom in which to place a cork, while hatpin holders are solid on the bottom.

18. . While researching for my Royal Bayreuth books at Antique Publications in Marietta, Ohio, I found interesting material on R.S. Prussia in the old Butler Bros. Co. catalogs.

19. There were over 300 Schlegelmilch pieces (RS, ES, OS, CS) displayed in the 1992 exhibit in Suhl, Germany.

20. You may see "GESEGZLICH GESCHUTZT" with a RSP mark. It means patented or trademark.

21. P.T. Tillowice, Poland factory name is now Zaklady Porcelitu Stolowego, Tillowice.

22. Do not pass up beautiful Schlegelmilch porcelain. Not every piece was marked. Know your Schlegelmilch designs, molds, decals, and textures.

It is my opinion that eBay auction prices are not a true evaluation of a piece of RSP. Auction companies that specialize in R.S. Prussia give more reliable and realistic prices and information. We all look for a bargain, and sometimes find one on eBay.

Happy hunting!

Dr. Reiner Schlegelmilch
of Bad Langensalza, Germany

Clifford Schlegelmilch mentions Reiner Schlegelmilch on page three of his book R.S. Prussia. I corresponded with Dr. Schlegelmilch over a period of two years. We decided to visit him in 1991 and 1992. He and his family were very gracious hosts and enlightened us on the genealogy of the Schlegelmilchs. He was kind enough to trace his family through various official records, both church and government, back to the mid-1600s. He pointed out that the earliest reference to the Schlegelmilch name was from the twelfth century in the Nuendorf area of Suhl. From this apparent area of origin, the family spread throughout what is known as the Thuringia area of Germany.

When asked about the link between the American Schlegelmilch family and his own, he stated that it goes back as far as the mid-1840s. When a direct relation of both families immigrated to America, Dr. Reiner believes that he and Clifford Schlegelmilch were very distant cousins (approximately fifth to seventh generations removed). I asked him if his Bad Langensalza family tree was related to either the Erdmann or Reinhold Schlegelmilch families of Suhl, and he was very adamant in saying that there were no perceptible family ties between these families of Suhl. His father had been a teacher in Langenviesen, and had also researched this issue pertaining to the R.S., O.S., and E.S. families. He found no family relationships.

Dr. Reiner's records were thoroughly documented. His family had been in the leather production and marketing trade. Their family had no involvement in the porcelain industry. He stated that his family and Clifford's family had only been in written correspondence and not direct contact. This was the only way to have contact because of the extremely restricted and controlled travel between East and West Germany during the Cold War.

We appreciate Dr. Schlegelmilch, a biochemist, and his family for providing the facts of their genealogy study. Also, to Clifford and Louise Schlegelmilch (now deceased) for their efforts in researching under very difficult conditions. Their book was the beginning for many of us, a guide on our search for this beautiful porcelain. Bob and I were privileged to have them visit our home and enjoyed an afternoon talking and learning about R.S. Prussia.

Dr. Reiner Schlegelmilch and family of Bad Langensalza, Germany (mentioned in Clifford and Louise Schlegelmilch's book). After visiting them in 1991 and returning in 1992, he displayed a well-documented genealogy of the family, both civil and church records. They show that he had no close ties to Reinhold or Erdmann Schlegelmilch, but, he and Clifford S. are cousins about seven generations removed.

Relocation of Schlegelmilch Factory
From Suhl, Germany, to Tillowitz, Poland

I had the pleasure of corresponding with Stefanie Heinrichs, a German lady from Neustrelit, about her connection with the Schlegelmilch factory. Her homeland was Upper Silesia. She is the granddaughter of an artist who was employed by the Schlegelmilch factories in Suhl and Tillowitz. I thought her story and love of R.S. Prussia was of great interest to those of us that collect and share her enthusiasm of this beautiful porcelain. She was kind enough to send me photos and explanations of this connection. It coincides exactly with the information gathered about the relocation of the Schlegelmilch factory from Suhl to Tillowitz. This is her story in her words:

Dear Mary,

In the past weeks, I have read your dear letter many times and am thankful, from the bottom of my heart. The letter gives me back a piece of my homeland, which has been lost since 1945. I want to start at the very beginning, so that you understand me.

My grandfather, Stiener (my mother's father), worked in the R.S. Schlegelmilch Porcelain Factory in Suhl, Germany and then was moved to Upper Silesia with the Schlegelmilch family in 1892. He was a porcelain painter/decorator in Suhl and lost his wife at the birth of their third child. He married again and received a house in Tillowitz from the Schlegelmilch firm (shown in my photos). Two girls were born from the second marriage, Luise Steiner (my mother) in 1905, and her sister Ruth Steiner in 1915. His second wife died in 1932 and grandfather a year later. My mother (23 at the time) lived there with her little sister, alone, in the house provided by the firm.

My mother graduated from a secondary school in Oppeln, and sister Ruth entered nursing training. In 1933, my mother married and moved to Oppeln with husband, Rudolf (my father). I was born in Oppeln in 1937. My father was called by the military and became a soldier.

I remember that there was wonderful porcelain from the Schlegelmilch factory in our home in Oppeln. Unfortunately, we had to leave our homeland on January 1, 1945. Our house was hit by a bomb and totally destroyed. All we had left was a trunk and a hat box (which I carried). We had nothing more. From Gorlitz, my mother and I were moving west with a Czech on the day of the bombing attack in Dresden (February 13, 1945) on west to Glauchau. In May, my father was released from a P.O.W. status and came to us. We began to build a new existence. My aunt found us and we were all happy to be alive.

After completing school, I became a surgical nurse and worked 20 years in my profession, the last years in Neustrehlitz. In 1980, I went to the mechanical school in our area as a member of the teaching staff for interns.

In 1961, I married my husband, Raimund Heinrichs, who for 35 years was very active as a singer and manager of a theater in our area.

In the course of time after the war, there were many painful departures in our family. Today there is only the one daughter of the oldest sister of my mother still living. She is 78 years old.

After the war, my mother began to collect Tillowitz porcelain. I have photographed what I have and am enclosing these pictures for you.

It would please me very much to share this source of joy with you, especially since you are so interested. Should you come to Germany again, we would be very pleased to have you visit.

Something to add would be that, since 1945, I have never visited Oppeln or Tillowitz. It was simply too painful. Since the reunification in 1989, the world stands open to us. We have been retired for a year and are making the best of it.

My dear, valued, beautiful homeland porcelain and I would like to end my letter for today with the hope of having helped you and your book a little further along.

I would be happy to hear from you again.

Sincerely heartfelt greeting from,

Stefanie

Stefanie's grandfather,
Herr Steiner.

Stefanie and family lived in this house in Tillowitz, Poland, built by the Schlegelmilchs for their workers.

Stefanie Heinrichs (white t-shirt), husband Raimund, and friends at their home in Germany.

A Photo Walk
Through Suhl, Germany, and Tillowitz, Poland

What an adventure and pleasure it has been to go to Germany several times between 1990 and 1998 to research the factories and sites of interest of our beautiful Schlegelmilch porcelain. Our first trip was taken in 1991, a year after the Berlin Wall came down. It was exciting to see not only the factories and homes of the Schlegelmilch families, but to meet and enjoy the wonderful hospitality of the German people. They were always eager to share their knowledge of this porcelain. Of course the factories had not been in production for many years, but the buildings are still there and have been in use as apartment buildings and places of business. The people were somewhat surprised that we (the United States) had an interest in their porcelain, which was not considered antique in Europe.

I hope you will enjoy these photos taken in the 1990s on several different occasions.

Suhl sticker, "SUHL Läbt nicht cool!"

Welcome to Suhl, Germany — city limits and entry to Suhl.

Rathaus (town hall), in early 1900s.

Streets of Suhl.

24

Rathaus as it is today, a farm market that provides fresh farm produce to city residents. Modern department stores are in the background.

Arms Museum. Suhl is known for its production of small arms.

View of downtown Suhl bus stop area.

Railway station located across from the Arnold Schlegelmilch villa in Suhl.

Entertainment for children
on the streets of Suhl.

School band performing
on the streets of Suhl.

Local band.

Typical sleeping room in pensions above an eating facility.

26

Main street or walkway of Suhl.

Armory. This was the Secret Service Building and Training School in earlier times. We were allowed to visit and view the Schlegelmilch porcelain, which was under lock and key.

Porcelain that we viewed in the Armory.

About 200 items were on display in locked cabinets.

A café in Suhl.

Herr Richter and Frau Eleonore Richter of Suhl, Germany. Eleonore, a historian of Suhl, invited us into her home. Notice the Schlegelmilch picture frame on the wall.

The villa of Arnold Schlegelmilch (son of Reinhold) across from the railway station in Suhl.

Today (1990s), the Schlegelmilch villa is a kindergarten.

Beautiful carved work on the main house in Arnold's villa.

Entry to Arnold Schlegelmilch villa.

Rear of villa with sunroom on the left. Shows a need for repair after the G.D.R. years of neglect.

Outside view of the stained glass window.

Inside view of the stained glass window.

Beautiful ornament decorating the top newel post.

Stairway to the landing which proceeds to a second floor.

Gas furnace (located on the first floor), said to be the original one, still in use.

Servants' quarters and horse stable at the Schlegelmilch villa.

Schlegelmilch horse and carriage.

R.S. Prussia Porcelain Factory in Suhl, Administration Building. Building on the right shows the beginning of the renovation of the old buildings that are now business offices or apartment buildings.

A souvenir of the original building before renovation.

Before renovation, one of many factory buildings (1869 – 1917).

After renovation.

Horse stables, before renovation.

Horse stables, after renovation.

Kiln building after renovation, now a training school and storage building for RSP pieces.

RSP Factory Administration Building (right) and main factory (left), 1869 – 1917, sold to the city of Suhl in 1921 and used as apartment buildings.

Building after renovation, now a television studio.

Part of RSP factory main building.

Kiln building, showing the importance of having a water source near the factory.

Rear of main factory building.

More renovation.

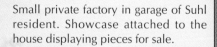

Small private factory in garage of Suhl resident. Showcase attached to the house displaying pieces for sale.

Leonhard Schlegelmilch (son of Erdmann) villa, in Suhl (E.S.).

E.S. Factory, named for Erdmann, father of founders Carl August Schlegelmilch, Leonhard Schlegelmilch, and Friedrich Schlegelmilch, now apartment buildings (since 1937). Erdmann died in 1844.

E.S. factory building.

E.S. factory building, also located near a stream of water.

Oscar Schlegelmilch (grandson of Erdmann Schlegelmilch) Factory in Langewissen, Germany. Founded in 1882 and closed in 1991.

Entry to O.S. factory.

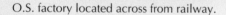

O.S. factory located across from railway.

Group of R.S. Prussia members of the International R.S. Prussia Club in the United States. Tour included the Suhl area and Tillowitz, Poland area. The old RSP factory is in the background. Tillowitz, Poland, is a very small village with a population of about 1,500 people.

Entry to old R.S.T. factory.

Above the door, R.S.T. — 1904. It was built just north of the 1894 factory.

Old RSP main factory building with original five-kiln smoke stacks. We were told that in 1991, these old kilns could still be used if needed. Notice the railway station beside it. The white building was built by the Polish after the 1945 take over.

Modern day kilns in the factory.

Kiln being dismantled in the old building.

Drying room and cooling area for the new molds.

Graveyard (present day) for the discarded molds.

Entry to the new factory.

The mark and logo of the "P.T." Tillowitz used by the present factory.

Employees headed to work in the old factory.

Present factory batch or mixing room. Very large area for various types of clay, in production preparation before being fired in the R.S.P. kilns.

Kilns in the old RSP factory in Tillowitz. New owners tore them down in the late 1990s.

P.T. mold room displaying glazed ceramic products made for worldwide export to more than 24 countries.

Cleaning the molds.

P.T. factory. Decorators working on the new "Porcelit" pieces.

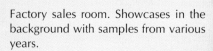

Factory sales room. Showcases in the background with samples from various years.

40

Displays in showroom.

Schlegelmilch building in Tillowitz, used for apartments now.

Houses built by the Schlegelmilchs for their factory workers that came from Suhl, Germany, to work in the Tillowitz factory (1869 – 1917).

Workers' homes.

Porzellanfabrik Schlegelmilch

Tillowitz O.-S.

Villa Schlegelmilch

Postcard showing the old factory and Schlegelmilch villa in the early 1900s.

Workers' homes.

Erhard Schlegelmilch's (son of Reinhold) old villa in Tillowitz. It is now used for the housing of young people with respiratory problems.

Back view of Erhard's villa during the early 1900s.

Outside view of indoor staircase.

Inside view of the famous chandelier hanging above the stairway.

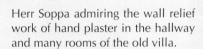

Herr Soppa admiring the wall relief work of hand plaster in the hallway and many rooms of the old villa.

Arnold Schlegelmilch's home, known as the "new" villa in Tillowitz.

Beautiful castle believed to have been a residence for the Schlegelmilch family during the late 1890s or early 1900s in Tillowitz.

Lutheran church built by the Schlegelmilchs for their factory workers that came from Suhl to work in the Tillowitz Factory (1869 – 1917).

Looking for gravestones in the unkempt cemetery located behind the church building. It shows years of neglect.

The Schlegelmilch family gravestone and separate stones of the sons of Reinhold.

Upper Silesia Museum, the Oberschlesisches Landesmuseum in Ratigen-Hosel (Peine near Essen).

Herr Gerhard Soppa, of Essen, had his wonderful collection on display in the museum during our visit. He is an avid collector and a great source of information on the history of this porcelain.

R.S. Tillowitz pieces displayed in the museum.

Ibex statue with R.S. Tillowitz mark.

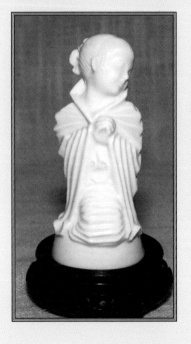

The Praying Girl with R.S. Til-lowitz mark.

Checkpoint or guard tower after WWII, displaying American banners (New Kids on the Block, musical group).

Ruins and dismantled G.D.R. border.

Another dismantled guardhouse seen through the barbed wire that still encircles part of the old GDR. Later these fences were torn down.

This area is now a modern gas station.

An information tower displaying WWII data from that area replaced the old guard tower.

47

Cobalt Porcelain

Cobalt is very popular and collectible in any form of antique porcelain or glass.

Schlegelmilch cobalt porcelain is featured in this book and many collectors were willing to share their pieces with us. I know you will enjoy seeing the large assortment exhibited throughout the entire book. Every collector's desire is to have at least one piece in his or her collection.

The largest collection of cobalt that I have seen is found in the home of John and Lavaun Headlee. It is displayed in massive cabinets throughout their home. Not only is it a beautiful sight to see, but it is very educational and informative for the R.S. Prussia collector and those interested in beautiful porcelain. Bob, Dave Richardson (photographer), and I were in the Headlee home for three days capturing the true beauty of their collection and it is shown in the following pages. I started looking into other collections for more cobalt (which is scattered throughout this book), and decided that people should see these other wonderful collections. Therefore, there are some duplications. Even though they are the same mold or pattern, many times they are different in color and iridescence. Many other collectors contributed to the cobalt pieces that are shown throughout the book. I hope you will enjoy seeing them as much as we did photographing them.

Chocolate set: Carnation mold, cobalt, gold handles and trim. Tankard, 11¼"h.; cup, 3"h.; saucer, 4½" d.; RSP (rm). $15,000.00 – 20,000.00 set.

Tankard and mug set, Carnation mold. Tankard, 11"h.; mugs, 3¼"h.; RSP (rm). $7,000.00 – 8,000.00 set.

Melon Boys by artist Bartolome Esteban Murillo

Row 1. Bowl: Dice players, 10½"d., RSP (rm). $4,500.00 – 5,200.00. Plate: Melon eaters, open-handled, 11"d., RSP (rm). $4,500.00 – 5,200.00. Bowl: Melon eaters, 10½"d., RSP (rm). $4,500.00 – 5,200.00.
Row 2. Plate: Melon eaters, open-handled, 9¾"d., RSP (rm). $2,800.00 – 3,200.00. Bun bowl: Melon eaters, open-handled, 13"l. x 8½"w., RSP (rm). $4,500.00 – 5,000.00. Plate: Dice players, 8¾"d., RSP (rm). $2,500.00 – 3,000.00.
Row 3. Pin tray: Melon eaters, 5½"l. x 3½"w., RSP (rm). $2,000.00 – 2,500.00. Creamer: Melon eaters, 4"h., RSP (rm). $1,200.00 – 1,500.00. Celery: Melon eaters, open-handled, 12¼"h., RSP (rm). $2,500.00 – 3,000.00. Relish: Dice players, open-handled, 9½"l. x 4¾"w., RSP (rm). $1,500.00 – 1,800.00.
Row 4. Coffeepot/lid: Melon eaters, 9"h., unmk. $4,000.00 – 4,500.00. Plate: Melon eaters, 8¾"d., RSP (rm). $2,500.00 – 3,000.00. Teapot/lid: Melon eaters, 6½"h., RSP (rm). $3,200.00 – 3,800.00. Chocolate pot/lid: Melon eaters, 10"h., RSP (rm). $5,000.00+.

Portraits by Madame Elisabeth Louise Vigee LeBrun

Row 1. Plate: Countess Potocka, 12"d., unmk. $2,200.00 – 2,800.00. Plate: Madame LeBrun (self-portrait, 1790), 12"d., unmk. $2,200.00 – 2,800.00. Plate: Madame Recamier, 12"d., unmk. $2,200.00 – 2,800.00.
Row 2. Bowl: Madame LeBrun, 10½"d. (gold steeple mark). $2,500.00 – 3,000.00. Bowl: Madame Recamier, 10"d., unmk. $3,000.00 – 3,500.00. Bowl: Madame LeBrun, stippled, 10½"d., unmk. $3,000.00 – 3,500.00.
Row 3. Vase: Madame Recamier, ornate handles, 9"h., unmk. $1,200.00 – 1,600.00. Vase: Madame LeBrun, ornate handles, 9½"h., unmk. $1,200.00 – 1,600.00. Vase: Madame LeBrun, ornate handles, 9¼"h., unmk. $900.00 – 1,200.00. Vase: Countess Potocka, ornate handles, 9¼"h. (Royal Vienna/crown). $900.00 – 1,200.00.

Row 1. Bowl: Madame LeBrun, five medallions, 10¾"d., RSP (rm). $3,500.00 – 4,000.00. Vase: The Cage, handles, 11"h., R.S. Suhl (bee-hive). $3,000.00 – 3,500.00. Plate: Madame Recamier, stippled, 11¾"d., unmk. $3,500.00 – 4,000.00. Bowl: Countess Potocka, five medallions, 10¾"d., RSP (rm). $3,500.00 – 4,000.00.
Row 2. Vase: Countess Litta, ornate handles, 9½"h., unmk. $2,400.00 – 2,800.00. Plate: Madame LeBrun, stippled, 8½"d., unmk. $2,800.00 – 3,200.00. Bowl: Countess Potocka, pleated mold, 10½"d., unmk. $2,000.00 – 2,500.00. Plate: Countess Potocka, 8½"d., unmk. $2,700.00 – 3,200.00.
Row 3. Cup/saucer: The Cage, cup, 2¾"h., saucer, 6½"d., R.S. Suhl. $400.00 – 600.00. Plate: The Cage, 7½"d., R. S. Suhl. $700.00 – 1,000.00. Dish: The Cage, ornate handles, 4½" x 5½", R.S. Suhl. $400.00 – 600.00. Vase: Lady/dog, ornate handles, 6½"h. x 4¾"w., unmk. $1,800.00 – 2,200.00. Vase: Lady/chickens, ornate handles, 6½"h. x 4¾"w., unmk. $1,800.00 – 2,200.00.
Row 4. Ewer: Cupids, 6"h., Saxe Altenburg. $600.00 – 800.00. Ewer: Lady/dog, 5"h. (Royal Vienna/crown). $600.00 – 800.00. Ewer: Lady/fan, 8¼"h., Saxe Altenburg. $1,000.00 – 1,200.00. Vase: Melon Boy (Melon eater), 10½"h., R. S. Suhl. $1,800.00 – 2,000.00. Vase: Countess Potocka, ornate handles, 9½"h., unmk. $1,200.00 – 1,600.00.

Row 1. Ewer: Flossie, iris handle, 11¾"h. (Royal Vienna). $4,000.00 – 5,000.00. Bowl: Summer season, stippled, 9"d., RSP (rm). $4,000.00 – 5,000.00. Plate: Fall season, stippled, 11½"d., RSP (rm). $5,000.00 – 5,500.00. Bun bowl: Summer season, stippled, open-handled, 11"l., RSP (rm). $5,000.00 – 5,500.00.

Row 2. Bowl: Floral, iris, 10"d. (Wheelock). $800.00 – 1,200.00. Bowl: Floral, iris mold, 10½"d., RSP (rm). $2,000.00 – 2,500.00. Plate: Floral, 10¾"d., RSP (rm). $800.00 – 1,200.00.

Row 3. Ewer: Lady/flowers, iris handle, 11¾"h., unmk. $4,000.00 – 5,000.00. Ewer: Lady/chickens, ornate handles, 12"h., unmk. $2,500.00 – 3,000.00. Ewer: Lady/dog, iris handle, 9"h., Royal Vienna. $2,500.00 – 3,000.00. Ewer: Peasant girl (Tillie), iris handle, 11¾"h., unmk. $4,000.00 – 5,000.00.

Row 1. Bowl: Spring season, 10"d., RSP (rm). $3,500.00 – 4,000.00. Coffeepot: Pheasant/pine trees, cobalt trim, 9½"h., RSP (rm). $1,800.00 – 2,200.00. Plate: Swans/pine trees, 10½"d., RSP (rm). $1,200.00 – 1,600.00. Bowl: Fall season, 10"d., RSP (rm). $3,500.00 – 4,000.00.
Row 2. Plate: Peasant girl (Tillie), 9½"d., RSG (gold steeple). $1,600.00 – 2,000.00. Plate: Swan/pine trees, cobalt trim, 10"d., RSP (rm). $1,200.00 – 1,600.00. Plate: Flossie, 11¼"d. (gold steeple – Germany). $1,800.00 – 2,200.00.
Row 3. Plate: Lady/dog, 7¾"d., unmk. $800.00 – 1,200.00. Celery: Swan/pine trees, cobalt trim, open-handled, 12¼"l. x 6"w., unmk. $1,000.00 – 1,400.00. Bowl: Pheasant/pine trees, cobalt trim, 9¼"d., RSP (rm). $1,200.00 – 1,600.00.
Row 4. Dresser tray: Pheasant/pine trees, cobalt trim, open-handled, 11½"l. x 7¼"w. RSP (rm). $1,000.00 – 1,400.00. Mug: Swan/pine trees, cobalt trim, 4"h., RSP (rm). $400.00 – 700.00. Toothpick holder: Swan/pine trees, cobalt trim, 2¼"h., unmk. $200.00 – 300.00. Creamer: Swan/pine trees, cobalt trim, 4"h., RSP (rm). $200.00 – 300.00. Dresser tray: Swan/pine trees, cobalt trim, open-handled, 11½"l. x 7¼"w., unmk. $1,000.00 – 1,400.00.

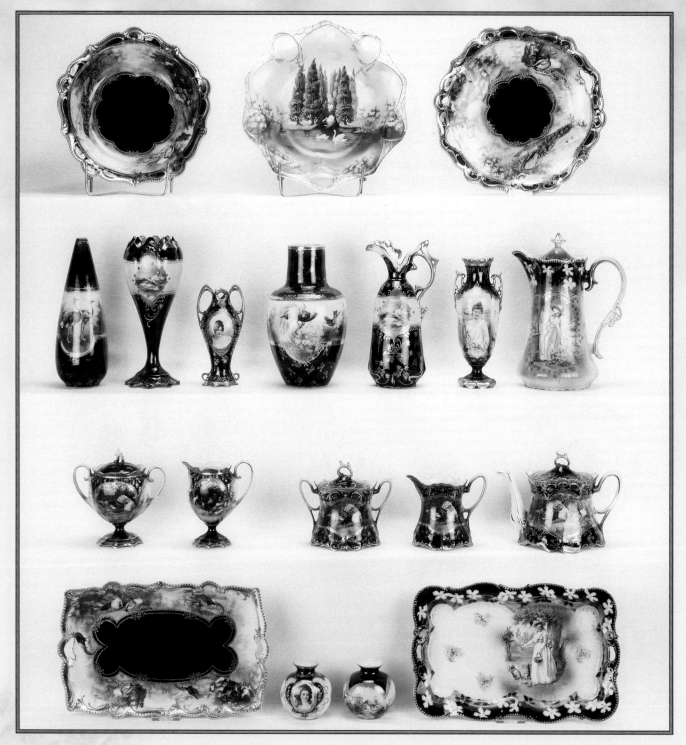

Row 1. Bowl: Barnyard scene, 10"d., RSP (rm). $2,500.00 – 3,000.00. Bowl: Swans/pine trees, 11"d., RSP (rm). $1,400.00 – 1,800.00. Plate: Barnyard scene, 11"d., unmk. $2,500.00 – 3,000.00.

Row 2. Vase: Ostrich, 9"h., unmk. $3,000.00 – 3,400.00. Vase: Reclining lady, 9"h. (Royal Vienna). $800.00 – 1,200.00. Vase: Madame Recamier, handles, 6"h., unmk. $800.00 – 1,200.00. Vase: Bird of paradise/hummingbird, 9"h. $2,400.00 – 2,800.00. Ewer: Reclining Lady/Diana the huntress, 9"h., Saxe Altenburg. $1,000.00 – 1,500.00. Vase: Spring season, 7½"h., RSP (rm). $800.00 – 1,200.00. Chocolate pot/lid: Lady/flowers, 9"h., unmk. $1,400.00 – 1,800.00.

Row 3. Sugar/lid: Barnyard scene, ftd., 5¼"h. (Wheelock), RSP. $400.00 – 600.00. Creamer: Barnyard scene, ftd., 4½"h. (Wheelock). $400.00 – 600.00. Sugar/lid: Barnyard scene, 4½"h., RSP (rm). $350.00 – 400.00. Creamer: Barnyard scene, 4½"h., RSP (rm). $350.00 – 400.00. Teapot: Barnyard scene, 5"h., RSP (rm). $1,200.00 – 1,600.00.

Row 4. Dresser tray: Barnyard scene, open-handled, 11½"l. x 7¼"w., RSP (rm). $1,400.00 – 1,800.00. Vase: Countess Potocka, 3"h., unmk. $250.00 – 400.00. Vase: Mill/cottage scene, 3"h., RSP (rm). $250.00 – 400.00. Dresser tray: Lady/chickens, open-handled, 11¼"l. x 7½"w., unmk. $1,200.00 – 1,600.00.

Row 1. Bowl: Floral, cobalt trim, blue jewels, gold trim, 10¾"d., RSP (rm). $800.00 – 1,200.00. Vase: Floral, medallions, jeweled, gold trim and handles, 8½"h., RSP (rm). $1,200.00 – 1,600.00. Ewer: Mill scene, pedestal, gold handle, 9¼"h., unmk. $1,200.00 – 1,600.00. Bowl: Floral, bowl-in-bowl, 10½"d., RSP (rm). $1,000.00 – 1,400.00.

Row 2. Plate: Madame LeBrun (blue ribbon), gold trim, 8½"h., RSP (rm). $3,200.00 – 3,600.00. Ewer: Madame Recamier, gold trim and handle, 8"h., unmk. $1,600.00 – 2,000.00. Bun bowl: Mill scene, four medallions, open-handled, 12"l. x 8½"w., unmk. $4,500.00 – 5,000.00. Vase: Peace Bringing Plenty, gold trim and handle, 11"h., RSP (rm), artist-signed, Boucher. $2,400.00 – 2,800.00.

Row 3. Syrup/lid: Floral, gold handle, blue jewels, 5"h., RSP (rm). $800.00 – 1,200.00. Vase: Floral, gold handle, pedestal, RSP (steeple). $600.00 – 1,000.00. Cup/saucer: Floral, cobalt trim, cup, 3"h.; saucer, 4½"h., RSP (rm). $200.00 – 400.00. Chocolate pot/lid: Floral, cobalt trim. $1,200.00 – 1,600.00. Clock: Floral, cobalt trim, 7¼"h., unmk. $800.00 – 1,200.00.

Row 4. Table set (miniature). Toothpick holder: Floral, cobalt trim, 2½"h., unmk. $150.00 – 300.00. Tray: Floral, open-handle, 8¾"L., RSP (steeple). $800.00 – 1,200.00. Creamer: Floral, cobalt trim, 2¼"h. $150.00 – 300.00. Sugar (open): Floral, 3½"l., RSG (steeple). $150.00 – 300.00. Hanging matchholder: Floral, shoe-shaped, 6⅞"l., RSG (steeple). $600.00 – 1,000.00. Pin tray: Floral, cobalt trim, 5¼"l., RSG (steeple). $300.00 – 500.00.

Plate, colonial medallions, 7"h., RSP (rm). $750.00 – 900.00.

Celery, floral, black band, jeweled, 15¾"l. x 2"h., RSP (rm). $800.00 – 1,200.00.

Bowl, melon eaters, cobalt/gold/green, 11"d. x 3½"h., RSP (rm). $4,500.00 – 5,200.00.

Powder box/lid, cobalt/gold trim, 5", E.S. (beehive). $350.00 – 450.00.

Bowl, Countess Potocka, floral, 10½"d. x 3½"h. $1,800.00 – 2,000.00.

Powder box/lid, Countess Potocka, floral, jeweled, cobalt/gold trim, 5¼"d. x 2"h. $400.00 – 600.00.

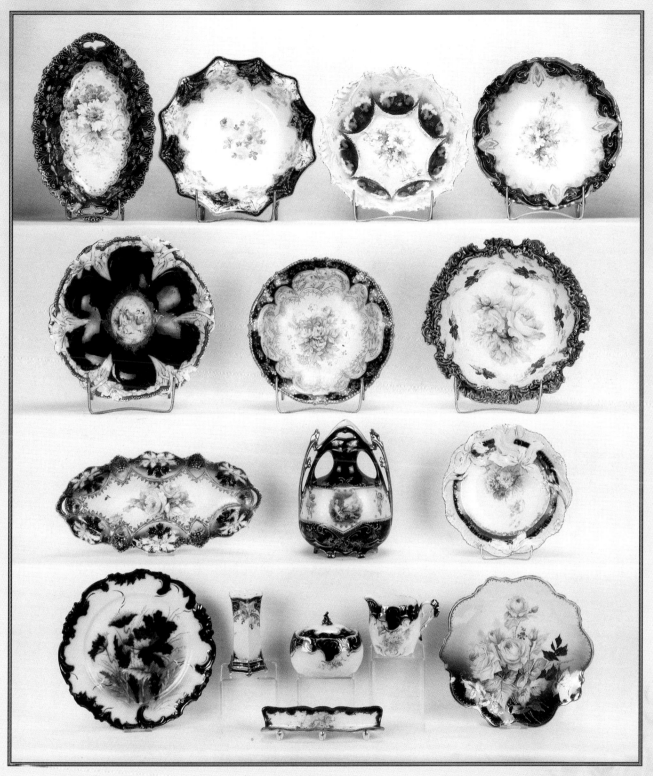

Row 1. Bun bowl: Floral, open-handled, 12½"l. x 8½"w., unmk. $600.00 – 800.00. Bowl: Floral, swag/tassel mold, 11"d., RSP (rm). $400.00 – 600.00. Bowl: Floral, 10½"d., unmk. $400.00 – 600.00. Bowl: Floral, 10"d., unmk. $400.00 – 600.00.

Row 2. Bowl: Colonial scene, reticulated border, 10½"d., unmk. $600.00 – 800.00. Bowl: Floral (decorations inside and outside), three legs, 9"d. (crown/VIERSA). $300.00 – 500.00. Bowl: Floral, 10½"d., unmk. $300.00 – 500.00.

Row 3. Celery: Floral, open-handled, 12¼"l. x 6"w., unmk. $400.00 – 500.00. Vase: Reclining lady (Diana), ornate handle, 7¾"l. x 5½"w. (Royal Vienna). $1,200.00 – 1,500.00. Plate: Hidden image, 7¾"d., unmk. $400.00 – 500.00.

Row 4. Plate: Floral, 9"d., unmk. $300.00 – 500.00. Hatpin holder: Floral, 4¾"h., RSP (rm). $200.00 – 250.00. Pen holder: Cupids, ftd., 6½"l., unmk. $100.00 – 200.00. Sugar/lid: Floral, unmk. $150.00 – 200.00. Creamer: Floral, unmk. $150.00 – 200.00. Plate: Floral, roses/gold leaves, 8¾"d., unmk. $400.00 – 600.00.

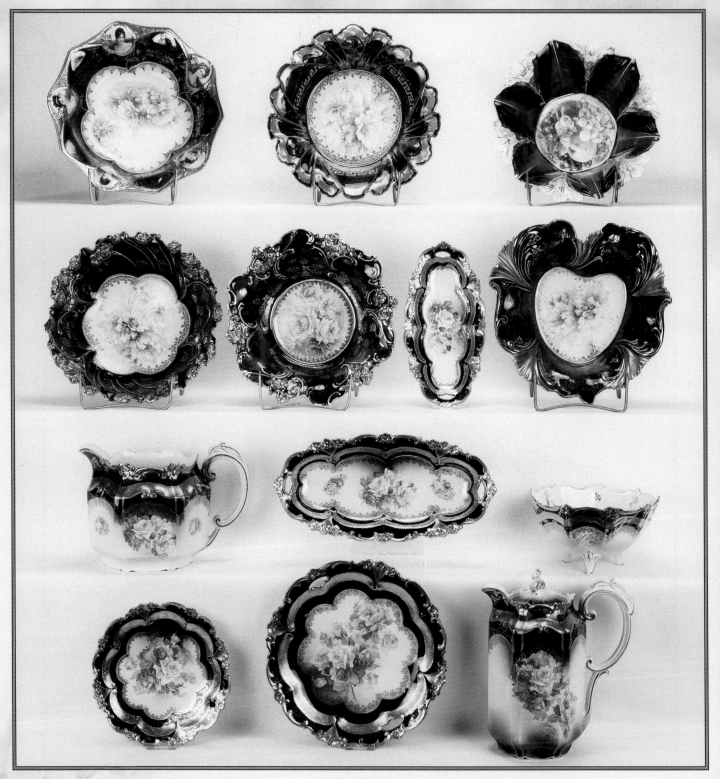

Row 1. Bowl: Madame LeBrun, five portrait medallions, floral center, 10¾"d., RSP (rm). $1,800.00 – 2,200.00. Bowl: Greek Key, 10½"d., unmk. $800.00 – 1,200.00. Bowl: Fruit, 10½"d., RSP (rm). $1,000.00 – 1,400.00.
Row 2. Bowl: Floral, 10"d., unmk. $600.00 – 1,000.00. Bowl: Floral, 10¼"d., RSP (rm). $800.00 – 1,200.00. Relish: Floral, open-handled, 9½"l. x 4¾"w., RSP (rm). $350.00 – 400.00. Bowl: Floral, heart-shaped, 10½"d., unmk. $600.00 – 1,000.00.
Row 3. Lemonade Pitcher: Floral, 6½"h., RSP (rm). $600.00 – 800.00. Celery: Floral, open-handled, 12"l. x 4¾"w., RSP (rm). $400.00 – 500.00. Bowl: Floral, ftd., 7"h., RSP (rm). $600.00 – 800.00.
Row 4. Plate: (underplate for Row 3 bowl), floral, 7"d., RSP (rm). $250.00 – 350.00. Plate: Floral, 9½"d., unmk. $800.00 – 1,000.00. Chocolate pot/lid: Floral, 10"h., RSP (rm). $800.00 – 1,200.00.

Carnation

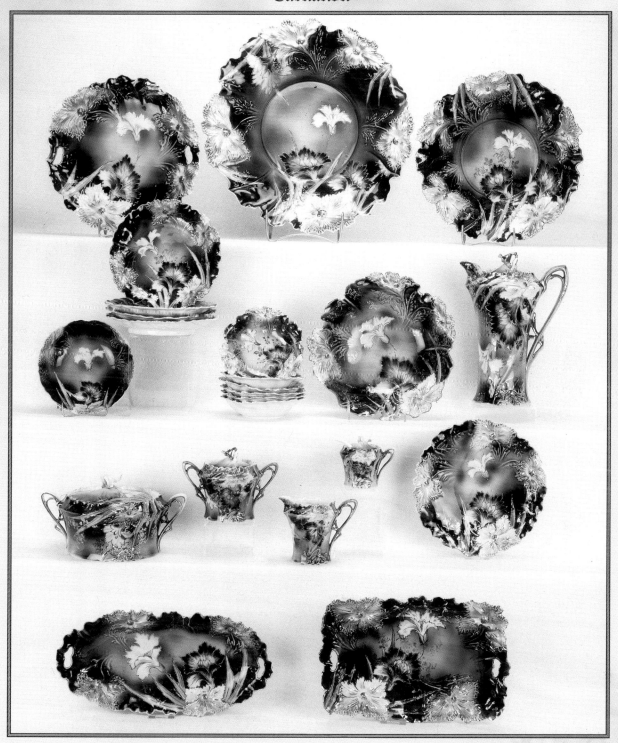

Row 1. Cake plate: Floral, open-handled, 10¾"d., RSP (rm). $3,000.00 – 3,500.00. Bowl: Floral, 15"d., unmk. $10,000.00 – 15,000.00. Bowl: Floral, 12"d., RSP (rm). $4,000.00 – 5,000.00.

Row 2. Bowl: Floral, 6⅜"d., unmk. $400.00 – 500.00. Plates: (go with cake plate Row 1) 8"d., RSP (rm). $500.00 – 600.00 each. Berry bowls: Floral, 5½"d., RSP (rm). $300.00 – 400.00 each. Berry master bowl: Floral, 10½"d., RSP (rm). $2,500.00 – 3,000.00. Chocolate pot/lid: Floral, 10"h., RSP (rm). $2,500.00 – 3,000.00.

Row 3. Cracker jar/lid: Floral, 5"h., RSP (rm). $2,500.00 – 3,000.00. Sugar/lid: Floral, 4½"h., RSP (rm). $1,200.00 – 1,600.00. Creamer: Floral, 4"h., RSP (rm). $1,200.00 – 1,600.00. Mustard pot/lid: Floral, 3½"h., unmk. $900.00 – 1,200.00. Plate: 9"d., RSP (rm). $800.00 – 900.00.

Row 4. Celery: Floral, open-handled, 13"l. x 6"w., RSP (rm). $1,800.00 – 2,200.00. Dresser tray: Floral, open-handled, 11½"l. x 7½"w., RSP (rm). $1,800.00 – 2,200.00.

Pastel Mixed Flowers

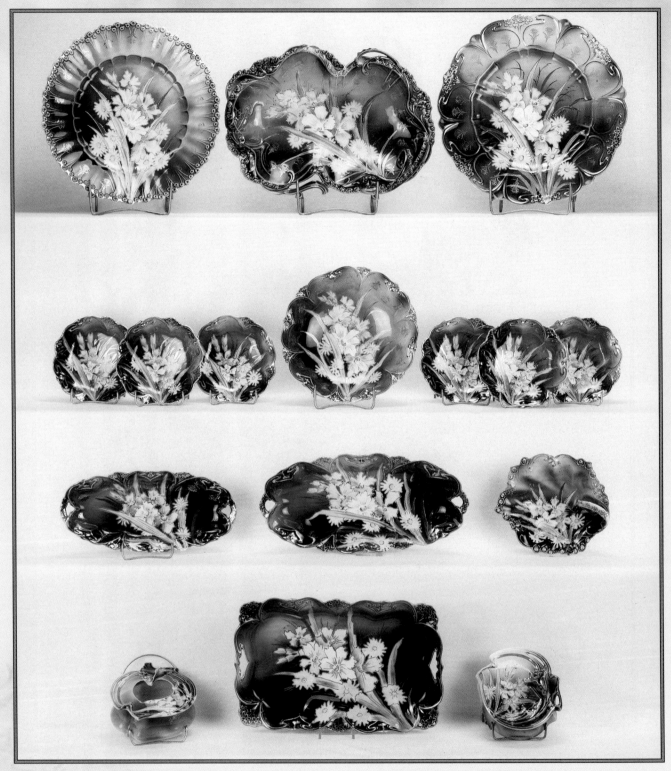

Row 1. Plate: 12"d., unmk. $800.00 – 1,200.00. Plate: Open-handled, 14"l. x 9"w. (red steeple). $2,400.00 – 2,800.00. Plate: Open-handled, 12"d., unmk. $800.00 – 1,200.00.

Row 2. Berry set (seven-piece): Lg. bowl: 8½"d., unmk., sm. bowls: 5½"d., Royal Coburg. $2,600.00 – 3,000.00 set.

Row 3. Relish: Open-handled, 10½"l. x 4½"w., unmk. $200.00 – 300.00. Celery: Open-handled, 12¼"l. x 5¾"w., unmk. $300.00 – 400.00. Leaf nappy: 6¾"l. x 5¾"w. (red steeple). $600.00 – 800.00.

Row 4. Covered box/lid: 4½"l. x 5"w., unmk. $300.00 – 500.00. Dresser tray: Open-handled, 11½"l. x 7½"w., unmk. $300.00 – 400.00. Covered box/lid: 4½"l. x 5"w., unmk. $300.00 – 500.00.

Pastel Mixed Flowers

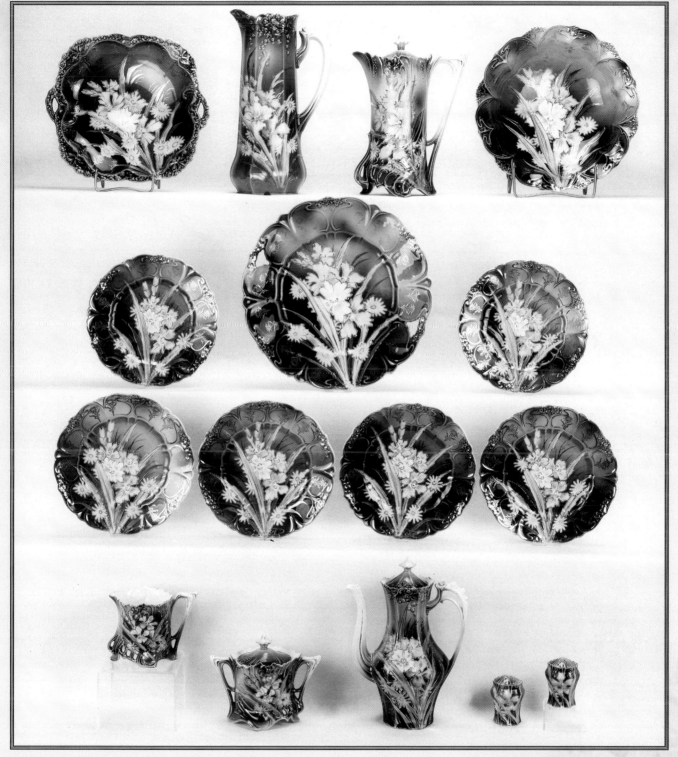

Row 1. Plate: Square cake plate, open-handled, 10¼"d., unmk. $700.00 – 1,000.00. Tankard: 11½"h., unmk. $3,800.00 – 4,400.00. Chocolate pot/lid: 9½"h., Royal Coburg ware, Germany (red steeple). $2,200.00 – 2,600.00. Bowl: 10½"d., unmk. $700.00 – 1,000.00.

Rows 2 & 3. Seven-pc. cake set: Lg. plate, open-handled, 11¼"d., unmk. $800.00 – 1,200.00. Sm. plates, 7¾"d., unmk. $300.00 – 350.00 each. Set, $2,500.00 – 3,000.00.

Row 4. Creamer: 3¾"h. (red steeple). $200.00 – 300.00. Sugar/lid: 4¾"h. (red steeple). $200.00 – 300.00. Demitasse pot/lid: 8¾"h. (red steeple). $1,800.00 – 2,200.00. Salt & pepper shakers: 2½"h., unmk. $350.00 – 400.00 each.

Row 1. Bowl: Berry sauce, floral, iris mold (goes with bowl shown to its right), 5¾"d., RSP (rm). $400.00 – 600.00 each. Bowl: Berry master, floral, iris mold, 10½"d., RSP (rm). $3,000.00 – 3.500.00. Bowl: Reflecting flowers, 11"d., unmk. $800.00 – 1,200.00. Bowl: Floral, plume mold, 11"d., RSP (rm). $800.00 – 1,200.00.

Row 2. Plate: Floral, iris mold, 11"d., RSP (rm). $1,800.00 – 2,200.00. Plate: Floral, iris mold, 11"d., RSP (rm). $1,800.00 – 2,200.00. Plate: Floral, water lilies, 9½"d., RSP (rm). $600.00 – 1,000.00.

Row 3. Plate: Mythological scene, 6"d., RS Suhl (red). $800.00 – 1,200.00. Sugar/lid: Floral, water lilies, 4½"h., RSP (rm). $200.00 – 400.00. Creamer: Floral, water lilies, 4"h., RSP (rm). $200.00 – 400.00. Cracker jar/lid: Floral, water lilies, 5½"h., RSP (rm). $1,000.00 – 1,400.00. Lemonade pitcher: Floral, water lilies, 6"h., RSP (rm). $1,000.00 – 1,400.00.

Row 4. Celery: Floral, water lilies, open-handled, 12"l. x 6"w., RSP (rm). $600.00 – 900.00. Candy dish: Floral, water lilies, ftd., 6½"d., RSP (rm). $400.00 – 500.00. Celery: Floral, water lilies, open-handled, 13½"l. x 6½", RSP (rm). $700.00 – 1,000.00.

Daffodil

Row 1. Bun tray: Open-handled, 12½"l. x 8¼"w., Saxe Altenburg (steeple). $400.00 – 500.00. Plate: Open-handled, 12"d., unmk. $500.00 – 600.00. Bun tray: Open-handled, 12½"l. x 8¼"w., Saxe Altenburg. $400.00 – 500.00.
Row 2. Berry set: Lg. bowl and six sm. bowls. $1,000.00 – 1,400.00 set.
Row 3. Bowl: 6¾"d., Saxe Altenburg. $350.00 – 400.00. Mustard/lid: Unmk. $300.00 – 400.00. Syrup/underplate: Steeple mark #8. $400.00 – 500.00. Sugar/lid: 5"h., unmk. $350.00 – 450.00. Creamer: 4¼"h., unmk. $350.00 – 450.00.
Row 4. Milk pitcher: 7½"h., unmk. $400.00 – 600.00. Cracker jar/lid: $500.00 – 700.00. Plate: 8"d., unmk. $400.00 – 500.00. Chocolate pot/lid: 9"h., unmk. $500.00 – 800.00.

Daffodil

Row 1. Plate: 9"d., Saxe Altenburg. $400.00 – 600.00. Bowl: 10"d., unmk. $400.00 – 600.00. Bowl: 10¼"d., unmk. $400.00 – 600.00. Bowl: 10"d., unmk. $400.00 – 600.00.
Row 2. Cake set: Lg. plate, 10½"d., unmk. $500.00 – 700.00. Sm. plates (four), 9"d., unmk. $300.00 – 500.00 each. Set, $1,400.00 – 1,800.00.
Row 3. Bowl: 6¾"d., unmk. $300.00 – 400.00. Relish: 9½"l. x 4"w., Saxe Altenburg. $200.00 – 300.00. Bun tray: Open-handled, 12" x 7½"w., Saxe Altenburg. $400.00 – 500.00.
Row 4. Bowl: 9"d., unmk. $400.00 – 600.00. Plate: 9"d., Saxe Altenburg. $400.00 – 600.00. Plate: 9"d., Saxe Altenburg. $400.00 – 600.00.

Row 1. Bowl: Floral, scrolled border, 10¼"d., unmk. $300.00 – 400.00. Tankard: Floral, scrolled, 10"h., unmk. $600.00 – 700.00. Bowl: Floral, fold-over side, 11½"d., unmk. $600.00 – 700.00.

Row 2. Cracker (biscuit) jar/lid: Floral, 7"h., unmk. $700.00 – 800.00. Plate: Floral, open-handled, 9¼"d., unmk. $400.00 – 500.00. Pitcher: Floral, 6½"h., unmk. $400.00 – 500.00. Dresser tray: Scrolled border, 10½"l. x 6"w., unmk. $300.00 – 400.00.

Row 3. Plate: Floral, scrolled border (same as Row 4), 6½"d., unmk. $200.00 – 300.00. Box/lid (matches): Floral, 3¾"l. x 2¼"w., unmk. $200.00 – 250.00. Creamer: Floral (with sugar), 2"h., unmk. $200.00 – 250.00. Pitcher: Floral, 3¼"h., unmk. $300.00 – 400.00. Sugar (open): Floral (with creamer), 1¼"h., unmk. $200.00 – 250.00. Box/lid (pins): Floral, 3" x 2½", unmk. $200.00 – 250.00.

Row 4. Plates (set of six, goes with Row 3, #1): Floral, scrolled border (goes with Row 3, first plate), 6½"d., unmk. $200.00 – 500.00 each.

Row 1. Bowl: Floral, cut-out handles, 10"d. (green steeple). $400.00 – 600.00. Plate: Floral, open-handled, 12"d. (green steeple) Germany. $500.00 – 600.00. Bowl: Floral, triangular leaf mold, 10¼"d. (green steeple). $400.00 – 600.00.

Row 2. Hatpin box/lid: Floral, 3¾"l. x 2¼"w. (steeple). $250.00 – 400.00. Creamer: Floral, 2"h. (steeple). $200.00 – 300.00. Sugar: Floral, 2½"h. (steeple). $200.00 – 300.00. Plate: Floral, 9"d. (green steeple). $400.00 – 500.00. Humidor: Floral, 7"h. (green steeple). $600.00 – 800.00.

Row 3. Relish: Floral, open-handled, 8½"l. x 4"w. (steeple). $200.00 – 300.00. Matchholder: Floral, 2½"h. x 4"w. (steeple). $300.00 – 400.00. Teapot/lid: Floral, 5"h. (crown) Germany. $500.00 – 700.00. Ink blotter: Floral, 4½"l. (steeple). $400.00 – 600.00. Creamer: Floral, 4"h. (steeple). $200.00 – 300.00.

Row 4. Dish: Floral, reticulated, 7¼"d. x 6¼" (steeple). $175.00 – 250.00. Dish: Floral, reticulated, 6" x 4¾" (steeple). $100.00 – 150.00. Dish: Floral, reticulated, 6½" x 5¼" (steeple). $150.00 – 200.00.

Row 1. Bowl: Floral, daffodil mold, 10½"d., unmk. $700.00 – 800.00. Bowl: Floral, carnation mold, 15"d., unmk. $12,000.00 – 15,000.00. Plate: Floral, carnation mold, 11½"d., RSP (rm). $3,000.00 – 3,500.00.

Row 2. Bowl: Floral, pansy & butterfly mold, 11"d., RSP (rm). $600.00 – 800.00. Bowl: Floral and urn, rope mold, 10½"d., RSP (rm). $600.00 – 800.00. Bowl: Floral, jeweled, 10¾"d., RSP (rm). $600.00 – 800.00.

Row 3. Hair receiver/lid: Floral, 2½"h. x 5¼"w., RSP (rm). $600.00 – 800.00. Relish: Floral, icicle mold, open-handled, 9½"l. x 4½"w., RSP (rm). $500.00 – 800.00. Dresser tray: Floral, open-handled, 11"l. x 7½"w., RSP (rm). $1,200.00 – 1,700.00.

Row 4. Plate: Floral, 9"d., unmk. $300.00 – 400.00. Bowl: Floral, ftd., jeweled, 7½"d., RSP (rm). $700.00 – 900.00. Plate: Floral (snowball, roses), jeweled, 8½"d., unmk. $700.00 – 900.00.

Row 1. Bowl: Floral, 10½"d., unmk. $200.00 – 400.00. Bun tray: Floral, open-handled, 12½"l. x 8¼"w. (steeple). $250.00 – 400.00. Bowl: Floral, 10¼"d. (steeple). $250.00 – 400.00.

Row 2 & 3. Set of eight plates (with Row 4, #1 & #3): Floral, 9"d. (steeple). $150.00 – 200.00 each; $1,400.00 – 1,600.00 set.

Row 4. Plates: (go with Rows 2 & 3 plates). Bowl (center item): Reclining lady, floral and cupids, handles, very ornate, 12"l. x 6"w., Saxe Altenburg. $1,800.00 – 2,300.00.

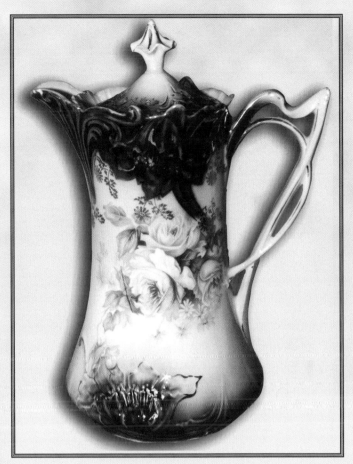

Chocolate pot, floral, 9", unmk. $1,800.00 – 2,200.00.

Clock, steeple mark. $800.00 – 1,200.00.

Scuttle (double) mug, floral, 4"h. x 5"w., RSP (rm). $300.00 – 450.00.

Toast rack, hidden image (house), 5"h. x 2¾"w., unmk., steeple mark. $250.00 – 350.00.
Bowl, hidden image (house), 10½"d., green RSP steeple mark. $600.00 – 900.00.
Pen rest, 7", unmk. $200.00 – 300.00. Bell, 4"h. $250.00 – 350.00.

Toast rack, floral, cobalt trim, 6½"l. x 3"w., RSP (rm). $250.00 – 350.00.

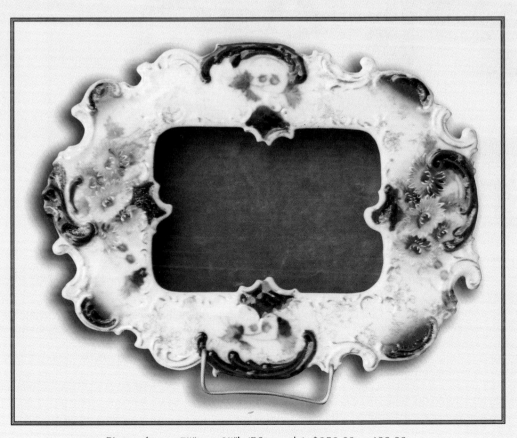

Picture frame, 7½"w. x 9½"l. (RS steeple). $250.00 – 400.00.

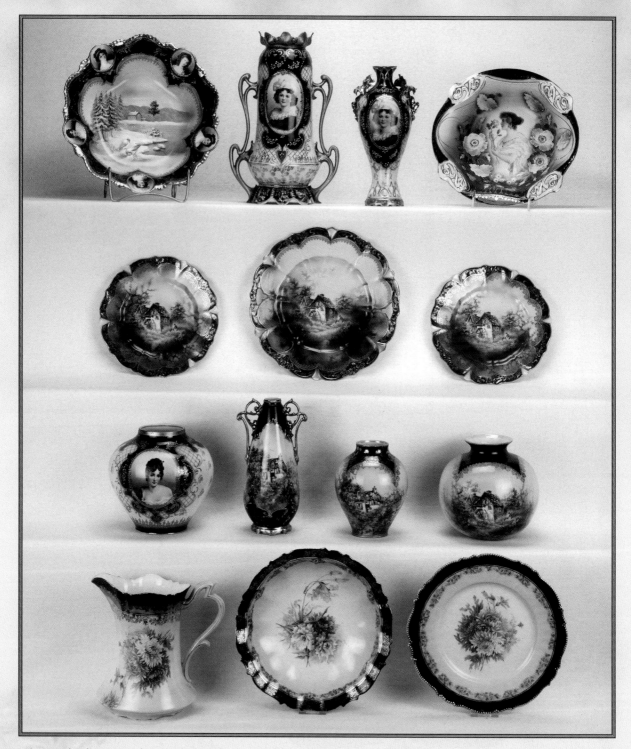

Row 1. Bowl: Snowbird (center), five Madame LeBrun medallions, 10½"d., RSP (rm). $6,000.00 – 7,500.00. Vase: Madame LeBrun (self-portrait), very ornate handles, ftd., 11"h., unmk. $2,500.00 – 3,000.00. Vase: Madame LeBrun, ornate handles, 9¼"h., Royal Vienna, Germany. $1,200.00 – 1,600.00. Bowl: Lady holding rose, cobalt trim, reticulated on four points of outer border, 9¾"d., Saxe-E.S. Germany. $700.00 – 1,000.00.
Row 2. Plate: Mill scene, cobalt trim, opal jewels, 7⅜"d., unmk. $900.00 – 1,200.00. Plate: Mill scene, jeweled, 9¾"d., crown, VIERSA. $1,200.00 – 1,500.00. Plate: Mill scene, cobalt trim, jeweled, 7⅜"d., unmk. $900.00 – 1,200.00.
Row 3. Vase: Double scene, Madame Recamier and cottage scene (on back), 6"h. x 6"w., Royal Vienna (crown). $1,200.00 – 1.600.00. Vase: Cottage scene, 8"h., RSP (rm). $800.00 – 1,200.00. Vase: Double scene, mill and cottage scene, 5½"h., RSP (rm). $800.00 – 1,200.00. Vase: Double scene, mill and cottage scene, 6"h. x 6"w., RSP (rm). $1,200.00 – 1,600.00.
Row 4. Tankard: Floral, cobalt trim, 7½"h., unmk. $300.00 – 500.00. Bowl: Floral, cobalt border, 9"d., unmk. $300.00 – 400.00. Plate: Floral, cobalt border, 9"d., unmk. $300.00 – 400.00.

Row 1. Plate: Floral, open-handled, 11¼"d., unmk. $300.00 – 500.00. Plate: Fruit, 13"d., Saxe Altenburg. $300.00 – 500.00. Bowl: Fruit, 10¼"d., E. S. Germany. $300.00 – 500.00.
Row 2. Bowl: Floral, scroll, 11"d., RSP (rm). $600.00 – 800.00. Bowl: Floral, 10¾"d., unmk. $500.00 – 800.00. Bowl: Floral (scattered flowers), 10½"d., RSP (rm). $600.00 – 900.00.
Row 3. Plate: Floral, cupid medallions, 8½"d. (steeple). $300.00 – 500.00. Plate: Floral, cupid medallions, 8½"d. (steeple). $300.00 – 500.00.
Row 4. Bowl: Floral, 9"d., unmk. $300.00 – 500.00. Plate: Floral, 9¾"d., Saxe Altenburg. $300.00 – 500.00. Bowl: Floral, 9"d., unmk. $300.00 – 400.00.

Row 1. Plate: Floral, open-handled, 11"d., unmk. $300.00 – 400.00. Bowl: Floral, carnation mold, 12"d., unmk. $2,000.00 – 2,500.00. Plate: Floral, 11"d., unmk. $200.00 – 400.00.
Row 2. Bowl: Floral, icicle mold, 10¾"d., RSP (rm). $800.00 – 1,200.00. Plate: Floral (scattered flowers), open-handled, 10½"d., RSP (rm). $600.00 – 900.00. Bowl: Floral, 10"d., unmk. $300.00 – 500.00.
Row 3. Plate: Floral, open-handled, 9¾"d., unmk. $500.00 – 800.00. Plate: Floral, 10"d., RSP (rm). $400.00 – 600.00.
Row 4. Bowl: Floral, iris mold, 10"d., RSP (rm). $1,800.00 – 2,200.00. Bowl: Floral, 10½"d., unmk. $1,200.00 – 1,600.00. Bowl: Floral, hidden image, 10"d., unmk. $800.00 – 1,200.00.

Row 1. Plate: Madame LeBrun, lily mold, 12"d., unmk. $1,200.00 – 1,600.00. Plate: Queen Louise portrait, open-handled, 12"d. (steeple). $800.00 – 1,200.00. Plate: Lady/dog, open-handled, 12"d., Royal Coburg. $1,800.00 – 2,200.00.
Row 2. Plate: Lady feeding chickens, open-handled, 12"d., unmk. $1,800.00 – 2,200.00. Plate: Floral, open-handled, 12"d. (steeple). $300.00 – 500.00.
Row 3. Plate (from cake set): Floral, blackberry, 7½"d. (steeple). $100.00 – 150.00. Tray: Floral, blackberry, 11½"l. x 8"w. (steeple). $200.00 – 300.00. Plate (from cake set): Floral, blackberry, 7½"d. (steeple). $100.00 – 150.00.
Row 4. Plate: Floral, blackberry, open-handled, 10"d. (steeple). $200.00 – 400.00. Plate: Floral, blackberry, open-handled, 11"d. (steeple). $300.00 – 500.00.

Row 1. Plate: Floral, leaf mold, open-handled, 11¼"d., unmk. $250.00 – 400.00. Plate: Floral, 11¾"d. (steeple). $600.00 – 800.00. Plate: Floral, open-handled, 12"d. (green Prussia steeple). $250.00 – 400.00.
Row 2. Bowl: Floral, blown-out hibiscus, 11"d., unmk. $150.00 – 250.00. Plate: Floral, 10¾"d. (green steeple). $200.00 – 400.00. Bowl: Floral, blown-out-mold, 11¼"d., unmk. $150.00 – 250.00.
Row 3. Bun bowl: Floral, blown-out-mold, 12"l. x 8½"w. (steeple). $300.00 – 500.00. Saucer: Floral, 6"d. (green steeple). $50.00 – 100.00. Celery: Floral, open-handled, 13¼"l. x 6¾"w. (steeple). $150.00 – 300.00.
Row 4. Bowl: Lady/floral medallion in center, blown-out mold, 10"d., unmk. (not RSP). Plate: Floral, open-handled, 9½"d. (steeple). $200.00 – 500.00. Bowl: Floral, blown-out mold, 10"d., unmk. (not RSP).

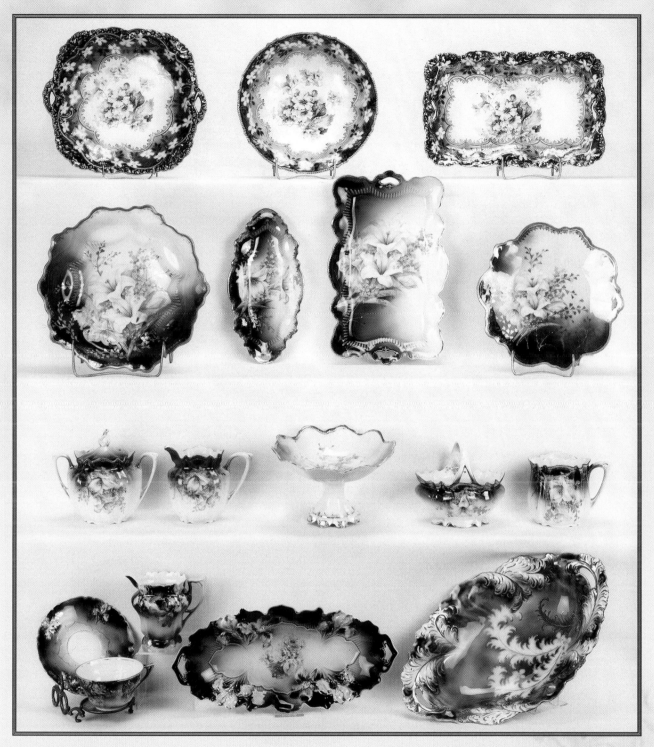

Row 1. Plate: Floral, square-shaped mold, open-handled, 9" x 9" (steeple). $300.00 – 400.00. Bowl: Floral, 9"d. (steeple). $250.00 – 400.00. Dresser tray: Floral, open-handled, 11½"l. x 7"w. (steeple). $200.00 – 400.00.
Row 2. Bowl: Floral, 10"d., RSP (rm). $600.00 – 900.00. Relish: Floral, open-handled, 9½"l. x 4¾"w., RSP (rm). $200.00 – 300.00. Dresser tray: Floral, open-handled, 12"l. x 7½"w., RSP (rm). $350.00 – 500.00. Plate: Floral, 9"d., unmk. $500.00 – 800.00.
Row 3. Sugar/lid: Floral, cobalt trim, 5"h., RSP (rm). $300.00 – 400.00. Creamer: Floral, cobalt trim, 4¼"h., RSP (rm). $300.00 – 400.00. Compote (open): Floral, cobalt trim, ftd., 7"h., RSP (rm). $700.00 – 1,000.00. Basket: Floral, handle, 5"w., RSP (rm). $500.00 – 700.00. Shaving mug: Floral, cobalt trim, 3½"h., RSP (rm). $500.00 – 700.00.
Row 4. Cup/saucer: Floral, iris mold. $400.00 – 600.00. Creamer: Floral, iris mold, unmk. $300.00 – 400.00. Celery: Floral, open-handled, 5"l. x 5½"w., RSP (rm). $1,200.00 – 1,500.00. Bun bowl: Floral, open-handled, plume mold, 13"l. x 8½"w., unmk. $800.00 – 1,200.00.

Row 1. Plate: Mythological scenes, floral, open-handled, 12"d., unmk. $300.00 – 500.00. Plate: Floral, open-handled, 12"d., unmk. $200.00 – 300.00. Plate: Mythological scenes, floral, open-handled, 11"d., unmk. $250.00 – 450.00.
Row 2. Bowl: Madame LeBrun medallions, lily mold, 10"d., unmk. $1,400.00 – 1,800.00. Cracker (biscuit) jar: Floral, 8"h., unmk. $300.00 – 500.00. Plate: Floral, 7¾"d. (steeple). $150.00 – 300.00. Plate: Floral, 9"d., unmk. $250.00 – 400.00.
Row 3. Sugar/lid: Floral, 4¼"h. (steeple, red). $150.00 – 300.00. Creamer: Floral, 4¼"h. (steeple, red). $150.00 – 300.00. Spooner: Floral, 4¼"h. (steeple, red). $150.00 – 300.00. Tray: Floral, 10"l. x 6¾"w. (steeple, red). $150.00 – 300.00.
Row 4. Cracker (biscuit) jar: Floral, 6¾"h. (steeple, red). $500.00 – 700.00. Chocolate pot/lid: Floral, lily mold, 9½"h., unmk. $1,800.00 – 2,200.00. Cracker jar: Floral, lily mold, 4¾"h., unmk. $1,700.00 – 2,000.00. Plate: Floral, open-handled, 9½"d. (steeple, red). $500.00 – 800.00.

Row 1. Plate: Floral, open-handled, rope mold, 11½"d., unmk. $700.00 – 900.00. Bowl: Floral, cartouche (scroll), 9"d., unmk. $500.00 – 800.00. Plate: Floral, 11"d. (steeple, red). $1,000.00 – 1,500.00.

Row 2. Bowl: Floral (blue bells), open-handled, 9¼"l., unmk. $500.00 – 700.00. Bun bowl: Floral (blue bells), open-handled, 13½"l. x 8¾"w., unmk. $900.00 – 1,200.00. Vase: Lady/dog, 9"h. (Royal Vienna, red). $800.00 – 1,200.00. Vase: Lady/chickens, 9"h. (Royal Vienna, red). $900.00 – 1,200.00.

Row 3. Celery: Floral (blue bells), open-handled, 12½"l., unmk. $600.00 – 800.00. Relish: Floral (blue bells), open-handled, 9½"l., unmk. $300.00 – 400.00. Mug: Floral, 3¾"h., unmk. $250.00 – 400.00.

Row 4. Cracker jar: Floral (blue bells), 5"h., unmk. $800.00 – 1,200.00. Butter dish/lid: Shield pattern, 7½"d., unmk. $900.00 – 1,200.00. Vase: Lady/flowers, 9"h., unmk. $900.00 – 1,200.00. Vase: Lady/dog, 6½"h., unmk. $600.00 – 900.00.

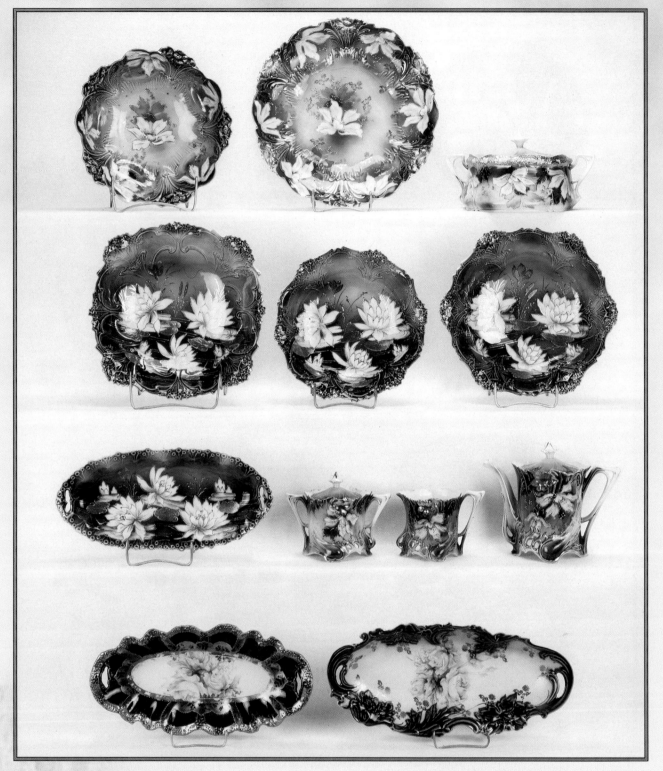

Row 1. Bowl: Floral, petticoat base, 10"d., unmk. $800.00 – 1,200.00. Plate: Floral, lily mold, 12"d., unmk. $700.00 – 1,000.00. Cracker jar: Floral, 9½"h., unmk. $800.00 – 1,200.00.

Row 2. Bowl: Floral (white lily and gold lily pads), 11¾"d., unmk. $800.00 – 1,200.00. Bowl: Floral (white lily and gold lily pads), 9½"d., unmk. $700.00 – 1,000.00. Bowl: Floral (white lily and gold lily pads), 10½"d., unmk. $800.00 – 1,200.00.

Row 3. Celery: Floral (white lily and gold lily pads), open-handled, 12½"l. x 5½"w., unmk. $600.00 – 800.00. Sugar/lid: Floral, 4¾"h., unmk. $400.00 – 500.00. Creamer: Floral, 3¾"h., unmk. $400.00 – 500.00. Teapot/lid: Floral, 6½"h., unmk. $800.00 – 1,200.00.

Row 4. Celery: Floral, open-handled, stippled mold, 12"l. x 6"w., unmk. $250.00 – 400.00. Celery: Floral, open-handled, 13"l. x 6"w., unmk. $250.00 – 400.00.

Row 1. Bowl: Floral, 10½"d., unmk. $300.00 – 400.00. Bowl: Floral, 11¼"d. (steeple). $300.00 – 500.00. Bowl: Floral, 10¼"d. (steeple). $300.00 – 400.00.

Row 2. Plate: Floral, open-handled, 11"d. (steeple). $300.00 – 500.00. Bowl: Floral, 12"l. x 9"w., unmk. $300.00 – 500.00. Plate: Floral, open-handled, 11"d., unmk. $300.00 – 500.00.

Row 3. Berry dishes (two): Floral, 5½"d. (steeple). $25.00 – 50.00 each. Plate: Floral, 7¾"d., unmk. $200.00 – 300.00.

Row 4. Plate: Floral, 8¾"d. (steeple). $300.00 – 500.00. Plate: Floral, open-handled, 9¾"d. (steeple). $300.00 – 500.00. Plate: Floral, 8¾"d. (steeple). $300.00 – 500.00.

Row 1. Dresser tray: Floral (daffodil), open-handled, 11½"l., unmk. $300.00 – 500.00. Relish: Floral (daffodil), open-handled, 9½"l. x 4"w., unmk. $200.00 – 300.00. Bowl: Floral (daffodil), 9"d., unmk. $400.00 – 600.00. Bowl: Floral (daffodil), 6¾"d., unmk. $300.00 – 400.00. Bowl: Floral (daffodil), 10¼"d., unmk. $400.00 – 500.00.

Row 2. Bun bowl: Floral, 12"l. x 8¼"w., unmk. $250.00 – 400.00. Bun bowl: Floral, 13½"l. x 8½"w., unmk. $500.00 – 600.00. Bowl: Floral, 9¼"d. (steeple). $250.00 – 400.00.

Row 3. Dresser tray: Floral, open-handled, 11½"l., unmk. $250.00 – 350.00. Dessert dish: Floral, 5½"d., unmk. $50.00 – 100.00. Dresser tray: Floral, open-handled, 11½"l. x 7½"w., unmk. $250.00 – 350.00.

Row 4. Celery: Floral, open-handled, 13½"l. x 6"w., unmk. $250.00 – 350.00. Celery: Floral, open-handled, 11½"l. x 5½"w. (steeple). $250.00 – 350.00.

Lily Mold

Row 1. Cake set (five-pc.): Floral, lg. plate (11½"d.), sm. plate (6"d.). $1,500.00 – 2,000.00 set. Tankard: Floral, skirted bottom, 15"h., unmk. $3,000.00 – 3,500.00.

Row 2. Plate: Floral, open-handled, 10½"d., unmk. $800.00 – 1,000.00. Plate: Floral, open-handled, 11"d., unmk. $800.00 – 1,200.00. Bowl: Floral, 10"d., unmk. $800.00 – 1,000.00.

Row 3. Celery: Floral, open-handled, 12"l. x 5½"w., unmk. $600.00 – 900.00. Mustard pot/lid: Floral, 4"h., unmk. $400.00 – 600.00. Syrup/lid & underplate: Floral, syrup (3½"h.), plate (6¼"d.). $600.00 – 800.00.

Row 4. Cracker (biscuit) jar/lid: Floral, 8"h., unmk. $1,200.00 – 1,600.00. Chocolate pot/lid: Floral, 11"h., unmk. $1,200.00 – 1,600.00. Cracker jar/lid: Floral, 5½"h., unmk. $1,200.00 – 1,600.00.

Vase, barnyard scene, gold trim, 8½"h., unmk. $1,200.00 – 1,400.00.

Reverse side of vase, golden pheasant.

Vase, barnyard scene, gold trim, 7¼"h., RSP (rm).
$1,200.00 – 1,400.00.

Reverse side of vase, golden pheasant.

Vase, The Cage, gold handles and trim, 17"h. $4,000.00 –
5,000.00.

Bowl, allegorical scene, maidens, gold trim, 10½"d., RS Suhl, Friedrich
II. $3,000.00 – 4,000.00.

Vase, allegorical scene, maidens, gold handles and trim, 17"h., R.S. Suhl. $4,000.00 – 5,000.00.

Vase, allegorical scene, maidens, gold handles and trim, 17"h. $4,000.00 – 5,000.00.

Vase/lid, Diana the huntress, 6"h. x 3"w. $800.00 – 1,200.00.

Vase, Peace Bringing Plenty, gold handles and trim, 17"h. $4,000.00 – 5,000.00.

Plate, Madame Recaimer, stipples, cobalt and gold border, 8"d., unmk. $2,000.00 – 2,400.00.

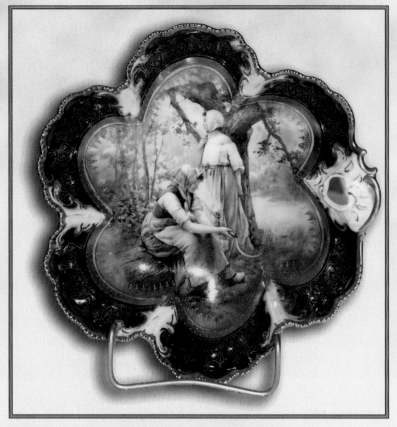

Candy dish, two women/sickle, open-handled, gold trim, 7½"d., RSP (rm).
$1,300.00 – 1,500.00.

Bowl, mill scene, cobalt and gold border, stippled, 10½"d., RSP (rm).
$3,000.00 – 3,500.00.

Bowl, peacock and bluebirds, 11"d., RSP (rm). $2,000.00 – 2,500.00.

Bowl, Floral, iris mold, gold irises, 10¼"d., RSP (rm). $3,000.00+.

Plate, four cows, gold trim, 7¾"d., unmk. $1,400.00 – 1,800.00.

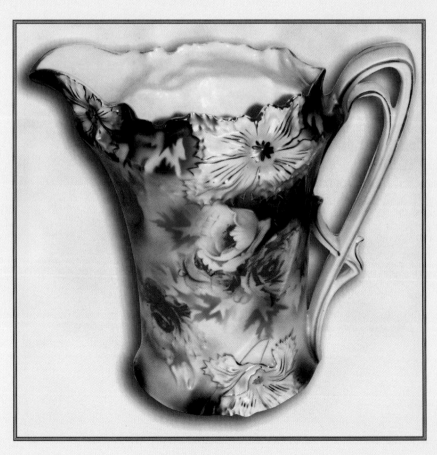

Lemonade pitcher, carnation mold, 9"h., RSP (rm). $2,500.00 – 2,800.00.

1

Bowl, floral, iris mold, light blue iris, 10½"d., RSP (rm). $3,000.00+.

Tea set, Victorian portraits. Teapot, 4¼"h. Creamer, 2¾"h. Sugar, 2¾"h. $2,000.00+ set.

Demitasse pot, lily mold, painted iris, 6¾"h., unmk. $1,800.00 – 2,000.00.

Demitasse pot, stippled with painted carnations, 7"h., RSP (rm). $2,500.00 – 3,000.00.

Teapot, carnation mold, 5½"h., RSP (rm). $2,500.00 – 3,000.00.

Mustard (no lid), runner duck, gold trim, 2½"h., RSP (rm). $750.00 – 850.00.

Chocolate set, lily mold, floral, unmk. Chocolate pot, 11"h. Cups, 3"h. Saucers, 4½"d. $1,800.00 – 2,000.00 set.

Lamp base, The Cage, gold trim, 10"h. Reverse side Peace Bringing Plenty. $1,500.00 – 1,800.00.

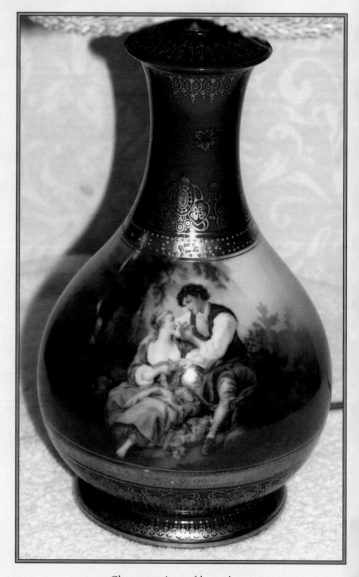

Close-up view of lamp base.

Row 1. Tankard: Floral, 13½"h., unmk. $2,400.00 – 2,800.00. Tankard: Floral, 13¾"h. (steeple, red). $4,000.00+. Tankard: Floral, 13½"h., RSP (rm). $4,000.00+. Tankard: Floral, carnation mold, 13½"h., unmk. $4,000.00+.
Row 2. Tankard: Floral, 10½"h., RSP (rm). $400.00 – 700.00. Tankard mug set: Carnation mold. Tankard (11"h.); mugs (3¾"h.). RSP (rm). $7,000.00 – 8,000.00 set.
Row 3. Plates (five): Desserts, floral, 5¾"d., RSP (rm). $150.00 – 200.00 each.
Row 4. Plate: (like Row 3), Floral, open-handled, 10"d., RSP (rm). $1,200.00 – 1,600.00. Plate: (like Row 3), floral, 5¾"d., RSP (rm). $150.00 – 200.00 each. Plates: (like Row 3), desserts, floral, 5½"d., unmk. $150.00 – 200.00 each. Plate: (like Row 3), floral, 10½"d., unmk. $1,200.00 – 1,500.00.

Row 1. Bowl: Floral, jeweled, 10¾"d., RSP (rm). $800.00 – 1,000.00. Plate: Madame LeBrun medallions, 10"d., unmk. $2,200.00 – 2,600.00. Plate: Madame LeBrun medallions, 11"d., unmk. $2,500.00 – 3,000.00.
Row 2. Plate: Floral, jeweled, 10½"d., RSP (rm). $600.00 – 900.00. Berry set: Madame LeBrun medallions, RSP (rm). Large bowl, 10¾"d. $2,000.00 – 2,500.00. Small desserts, 5½"d. $400.00 – 500.00 each. $4,000.00 – 4,500.00 set.
Row 3. Cracker (biscuit) jar/lid: Floral, jeweled, 7"h., RSP (rm). $800.00 – 1,200.00. Relish: Floral, colonial medallions, 9⅓"l. x 4½"w., unmk. $500.00 – 800.00. Bun bowl: Madame LeBrun medallions, 13"l. x 7¾"w., unmk. $2,500.00 – 3,000.00.
Row 4. Cup/saucer: $100.00 – 200.00. Coffeepot/lid: Floral, jeweled, 9"h., RSP (rm). $900.00 – 1,200.00. Plate: Floral, colonial medallions, 6"d., unmk. $750.00 – 900.00. Bowl: Floral, Madame LeBrun medallions, ftd., 7"d., unmk. $750.00 – 1,000.00.

Row 1. Plate: Madame LeBrun medallions, floral, 11¼"d., RSP (rm). $2,000.00 – 2,500.00. Plate: Madame LeBrun medallions, floral, 10"d., RSP (rm). $1,800.00 – 2,200.00. Bowl: Madame LeBrun medallions, floral, 11"d., RSP (rm). $2,000.00 – 2,500.00.
Row 2. Berry set: Madame LeBrun medallions, floral, lg. bowl (9¼"d.), sm. bowl (5½"d.), RSP (rm). $3,500.00 – 4,000.00 set. Coffeepot/lid: Madame LeBrun medallions, floral, 9"h., unmk. $2,700.00 – 3,200.00. Chocolate pot/lid: Madame LeBrun medallions, floral, 10¾"h., RSP (rm). $3,000.00 – 3,500.00.
Row 3. Cracker jar/lid: Madame LeBrun medallions, floral, 8½"d. x 5½"h., RSP (rm). $1,800.00 – 2,200.00. Celery: Madame LeBrun medallions, floral, open-handled, 14"l. x 7"w., RSP (rm). $1,800.00 – 2,200.00. Relish: Victorian people medallions, floral, open-handled, 9¾"l. x 5"w., RSP (rm). $800.00 – 1,200.00.
Row 4. Dresser tray: Madame LeBrun medallions, floral, 11¾"l. x 7⅝"w., unmk. $1,200.00 – 1,600.00. Relish: Victorian people medallions, floral, open-handled, 9¾"l. x 5"w., RSP (rm). $800.00 – 1,200.00. Bowl: Madame LeBrun medallions, floral, 8⅜"d., unmk. $1,700.00 – 2,000.00.

Row 1. Bowl: Floral, jeweled, 11"d., RSP (rm). $600.00 – 1,000.00. Dresser tray: Floral, jeweled, open-handled, 11¾"l. x 7¾"w., RSP (rm). $600.00 – 800.00. Bowl: Floral, jeweled, 11"d., RSP (rm). $600.00 – 1,000.00. Bowl: Floral, eight cobalt panels, 10"d., RSP (rm). $800.00 – 1,200.00.

Row 2. Berry set: Floral (snowball), lg. bowl (10¾"d.). $600.00 – 800.00; sm. bowl (5½"d.), RSP (rm). $150.00 – 200.00. Bowl: Floral (snowball), jeweled, 10½"d., RSP (rm). $1,000.00 – 1,200.00. Bowl: Floral (scattered flowers), 10½"d., RSP (rm). $800.00 – 1,000.00.

Row 3. Bun tray: Floral, jeweled, open-handled, 13"l. x 9½"w., RSP (rm). $600.00 – 900.00. Bun tray: Floral, icicle mold, 13"l. x 8⅜"w., unmk. $600.00 – 800.00.

Row 4. Plate: Floral, iris, 9½"d., RSP (rm). $1,500.00 – 1,800.00. Mug: Floral, iris, 4"h., RSP (rm). $400.00 – 600.00. Relish: Floral, open-handled, 9½"l. x 4½"w., unmk. $300.00 – 400.00. Cup/saucer: Floral, cup (3"h.), saucer (4½"d.). $300.00 – 400.00. Chocolate pot/lid: Floral, 8¾"h. $1,500.00 – 1,800.00.

Row 1. Bowl: Floral, black trim, 10½"d., unmk. $1,400.00 – 1,800.00.
Row 2. Plate: Floral, jeweled, 11"d., RSP (rm). $1,500.00 – 2,000.00. Celery: Floral, open-handled, four medallions (Madame Recamier, Madame LeBrun, Countess Potocka). $1,500.00 – 2,000.00. Bowl: Floral, black and gold trim, 11"d., RSP (rm). $1,400.00 – 2,000.00.
Row 3. Chocolate set. Chocolate pot/lid: Floral, carnation mold, gold handle and trim, 10¼"h., RSP (rm). Cup/saucer: Floral, carnation mold, cup (3"h.), saucer (4½"d.), RSP (rm). Cup/saucer: Floral, carnation mold, cup (3"h.), saucer (4½"d.), RSP (rm). Chocolate pot/lid: Floral, carnation mold, gold handle and trim, 11¾"h., RSP (rm). $15,000.00 – 20,000.00 set.
Row 4. Cups/saucers (four): Floral, carnation mold, cup (3"h.), saucer (4½"d.), RSP (rm). $800.00 – 1,000.00 each set.

Tankard, Lady with fan, gold trim, rosebud mold on handle, 14"h. (RS Germany). $3,200.00 – 3,800.00.

Chocolate pot/lid, Madame LeBrun (blue ribbon), gold trim, 11½"h., unmk. $3,200.00 – 3,500.00.

Vase, Reclining Lady, Diana the huntress (reverse side), gold trim, ornate handles, 10½"h. (Germany, Saxe Altenburg). $1,800.00 – 2,000.00.

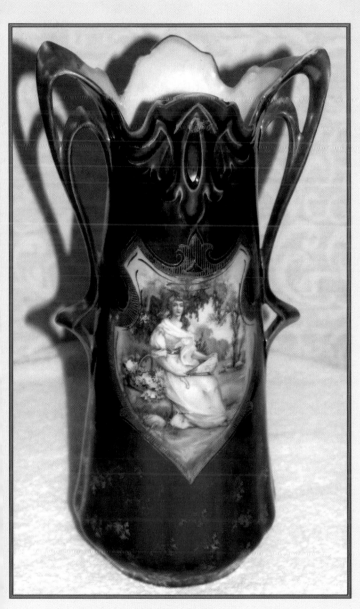

Vase, Lady with fan, gold trim, ornate handles, 13½"h. (red Royal Crown, Vienna). $2,700.00 – 3,000.00.

Vase, Madame Recamier portrait, gold trim, ornate handles, 10½"h. (gold crown, Royal Vienna). $1,800.00 – 2,000.00.

Vase, Countess Potocka (blue ribbon), gold trim, ornate handles, 11¾"h. (gold crown, Royal Vienna). $1,800.00 – 2,000.00.

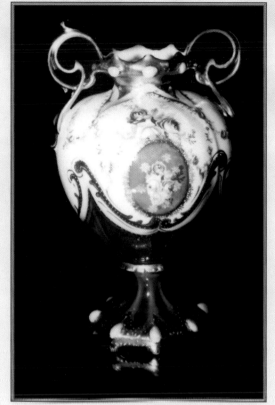

Vase, floral, gold trim, ornate handles, pedestal (14 opal jewels), 7¼"h. (Royal Vienna, Germany). $800.00 – 1,000.00.

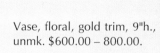

Vase, floral, gold trim, 9"h., unmk. $600.00 – 800.00.

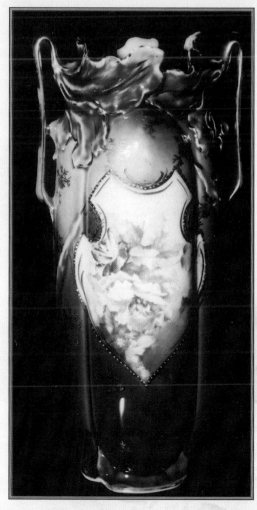

Vase, Countess Potocka (blue ribbon), 8"h., RSP (rm). $900.00 – 1,200.00.

Bowl-in-bowl, iris, tiffany, black trim, lots of gold, 10¼"d., RSP (rm). $1,800.00 – 2,200.00.

Plate, Spring season, Greek Key, red and green, 6"d., RSP (rm). $600.00 – 800.00.

Bowl, floral, iris border, 10½" d., RSP (rm). $800.00 – 1,200.00.

Plate, floral, plume border, tapestry, open-handled, gold trim, 8½"d., RSP (rm). $600.00 – 800.00.

Plate, floral, gold and light blue trim, open-handled, red jewels, 10½"d., RSP (rm). $800.00 – 1,200.00.

Bowl, floral, 9"d. (VIERSA and red crown). $400.00 – 600.00.

Desk set, cobalt scroll. Blotter, 4"l. x 3"w. Edges for pad, 3½"l. x 1¾"h. Stamp box/lid, 4"l. x 1"w. Pen holder and inkwell, 3½"h. x 6"l. Calendar holder, 4"h. x 2½"w. $1,500.00 – 1,800.00 set.

Relish, floral, gold trim, open-handled, 12"l. x 6"w., RSP (rm). $400.00 – 500.00.

Relish, cupids in medallions, floral, tiffany and gold trim, open-handled, 9½"l. x 4"w., RSP (rm). $700.00 – 800.00.

Vase, Madame Recamier, tiffany, gold trim, pedestal, ornate handles, 9"h., RSP (rm). $1,200.00 – 1,600.00.

Mustard, floral, tiffany, gold trim, jewels, satin finish, 3½"h. x 3"w., RSP. $300.00 – 350.00.

Chocolate pot, Spring season, tiffany with gold trim, ball feet, 9½"h. x 6½"w., RSP (rm). $5,000.00+.

Vase, floral, cobalt trim, 6½"h., gold handles (R.S. Poland). Small, $300.00 – 500.00. Large, $500.00 – 800.00.

Vases, maidens, gold trim, 4⅜"h. (RS Suhl, green), $400.00 – 600.00 each.

Vase, floral, cobalt and gold trim, 8½"h.,
RSP (rm). $500.00 – 800.00.

Bowl, floral, iris mold, ten light blue iris flowers, 10"d., RSP (rm). $800.00 – 1,000.00.

Bowl, floral, gold trim, 10½"d., RSP (rm). $800.00 – 1,000.00.

Bowl, floral, light blue and gold trim, 11"d., RSP (rm). $800.00 – 1,000.00.

Bowl, floral, five panels, 10½"d., RSP (rm). $800.00 – 1,000.00

Plate, floral, black (six panels), gold trim, open-handled, 10"d., unmk. $1,500.00 – 1,800.00.

Plate, floral, cobalt and green, blue jewels, 9"d., RSP (rm). $500.00 – 800.00.

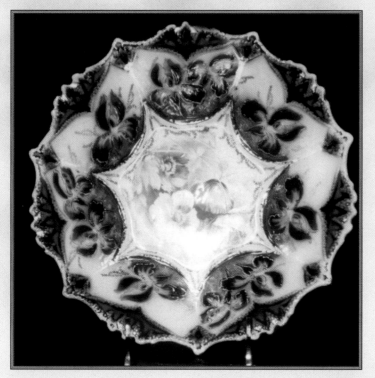

Bowl, floral, iris flowers and trim, 10"d., RSP (rm). $800.00 – 1,000.00.

Bowl, floral, iris mold, gold trim, 10½"d., RSP (rm). $900.00 – 1,200.00.

Shaving mug, hidden image, cobalt trim, 3½"h. x 5"d. $250.00 – 350.00.

Vase, Fall season, pedestal, ornate handles, gold trim, RSP (rm). $900.00 – 1,200.00.

Photo Gallery

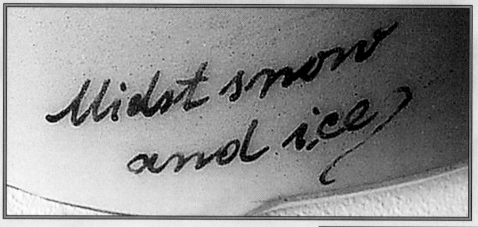

The phrase "Midst snow and ice" is written on each Admiral Perry piece.

Mustard/spoon, Admiral Perry (bear, dog, tent), inscribed "Midst snow and ice," 2¾"h. (RSP rm and Germany, red). Very rare. $4,500.00 – 5,000.00.

Lamp, hummingbirds. $1,500.00 – 1.800.00.

Bowl, Admiral Perry piece, 10¾"d., RSP (rm). $14,000.00 – 17,000.00.

Relish, Admiral Perry (two men, igloo, furs, U.S. flag), open-handled, inscribed "Midst snow and ice," RSP (rm). $7,000.00 – 10,000.00.

Relish, Admiral Perry (man on skis, polar bear, dogs, tent), 10¾"l., "Midst snow and ice," RSP (rm). $7,000.00 – 10,000.00.

Bun tray, Admiral Perry (bear and cub, dogs, man on skis, tent), "Midst snow and ice," 13¼"l. (RSP rm and Germany, red). $10,000.00 – 12,000.00.

Bowl, Admiral Perry (two men, furs, igloo, U.S. flag), 9½"d. (RSP rm and Germany, red). $12,000.00 – 16,000.00.

Wall plaque, Victorian lady/dog, 9½"d., unmk. $2,000.00 – 2,400.00.

Wall plaque, snowbirds, 11"d., unmk. $2,800.00 – 3,200.00.

Wall plaque, swans on lake, mill scene, 11"d., unmk. $2,800.00 – 3,200.00.

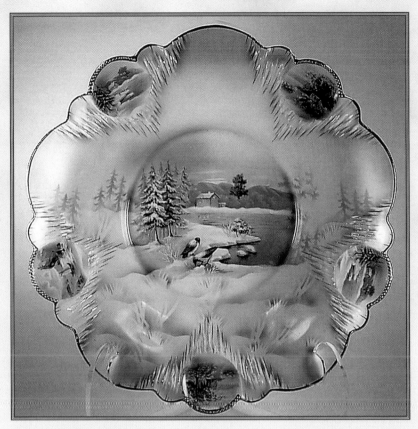

Bowl, snowbirds, five scenic medallions (old man/mountain, snowbirds, sheepherder), icicle mold, 15"d., RSP (rm). Very rare. $15,000.00 – 18,000.00.

Bun tray, snowbirds, open-handled, 15¼"l. x 5½"w. (RSG). $800.00 – 1,000.00.

Wall plaque, three scenes (ducks, swallows, swans), miniature, 4¾"d., RSP (rm). $700.00 – 900.00.

Tankards. Set of four animals (very rare). Tigers, giraffes (only piece known in this pattern), lions, and gazelles (only tankard known). RSP (rm). See next page.

Giraffes, 10¾"h. Only one known in any mold.
$20,000.00+.

Lions, 10¾"h. $12,000.00 –15,000.00.

Tigers, 10¾"h. $12,000.00 – 15,000.00.

Gazelles, 11½"h. $15,000.00+.

Tankard: Swan scene, icicle mold, 13¼"h., unmk. $3,500.00 – 4,000.00. Tankard: Barnyard scene, icicle mold, 13¼"h., RSP (rm). $3,200.00 – 3,500.00. Tankard: Snowbird scene, icicle mold, 13¼"h., unmk. (only one known). $8,500.00 – 9,500.00. Tankard: Turkey scene, icicle mold, 13¼"h., RSP (rm). $2,500.00 – 3,000.00. Tankard: Lady feeding chickens, tiffany and gold, 13½"h., RSG (red steeple). $4,500.00 – 5,000.00. Tankard: Man/mountain & swans (cove scene), 13"h., unmk. $4,500.00 – 5,000.00. Tankard: Three-part scene (birds, swans, ducks), ftd., 13"h., RSP (rm). $4,500.00 – 5,000.00. Tankard: Melon Boys (melon eaters), 14"h., unmk. $8,000.00 – 10,000.00.

Row 1. Tankard: Ostriches, 10"h., RSP (rm). $15,000.00+. Tankard: Parrots, 11¼"h., RSP (rm). $15,000.00+. Tankard: Hummingbirds, 9¾"h., RSP (rm). $10,000.00+.

Row 2. Tankard: Lions, 10½"h., RSP (rm). $15,000.00+. Tankard: Giraffes (only one known), 10½"h., RSP (rm). $20,000.00+. Tankard: Tigers, 10½"h., RSP (rm). $15,000.00+.

Row 3. Bowl: Gazelles, ftd., 6½"d., RSP (rm). $3,000.00 – 3,500.00. Pin tray: Lions (single), 5½"l. x 3½"w., RSP (rm). $2,500.00 – 3,000.00. Box/lid: Gazelles, 4" x 4", RSP (rm). $2,500.00 – 3,000.00.

Row 4. Vase: Gazelles, pastel, satin, 5¾"h., unmk. $1,500.00 – 2,000.00. Vase: Lions, handles, 8"h., RSP (rm). $2,000.00 – 2,500.00. Vase: Lions, handles, 14"h., unmk. $14,000.00+. Vase: Ostriches, handles, 8¾"h., R.S. Suhl. $1,400.00 – 1,800.00. Vase: Parrots, handles, 8"h., RSP (rm). $1,400.00 – 1,800.00.

Row 1. Tankard: Tigers, brown tones, 11"h., RSP (rm). $15,000.00+. Tankard: Tigers, brown tones, skirted, 11½"h., RSP (rm). $15,000.00+. Tankard: Tigers, bulbous, 1"h., RSP (rm). $15,000.00+. Vase: Parrots, ornate handle, 10¾"h., unmk. $18,000.00+.

Row 2. Vase: Black swans, bulbous, 4"h., unmk. $500.00 – 600.00. Salt shaker: Hummingbird (single), 2½"h., RSP (rm). $800.00 – 1,000.00. Toothpick holder: Duck, handles, ftd., 2½"h., unmk. $500.00 – 600.00. Cup/saucer: Bird of paradise, brown tones, cup (3"h.), saucer (4½"d.), unmk. $400.00 – 600.00. Chocolate pot/lid: Bird of paradise, brown tones, ftd., 9½"h., RSP (rm). $3,500.00+. Syrup/lid: Tigers, brown tones, 5½"h., RSP (rm). $1,800.00 – 2,200.00. Vase: Pheasants, handles. $350.00 – 400.00. Hatpin holder: Ostriches, ftd., brown tones, RSP (rm). $1,800.00 – 2,200.00. Vase: Hummingbird (single), handles, green tones, unmk. $500.00 – 700.00.

Row 3. Berry set. Bowl: Stag, satin, 11"d., RSP (rm). $1,800.00 – 2,000.00. Dessert bowls (six): Stag, satin, 5½"d., RSP (rm). $300.00 – 400.00 each.

White Satin

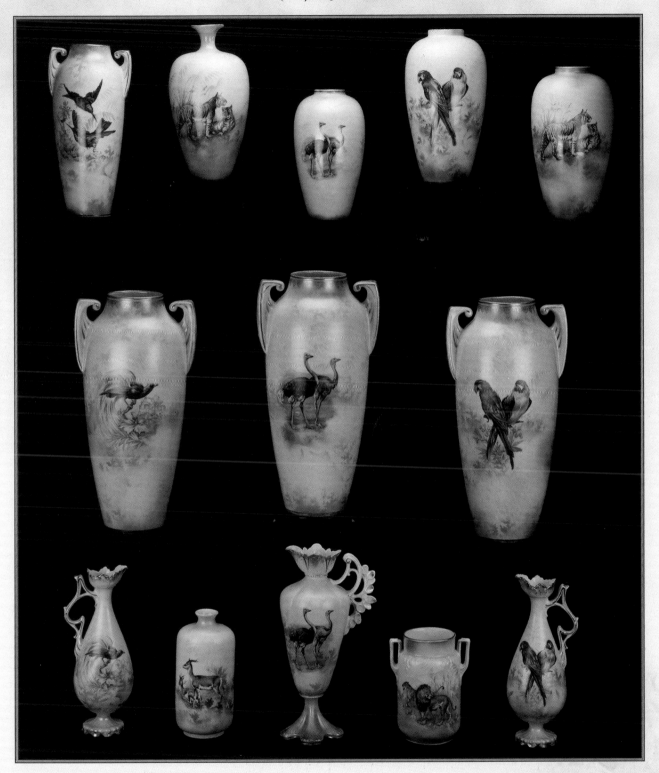

Row 1. Vase: Hummingbirds, handled, 9¾"h., unmk. $1,500.00 – 2,000.00. Vase: Tigers, stick spout, 8¾"h., unmk. $3,000.00 – 3,500.00.
Vase: Ostriches, 7¼"h., unmk. $1,200.00 – 1,600.00. Vase: Parrots, 8¾"h., unmk. $1,400.00 – 1,800.00. Vase: Tigers, 8¾"h., unmk.
$4,000.00 – 4,500.00.
Row 2. Vase: Bird of paradise, handled, 12"h., unmk. $4,000.00 – 5,000.00. Vase: Ostriches, handled, 12"h., unmk. $4,000.00 – 5,000.00.
Vase: Parrots, handled, 12"h., unmk. $4,000.00 – 5,000.00.
Row 3. Ewer: Bird of paradise, ornate handle, pedestal, ftd., 8"h., unmk. $1,500.00 – 2,000.00. Vase: Gazelles, stick spout, 6¼"h., unmk.
$1,500.00 – 2,000.00. Ewer: Ostriches, ornate handle, pedestal, ftd., 9"h., unmk. $2,500.00 – 3,000.00. Vase: Lions, handled, 5"h., unmk.
$3,000.00 – 3,500.00. Ewer: Parrots, ornate handle, pedestal, ftd., 8"h., RSP (rm). $1,500.00 – 2,000.00.

Row 1. Vase: Lions, white satin, ornate handles, 10"h., unmk. $7,500.00 – 9,000.00. Vase: Women gathering grain, 12"h., handles, RS Suhl. $1,200.00 – 1,400.00. Vase: Hummingbirds, white satin, handles, 12"h., unmk. $4,500.00 – 5,500.00. Vase: Lions, handles, 9¼"h., RSP (rm). $5,000.00 – 6,000.00.

Row 2. Vase: Cove (man on mountain), swans, handles, 9½"h., RSP (rm). $800.00 – 1,200.00. Vase: Gibson Girl (Mary), 9½"h., RS Suhl. $1,400.00 – 1,600.00. Vase: Fall season, reticulated base, 9"h., RSP (rm). $1,000.00 – 1,400.00. Vase: Melon Boys (dice throwers), ornate handles, 9½"h., jeweled, pedestal, RSP (rm). $1,600.00 – 2,000.00. Vase: Melon Boys (dice throwers), ornate handles, red trim, jeweled, 10"h., RSP (rm). $1,800.00 – 2,200.00.

Row 3. Cracker jar/lid: The Cage/Peace Bringing Plenty, red trim, RSP (rm). $2,300.00 – 2,500.00. Cracker jar/lid: Swan, hand-painted, 6½"h., unmk. $800.00 – 1,200.00. Cracker jar/lid: Melon Boys (melon eaters), black trim, 5½"h. x 6"w., RSP (rm). $2,300.00 – 2,500.00.

Row 4. Plate: Gibson Girl (Gretta, yellow hat), gold trim, 8"d., RSP (rm). $2,000.00 – 2,500.00. Plate: Fall season, open-handled cake plate, 9¾"d., RSP (rm). $1,000.00 – 1,200.00. Bowl: Madame Recamier, ftd., 7¼"d., unmk. $900.00 – 1,200.00

Row 1. Vase: Black swans, bulbous, 6"h., RS Poland (red). $800.00 – 1,200.00. Vase: Lions, bulbous, 6"h., unmk. $2,000.00 – $2,500.00. Bun Tray: Ostriches, open-handled, 13"l., RSP (rm). $3,000.00 – $3,500.00.
Row 2. Vase: Hummingbirds, 9"h., unmk. $1,600.00 – 2,000.00. Vase: Ostriches, 9"h., unmk. $1,600.00 – 2,000.00. Vase: Ostriches, 13"h., unmk. $3,500.00 – 4,000.00. Vase: Parrots, 10¾"h., unmk. $1,800.00 – 2,200.00. Vase: Tigers, 9"h., unmk. $2,000.00 – 2,500.00.
Row 3. Bowl: Chinese pheasants, 10½"d., unmk. $1,600.00 – 2,000.00. Compote: Bird of paradise, pedestal skirt, 7"l. x 4"w., unmk. $800.00 – 1,200.00. Bowl: Crown cranes, 10½"d., unmk. $4,000.00 – 5,000.00.
Row 4. Vase: Ostriches, ring handles, 4"h., RSP (rm). $1,200.00 – 1,600.00. Vase: Ostriches, ftd., 8"h., unmk. $1,600.00 – 2,000.00. Vase: Hummingbirds, ring handles, 6"h., unmk. $1,200.00 – 1,600.00. Sugar/lid: Chinese pheasants, 4"h., RS Germany. $250.00 – 400.00. Creamer: Pheasants, 3½"h., RS Germany (green). $250.00 – 400.00.

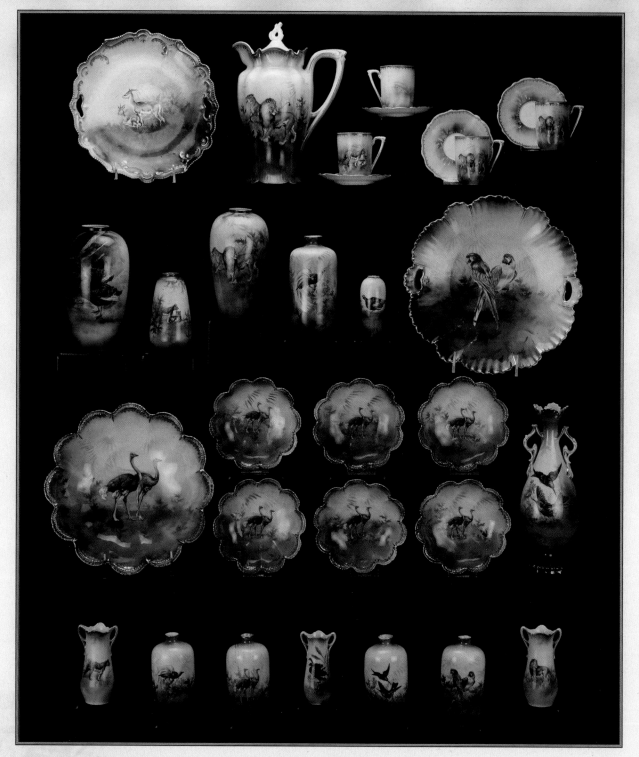

Row 1. Plate: Gazelles, open-handled, 9¾"d., RSP (rm). $3,500.00 – 4,000.00. Chocolate pot/lid: Lions (only one known), 10"h., RSP (rm). $6,000.00 +. Cups/saucers: Lion and tiger (goes with chocolate pot), cup (3"h.), saucer (4¼"d.), RSP (rm). $1,000.00 – 1,500.00 each.
Row 2. Vase: Black geese, 7½"h., RS Poland. $600.00 – 800.00. Vase: Tiger (single), 4"h., unmk. $1,000.00 – 1,500.00. Vase: Lion, 6½"h., unmk. $1,400.00 – 1,800.00. Vase: Bird of paradise, 6"h., unmk. $600.00 – 1,000.00. Vase: Turkey, 3¾"h., unmk. $400.00 – 600.00. Plate: Parrots, handles, 10½"h., RSP (rm). $1,500.00 – 2,000.00.
Row 3. Berry set: Bowl: Ostriches, brown tones, 9½"d., RSP (rm). $3,000.00. Dessert bowls (six): Ostriches, 5¼"d., RSP (rm). $1,500.00 – 2,000.00. Set, $5,500.00. Vase: Hummingbirds, ornate handle, pedestal, 9¼"h., unmk. $1,600.00 – 1,800.00.
Row 4. Vase: Tiger (single), miniature, pastel white, handles, 4"h., unmk. $1,000.00 – 1,500.00. Vase: Bird of paradise, miniature, brown tones, 4½"h., unmk. $600.00 – 800.00. Vase: Ostriches, miniature, brown tones, 4½"h., unmk. $600.00 – 800.00. Vase: Black geese, miniature, brown tones, 3¾"h., unmk. $500.00 – 700.00. Vase: Hummingbirds, miniature, brown tones, 4½"h., unmk. $600.00 – 800.00. Vase: Parrots, miniature, brown tones, 4½"h., unmk. $500.00 – 700.00. Vase: Lion (single), pastel white, handles, 4"h., unmk. $1,000.00 – 1,500.00.

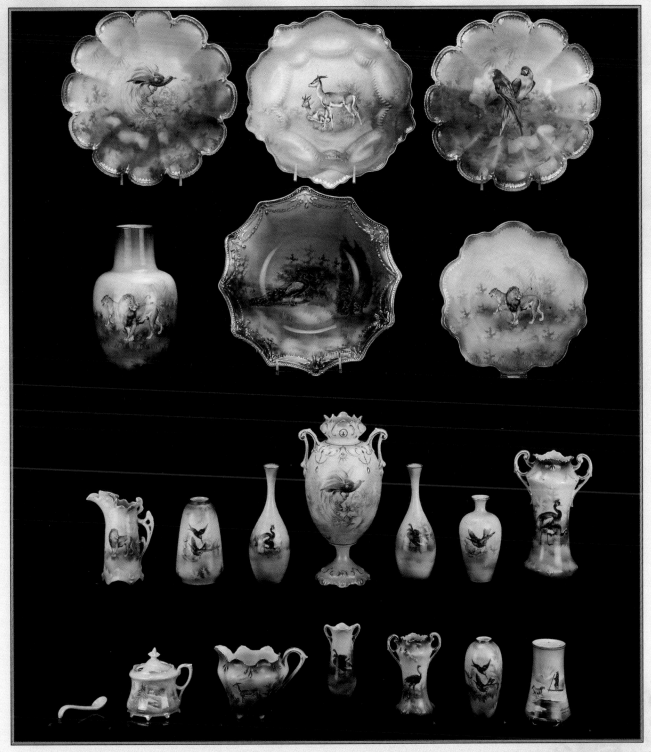

Row 1. Bowl: Bird of paradise, 11"d., RSP (rm). $3,500.00 – 4,500.00. Bowl: Gazelles, 11"d., RSP (rm). $5,000.00 – 6,000.00. Bowl: Parrots, 11"d., RSP (rm). $3,500.00 – 4,500.00.

Row 2. Vase: Lions, 9"h., RSP (rm). $4,000.00 – 5,000.00. Bowl: Peacock, 11"d., RSP (rm). $2,000.00 – 2,500.00. Plate: Lions, 8½"d., RSP (rm). $2,500.00 – 3,500.00.

Row 3. Ewer: Lion (single), 5"h., unmk. $1,600.00 – 2,000.00. Vase: Hummingbirds, 4"h., unmk. $500.00 – 600.00. Vase: Crown cranes, 6"h., RS Poland (rm). $600.00 – 800.00. Vase: Bird of paradise, white pastel, satin, handles, 9"h., RSP (rm). $2,500.00 – 3,000.00. Vase: Black geese, 6"h., unmk. $600.00 – 800.00. Vase: Hummingbird (single), 4"h., unmk. $600.00 – 800.00. Vase: Crown cranes, handles, 6¾"h., RS Poland (rm). $800.00 – 1,000.00.

Row 4. Mustard/spoon: Snowbird, 3¼"h., unmk. $300.00 – 350.00. Syrup: Gazelle (single), 3¼"h., RSP (rm). $1,500.00 – 2,000.00. Vase: Black geese, 3¼"h., RS Poland (rm). $600.00 – 700.00. Vase: Ostrich, handles, 4¼"h., unmk. $700.00 – 900.00. Vase: Hummingbirds, 4½"h., unmk. $600.00 – 800.00. Hatpin holder: Admiral Perry (dog, igloo, bear, man), 3¾"h., RSP (Germany over mark). $4,000.00 – 5,000.00.

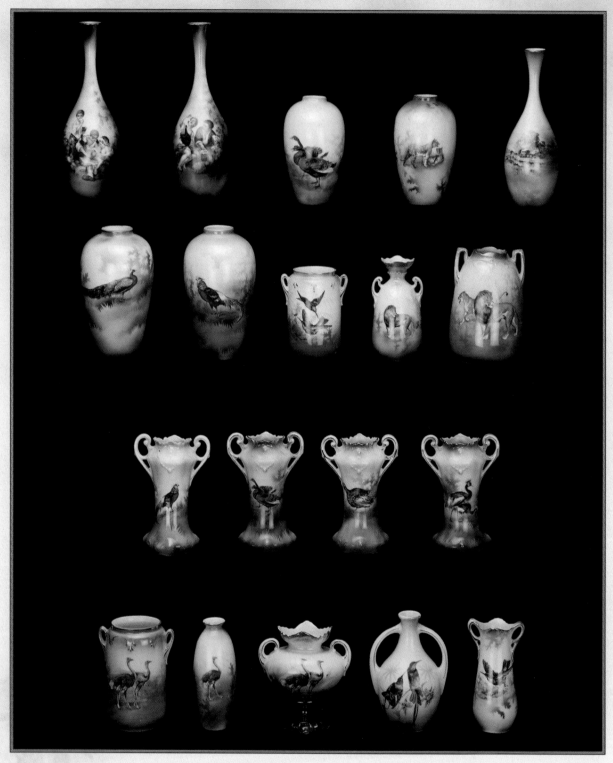

Row 1. Vase: Melon Boys (dice players), 7"h., unmk. $700.00 – 800.00. Vase: Melon Boys (melon eaters), 7"h., unmk. $700.00 – 800.00. Vase: Black geese, 4"h., R. S. Poland. $600.00 – 700.00. Vase: Tigers, 4½"h., RSP (rm). $1,000.00 – 1,500.00. Vase: Farm scene, 6¼"h., R. S. Poland. $200.00 – 250.00.

Row 2. Vase: Peacock, 5"h., unmk. $400.00 – 500.00. Vase: Chinese pheasant, 5"h., unmk. $400.00 – 500.00. Vase: Hummingbirds, handles, 3½"h., RSP (rm). $450.00 – 600.00. Vase: Lion, handles, 4"h., RSP (rm). $1,400.00 – 1,600.00. Vase: Lions, handles, 4½"h., RSP (rm). $1,400.00 – 1,600.00.

Row 3. Vase: Chinese pheasant, handles, 4¼"h., R. S. Poland. $500.00 – 700.00. Vase: Black geese, handles, 4¼"h., R. S. Poland. $500.00 – 700.00. Vase: Turkey, handles, 4½"h., RSP (rm). $500.00 – 700.00. Vase: Crown cranes, handles, 4½"h., R. S. Poland. $600.00 – 800.00.

Row 4. Vase: Ostriches, handles, 3½"h., RSP (rm). $600.00 – 1,000.00. Vase: Ostrich (single), 3½"h., unmk. $600.00 – 1,000.00. Vase: Ostriches, handles, 3⅜"h., unmk. $600.00 – 1,000.00. Vase: Hummingbirds, handles, 4"h., RSP (rm). (Decal also seen on Royal Bayreuth). $500.00 – 600.00. Vase: Hummingbird, handles, 4"h., unmk. $500.00 – 600.00.

Miniatures

Row 1. Ewer: Mill scene, handles, 5¾"h., unmk. $800.00 – 1,000.00. Ewer: Parrots, 5¾"h., unmk. $800.00 – 1,000.00. Vase: Countess Potocka, handles, 3⅜"h., unmk. $700.00 – 900.00. Vase: Chinese pheasants, handles, 3½"h., R. S. Poland. $400.00 – 600.00. Vase: Chinese pheasants, handles, 4"h., unmk. $400.00 – 600.00.
Row 2. Vase: Black swans, 4"h., unmk. $800.00 – 1,000.00. Vase: Swans/pine trees, 4"h., RSP (rm). $400.00 – 500.00. Vase: Crown cranes, 4"h., unmk. $600.00 – 800.00. Vase: Bird of paradise, 4"h., unmk. $600.00 – 800.00. Vase: Turkey, 4"h., RSP (rm). $500.00 – 700.00.
Row 3. Salt shaker: Parrot, 2½"h., RSP (rm). $800.00 – 1,000.00. Salt shaker: Hummingbird, 2½"h., RSP (rm). $800.00 – 1,000.00. Mustard/lid/spoon: Ostrich, 3"h., RSP (rm). $1,200.00 – 2,000.00. Mustard/lid/spoon: Tiger, 3"h., RSP (rm). $2,400.00 – 2,800.00.

Vase, gazelles, pedestal, ornate handles, 7¾"h. RSP (rm). $3,000.00 – 4,000.00.

Vase, lions, white satin, ornate handles. $3,000.00 – 4,000.00.

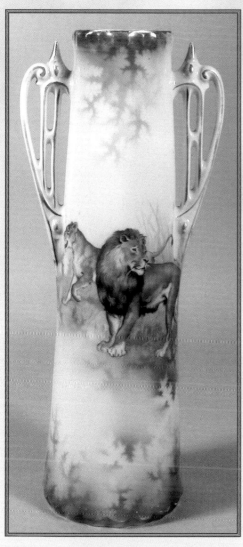

Vase, lions, ornate handles, 10¾"h., unmk. $1,200.00 – 1,600.00.

Vase, lions, white satin, 11½"h., RSP (rm). $8,000.00 – 10,000.00.

Creamer/sugar, runner duck. Creamer (3"h. x 3½"w.), sugar (3½"h. x 4¼"w.), RSP (rm). $400.00 – 600.00.

Powder box/lid, pheasant, white satin, 4¼"d x 2"h., RSP (rm). $400.00 – 500.00.

Vase, crown cranes, handles, gold trim, 12"h. (Poland China). $2,000.00 – 2,400.00.

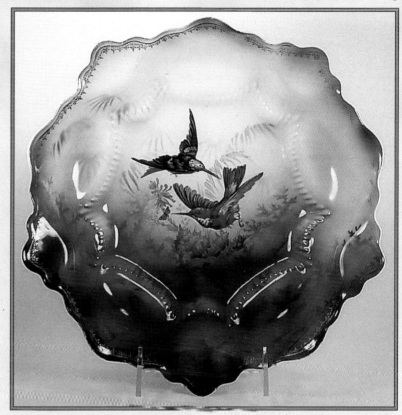

Bowl, hummingbirds, brown tones, 11"d., unmk. $3,000.00 – 3,500.00.

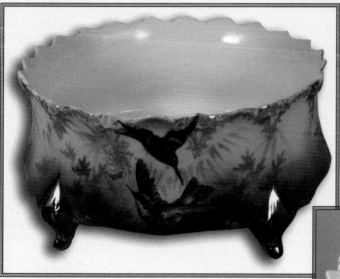

Fernery, parrots/hummingbirds (double scene), ftd., brown tones, 6½"d. x 3¾"w. RSP (rm). Front and back views. $2,800.00 – 3,200.00.

Bowl, swans in four medallions, bluebirds border, tapestry, 10"d., RSP (rm).
$900.00 – 1,200.00.

Bowl, carnation mold, hanging basket, silver satin finish, 12"d., RSP (rm).
$1,200.00 – 1,600.00.

Bowl, carnation mold, gold/light blue trim, satin finish, 15"d., RSP (rm) $4,500.00+.

Bowl, leaf mold, floral, gold leaf and border, satin finish, 10"d., 3"h., RSP (rm). $800.00 – 1,000.00.

Plate, leaf mold, floral, gold trim, 11"d., RSP (rm). $800.00 – 1,000.00.

Plate, floral, gold panels/pink roses and trim, 10"d., RSP (rm). $450.00 – 600.00.

Plate, rosebud mold, floral, aqua blue, gold trim, 8½"d., unmk. $200.00 – 300.00.

Bowl, five-panel daisy mold, floral, turquoise, 10"d., RSP (rm). $400.00 – 600.00.

Bowl, floral, lily mold, oval, light blue, 12½"l. x 8"w., unmk. $400.00 – 600.00.

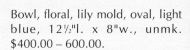

Bowl, daisy mold, floral, yellow and blue, 10"d. (Wheelock). $400.00 – 600.00.

Plate, floral, gold and green tiffany border, 10"d., RSP (rm). $500.00 – 700.00.

Bowl, floral, eight panels with four large peach roses, tiffany and gold trim, 10¾"d., RSP (rm). $500.00 – 700.00.

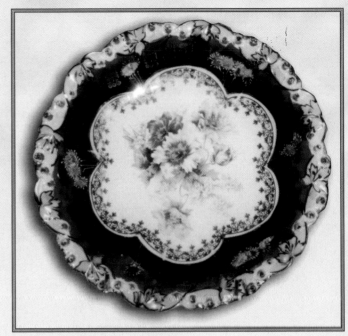

Plate, rosebud mold, floral, purple tiffany, 8½"d., RSP (rm). $200.00 – 350.00.

Plate, point/clover mold, floral, pink satin finish, 10½"d., RSP (rm). $400.00 – 600.00.

Bowl, floral, wheat in six panels, gold trim, 10"d., RSP (rm). $400.00 – 600.00.

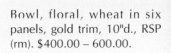

Bowl, floral, five medallions with pink roses, gold trim, 11"d. x 3½"h., RSP (rm). $450.00 – 650.00.

Relish, point/clover mold, floral, red tiffany border, opal jewels, 13½"l. x 6¾"w., RSP (rm). $400.00 – 500.00.

Bowl, floral, wheat in six panels, red border with gold trim, 10"d., RSP (rm). $350.00 – 500.00.

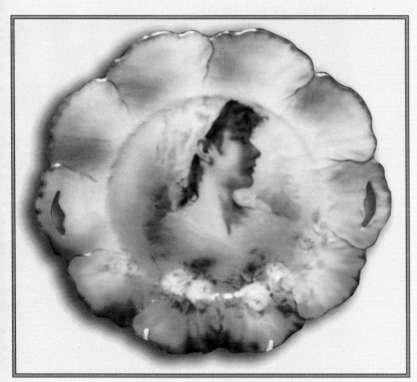

Plate, morning glory mold, floral, "Tillie," open-handled, 9½"d., RSP (rm). $700.00 – 900.00.

Plate, point/clover mold, floral, six black petals with opal jewels, gold trim, 9"d., RSP (rm). $400.00 – 600.00.

Chocolate pot/lid, Summer season, tiffany, gold ball feet and trim, 9"h., RSP (rm). $5,000.00+.

Chocolate set, Summer season, iris mold, pink with gold trim, RSP (rm), chocolate pot/lid (10¼"h.), cup (3"h.), saucer (4½"d.). $16,000.00+ set.

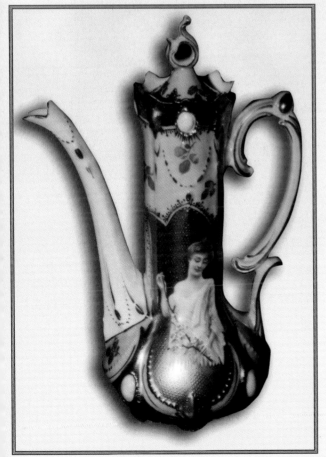

Demitasse coffeepot/lid, Spring season in gold tapestry, jewels, ornate handle, gold trim, 9½"h., RSP (rm). $5,000.00+.

149

Row 1. Bowl: Winter season, six medallions, Madame LeBrun, Countess Potocka, and Madame Recamier, 10½"d., RSP (rm). $3,000.00 – 3,500.00. Bowl: Summer season, six medallions, Madame LeBrun, Countess Potocka, and Madame Recamier, 10½"d., RSP (rm). $3,000.00 – 3,500.00. Bowl: Spring season, fleur-de-lis, bowl-in-bowl, red trim, 10½"d., unmk. $2,500.00 – 3,000.00.
Row 2. Chocolate pot/lid: Winter season, iris mold, satin, 10½"h., RSP (rm). $2,800.00 – 3,000.00. Plate: Summer season, six medallions, gold background, open-handled, 10½"d., unmk. $3,000.00 – 3,500.00. Vase: Fall season, ornate handle, ftd., 9"h., RSP (rm). $1,000.00 – 1,500.00. Cracker jar/lid: Winter season, iris mold, satin, 7"h., RSP (rm). $1,500.00 – 1,800.00.
Row 3. Bowl and dessert: Winter season, iris mold, satin, bowl (10½"), dessert (5½"), RSP (rm). $3,500.00+ set. Syrup/underplate: Winter season, iris mold, satin, syrup (4¾"h.), underplate (6"d.), RSP (rm). $1,000.00 – 1,500.00. Coffeepot/lid: Winter season, iris mold, satin, RSP (rm). $2,800.00 – 3,000.00. Cup/saucer: Winter season, iris mold. $400.00 – 600.00. Tankard: Summer season, carnation mold, satin, 13"h., RSP (rm). $8,000.00 – 10,000.00.
Row 4. Dresser tray: Spring season, iris mold, open-handled, 11"l., RSP (rm). $2,500.00 – 2,800.00. Dresser tray: Winter season, iris mold, open-handled, 11"l., RSP (rm). $2,000.00 – 2,500.00.

Tea set, Summer season, ball feet, tiffany, RSP (rm). $4,000.00+.

Bowl, portrait medallions (two Spring season and two Fall season), 10¼"d., RSP (rm). $2,500.00 – 3,000.00.

Bowl, Fall and Winter seasons, very ornate, gold trim, 10¼"d. x 4"h., RSP (rm). $2,500.00 – 3,000.00. Goes with bowl shown below.

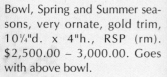

Bowl, Spring and Summer seasons, very ornate, gold trim, 10¼"d. x 4"h., RSP (rm). $2,500.00 – 3,000.00. Goes with above bowl.

Plate, dual scene, Summer season, cottage scene, iris mold, 8¾"d., RSP (rm). $800.00 – 1,200.00.

Vase, Spring season, tiffany, ornate gold handles and trim, ftd., 8½"h., RSP (rm). $900.00 – 1,200.00.

Vase, Fall season, pedestal base, ornate gold handles and trim, 9"h. x 4½"w., RSP (rm). $700.00 – 900.00.

Vase, Spring season, pedestal base, ornate gold handles and trim, 8¾"h. x 4½"w., RSP (rm). $700.00 – 900.00.

Vase, Winter season, ornate handles and trim, 9½"h. x 4¾"w., RSP (rm). $700.00 – 900.00.

Row 1. Bowl: (Row 1 and first bowl of Row 2 make complete set of four seasons.) Summer season, iris mold, satin, 10½"d., RSP (rm). $10,000.00 set of four. Bowl: Fall season, iris mold, satin, 10½"d., RSP (rm). $2,500.00 – 3,000.00. Bowl: Winter season, iris mold, satin, 10½"d., RSP (rm). $1,800.00 – 2,200.00.

Row 2. Bowl: (with Row 1) Spring season, iris mold, satin, 10½"d., RSP (rm). $2,500.00 – 3,000.00. Plate: Spring season (keyhole), 9"d., RSP (rm). $1,200.00 – 1,400.00. Plate: Winter season (keyhole), 9"d., RSP (rm). $900.00 – 1,200.00.

Row 3. Plate: Fall season (keyhole), 9"d., RSP (rm). $1,200.00 – 1,400.00. Plate: Summer season (keyhole), 9"d., RSP (rm). $1,400.00 – 1,800.00. Plate: Fall season (keyhole), open-handled cake plate, black trim, 9½"d., RSP (rm). $1,800.00 – 2,200.00.

Row 4. Chocolate set: Spring season, tiffany, ball feet, pot (9"h.), cup (3"h.), saucer (4½"d.), RSP (rm). $8,000.00 – 12,000.00 set. Tea set: Spring season, tiffany, ball feet, pot (4½"h.), sugar/lid (4"h.), creamer (3"h.), RSP (rm). $4,000.00 – 6,000.00.

Row 1. Plate: Fall season, iris mold, open-handled, 10½"d, RSP (rm). $2,200.00 – 2,700.00. Plate: Winter season, iris mold, open-handled, 10½"d., RSP (rm). $1,800.00 – 2,400.00. Plate: Summer season, iris mold, open-handled, 10½"d., RSP (rm). $2,500.00 – 3,000.00.
Row 2. Plate: Summer season, carnation mold, open-handled, 10½"d., RSP (rm). $2,800.00 – 3,200.00. Cracker jar/lid: Summer season, silver lid and handle, 7½"h., RSP (rm). $2,800.00 – 3,200.00. Plate: Fall season, carnation mold, open-handled, 10½"d., RSP (rm). $2,400.00 – 3,000.00.
Row 3. Tankard: Summer season, carnation mold, 11"h., RSP (rm). $8,500.00 – 12,000.00. Sauce dishes: Spring, Summer, Fall and Winter seasons, carnation mold, 5½"d., RSP (rm). $600.00 – 800.00 each.

Row 1. Bowl: Season medallions, floral center, 10½"d., RSP (rm). $2,500.00 – 3,000.00. Bowl: Season medallions, floral center, 10½"d., RSP (rm). $2,500.00 – 3,000.00. Bowl: Season medallions, floral center, 10½"d., RSP (rm). $2,500.00 – 3,000.00.
Row 2. Bowl: Spring season, 10½"d., RSP (rm). $2,500.00 – 3,000.00. Bowl: Summer/cottage scene, 10½"d., RSP (rm). $2,500.00 – 3,000.00.
Row 3. Bowl: Fall season, iris mold, 10½"d., RSP (rm). $2,500.00 – 3,000.00. Tankard: Summer, very ornate, ftd., 16"h., RSP (rm). $10,000.00 – 15,000.00. Bowl: Spring season, 10½"d., RSP (rm). $2,500.00 – 3,000.00.
Row 4. Plate: Fall "Charmer," 8½"d., RSP (rm). $1,800.00 – 2,000.00. Plate: Summer "Charmer," 8½"d., RSP (rm). $2,000.00 – 3,000.00. Plate: Spring "Charmer," 8½"d., RSP (rm). $1,800.00 – 2,000.00.

Row 1. Chocolate pot/lid: Fall season, iris mold, satin, 10"h., RSP (rm). $3,000.00 – 4,000.00. Plate: Summer season, carnation mold, open-handled cake plate, RSP (rm). $3,000.00 – 3,500.00. Cup/saucer: Summer season, carnation mold, satin, cup (3"h.), saucer (4¼"d.), unmk. $500.00 – 700.00. Chocolate pot/lid: Summer season, carnation mold, satin, 10¼"h., RSP (rm). $3,000.00 – 4,000.00.
Row 2. Bowl: Summer season, carnation mold, satin, 11"d., RSP (rm). $3,000.00 – 3,500.00. Chocolate pot/lid: Spring season, iris mold, satin, 10"h., RSP (rm). $3,000.00 – 4,000.00. Bowl: Fall season, carnation mold, satin, 11"d., RSP (rm). $3,000.00 – 3,500.00.
Row 3. Chocolate pot/lid: Winter season, iris mold, satin, 10"h., RSP (rm). $2,800.00 – 3,000.00. Bowl: Winter season, carnation mold, satin, 11"d., RSP (rm). $3,000.00 – 3,500.00. Chocolate pot/lid: Summer season, iris mold, 10"h., RSP (rm). $3,500.00 – 4,500.00.

Tankard, Madame LeBrun (blue ribbon), skirted, floral, gold trim, 15"h., RSP (rm). $3,500.00+.

Biscuit jar/lid, Madame Recamier, cobalt, skirted, 7"h., unmk. $1,500.00 – 1,800.00.

Cracker jar/lid, Madame LeBrun in gold tapestry frame, jewels, gold trim, 4½"h., RSP (rm). $2,500.00 – 3,000.00.

Vase, Madame LeBrun portrait, Greek Key, ftd., ornate handles, gold trim, 9"h., RSP (rm). $1,500.00 – 1,800.00.

Bowl, Madame Recamier, pastels, 10¼"d. x 3"h., RSP (rm). $1,600.00 – 1,800.00.

Bowl, Countess Potocka, gold, 9"d. x 2½"h. (RSP). $1,600.00 – 1,800.00.

Bowl, Madame Recamier, colonial scenes in five medallions, 11"d. x 3½"h. (RSP). $2,500.00 – 3,000.00.

Bowl, Madame Recamier, green/gold, ftd., 7¼"d. x 2½"h. (RSP). $800.00 – 1,000.00.

Set of bowls, top: Countess Potocka and Madame Recamier. Bottom, both Madame LeBrun, unmk. $1,800.00 – 2,200.00 each.

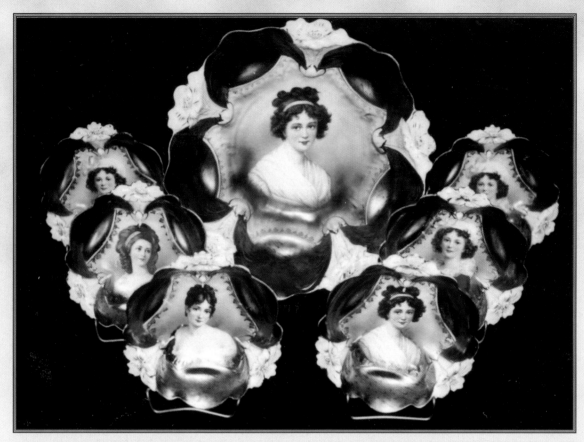

Berry set. Large bowl (Madame LeBrun), 10½"d., unmk. Dessert bowls (Madame LeBrun, Countess Potocka, and Madame Recamier), 5¾"d., unmk. $4,000.00+ set.

Chocolate set. Madame LeBrun portrait. Chocolate pot: jewels, gold trim, tiffany, RSP (rm). Cup, 3"h. Saucer, 4"d. Set (six cups & six saucers), $15,000.00+.

Dresser tray, Countess Potocka, 11½"l. x 7"w., unmk. $1,200.00 – 1,500.00.

GIBSON GIRLS
Red hat – Evelyn
Blue hat w/blue ribbon, facing right – Mary
Yellow hat – Gretta
Dark blue hat, looking forward – Emma
Ecru hat w/pink flowers – Sally
Blue hat looking right – Gina

Gibson Girl party fan, paper, value unknown.

Gibson Girls
Mark: Red flying horse, Prussia, hand-painted

Row 1. Plate: Emma, gold rim, 8½"d. $800.00 – 1,200.00. Plate: Sally, gold rim, 8½"d. $800.00 – 1,200.00. Plate: Mary, gold rim, 8½"d. $800.00 – 1,200.00.

Row 2. Plate: Gretta, gold rim, 8½"d. $800.00 – 1,200.00. Bowl: Gina, 10½"d. $1,200.00 – 1,600.00. Plate: Evelyn, gold rim, 8½"d. $800.00 – 1,200.00.

Row 3. Sugar/lid: Evelyn, pedestal, 5"h. $300.00 – 350.00. Creamer: Emma, pedestal, 4½"h. $300.00 – 350.00. Bowl: Sally, gold rim, 8"d. $800.00 – 1,200.00. Plate: Gina, gold rim, 8½"h. $800.00 – 1,200.00.

Row 4. Saucer: Evelyn, 5"d. $400.00 – 700.00. Saucer: Sally, 5"d. $400.00 – 700.00. Saucer: Emma, 5"d. $400.00 – 700.00. Saucer: Gina, 5"d. $400.00 – 700.00.

Row 1. Bowl: Parrots, 11"d., RSP (rm). $3,500.00 – 4,500.00. Bowl: Four Madame LeBrun medallions, 50th Anniversary in the center, 10¼"d., RSP (rm). $2,500.00 – 3,000.00. Bowl: "Belles of Linden," 11"d., RSP (rm). $7,000.00 – 8,000.00.
Row 2. Gibson Girl set: Large plate and six small plates. $3,500.00 – 4,000.00 set. Fan with Gibson Girl paper party decoration, value unknown.
Row 3. Candle lamps: Owls, 5¼"h., RSG (green). $350.00 – 400.00 each. Covered box/lid: Admiral Perry scene on base and lid, bone shaped, RSP (rm). $8,000.00 – 9,000.00. Bowl/underplate: Admiral Perry scene, bowl (8"d.), underplate (9½"d.), "Midst snow and ice," RSP (rm). $12,000.00 – 14,000.00. Cake set: Snowbirds, lg. plate, open-handled, 10½"d., RSG (green). Sm. plate, 6¼"d., RSG (green). $2,200.00 – 2,600.00, set of six.

Row 1. Vase: Four maidens, 14½"h., R.S. Suhl. $2,400.00 – 2,800.00. Bowl: Diana the huntress, floral, gold trim, 10¼"h., unmk. $1,400.00 – 1,600.00. Vase: Reverse side of four maidens, R. S. Suhl. $2,400.00 – 2,800.00.
Row 2. Plate: Snipe scene, floral, 8¼"d., RSP (rm). $900.00 – 1,200.00. Plate: Cove scene (man on mountain), scenic medallions, black trim, 7½"d., RSP (rm). $1,500.00 – 2,000.00.
Row 3. Plate: Summer "Charmer," 8½"d., RSP (rm). $1,800.00 – 2,000.00. Plate: Fall "Charmer" (Apple Girl), 8½"d., RSP (rm). $2,800.00 – 3,000.00. Plate: "Winter "Charmer," 8½"d., RSP (rm). $1,700.00 – 2,000.00.
Row 4. Vase: Spring season, ornate handles, 4½"h., RSP (rm). $600.00 – 900.00. Vase: Fall season, three-handled, ftd. base, 6½"h., RSP (rm). $2,000.00 – 2,500.00. Egg: Hummingbirds, ftd., 6"l. x 3"h., RSP (rm). $1,000.00 – 1,500.00.

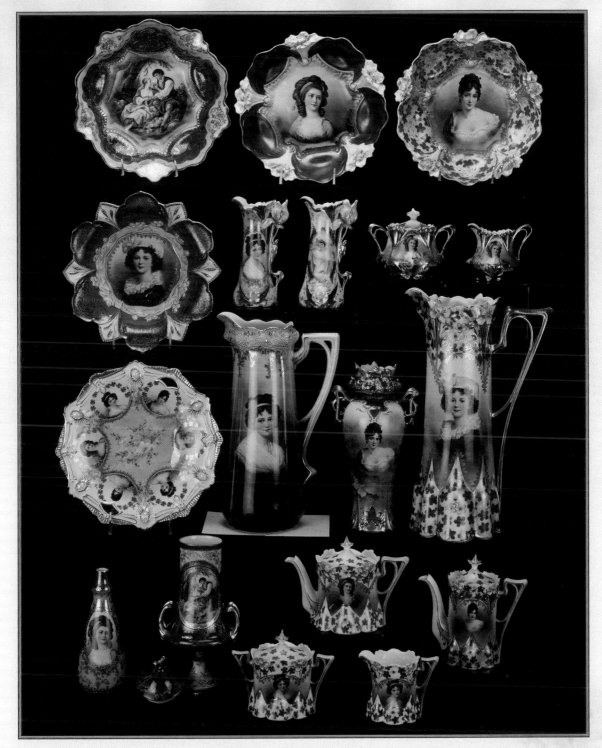

Row 1. Bowl: The Cage, red trim, 11"d., unmk. $2,000.00 – 2,400.00. Bowl: Countess Potocka, lily mold, 10½"d., unmk. $1,800.00 – 2,200.00. Bowl: Madame Recamier, 10½"d., unmk. $1,800.00 – 2,200.00.

Row 2. Bowl: Madame LeBrun (white hair), bowl-in-bowl, six petals, green tiffany, 10½"d., unmk. $1,800.00 – 2,200.00. Ewer: Madame LeBrun (ribbon), ornate iris handle, tiffany, 7"h., unmk. $2,500.00 – 2,800.00. Ewer: Summer season, ornate iris handle, tiffany, 7"h., unmk. $2,500.00 – 2,800.00. Sugar/lid: Countess Potocka, red trim, 4½"h., gold mark. $400.00 – 500.00. Creamer: Countess Potocka, red trim, 3½"h., unmk. $400.00 – 500.00.

Row 3. Plate: Floral with (six) medallions (Madame LeBrun, Countess Potocka, Madame Recamier), jeweled, 10½"d., unmk. $1,800.00 – 2,200.00. Tankard: Madame LeBrun (ribbon), 13"h., unmk. $1,800.00 – 2,200.00. Vase: Madame Recamier, ornate handles, red, gold trim, unmk. $1,800.00 – 2,200.00. Tankard: Madame LeBrun (white hat), skirted, gold, 15"h., RSP (rm). $3,500.00 +.

Row 4. Vase: Countess Potocka, stick spout, green tiffany, gold trim, unmk. $600.00 – 800.00. Urn/lid: The Cage, red, gold handles, pedestal, 11"h., RSP (rm). $1,500.00 – 2,000.00. Sugar/lid: Madame LeBrun (ribbon), gold handles, skirted, 4½"h., unmk. Teapot/lid: Countess Potocka, gold-handled, skirted, 5½"h., unmk. Creamer: Madame LeBrun (ribbon), gold handles, skirted, 3½"h., unmk. Set (sugar, teapot, and creamer) $1,400.00 – 1,600.00. Demitasse pot: Madame Recamier, gold handle, skirted, 6½"h., unmk. $800.00 – 1,200.00.

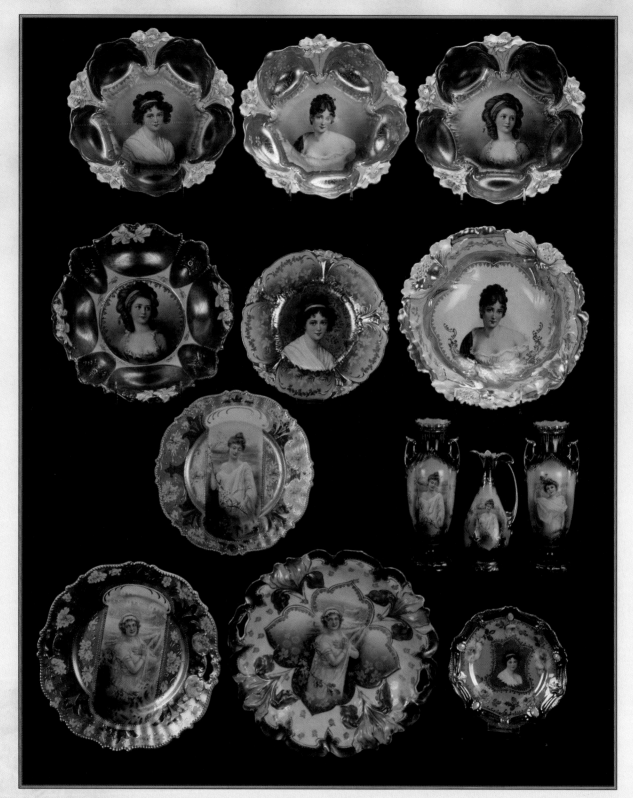

Row 1. Bowl: Madame LeBrun (blue ribbon), tiffany, 10¼"d., unmk. $1,800.00 – 2,200.00. Bowl: Madame Recamier, gold trim, 10¼"d., unmk. $1,600.00 – 1,800.00. Bowl: Countess Potocka, green tiffany, 10¼"d., unmk. $1,800.00 – 2,200.00.

Row 2. Bowl: Countess Potocka, tiffany, 10¼"d., unmk. $1,800.00 – 2,000.00. Plate: Madame LeBrun (blue ribbon), blue shading, 8½"d., unmk. $800.00 – 1,200.00. Bowl: Madame Recamier, gold, 10½"d., unmk. $1,800.00 – 2,000.00.

Row 3. Plate: Spring season, red trim, 8¾"d., RSP (rm). $900.00 – 1,200.00. Vase: Spring season, cobalt, handles, 8"h., RSP (rm). $900.00 – 1,200.00. Ewer: Spring season, cobalt, 6"h., RSp (rm). $1,800.00 – 2,200.00. Vase: Summer season, cobalt, handles, 8"h., unmk. $1,000.00 – 1,400.00.

Row 4. Plate: Winter season, open-handled, red trim, 9¼"d., RSP (rm). $1,200.00 – 1,600.00. Plate: Winter season, open-handled, iris, green, 11"d., RSP (rm). $1,600.00 – 2,000.00. Plate: Madame LeBrun, jeweled, 6"d., RSP (rm). $700.00 – 1,000.00.

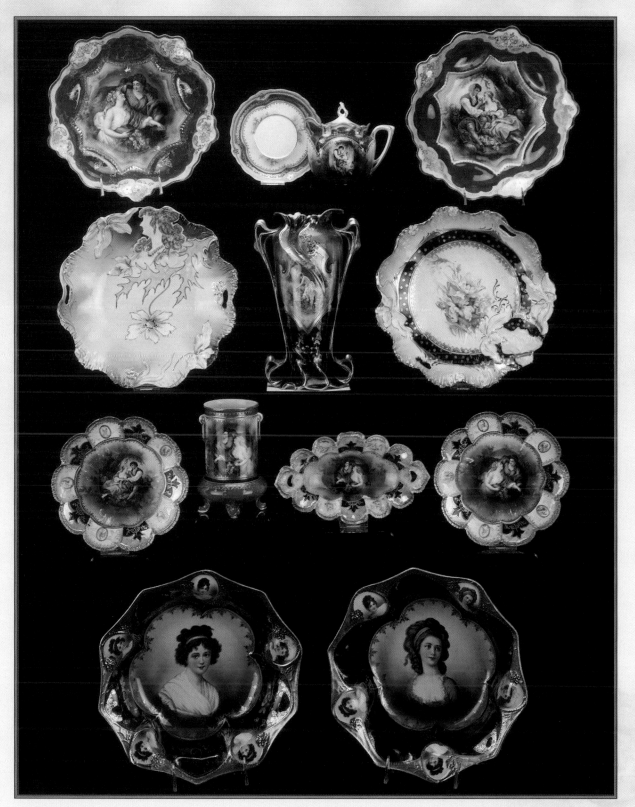

Row 1. Bowl: Peace Bringing Plenty, red trim, 11"d., RSP (rm). $2,000.00 – 2,400.00. Syrup/underplate: The Cage, red trim, syrup (5"h.), underplate (6"d.), unmk. $800.00 – 1,200.00. Bowl: The Cage, red trim, 11"d., unmk. $1,200.00 – 1,600.00.
Row 2. Plate: Hidden image, open-handled, 10½"d., unmk. $600.00 – 1,000.00. Vase: Portrait, cobalt, ornate handles, gold trim, 10½"h., Royal Colburg. $1,600.00 – 2,000.00. Plate: Hidden image, open-handled, cobalt trim, 10½"d., unmk. $800.00 – 1,200.00.
Row 3. Plate: The Cage, black trim, 6"d., $600.00 – 1,000.00. Vase: Peace Bringing Plenty, ftd., teal base, handles, unmk. $800.00 – 1,200.00. Relish: Peace Bringing Plenty, black trim, unmk. $400.00 – 800.00. Plate: Peace Bringing Plenty, black trim, 6"d., unmk. $600.00 – 1,000.00.
Row 4. Bowl: Madame LeBrun, portrait medallions, 10½"d., unmk. $2,400.00 – 3,000.00. Bowl: Countess Potocka, portrait medallions, 10½"d., unmk. $2,400.00 – 3,000.00.

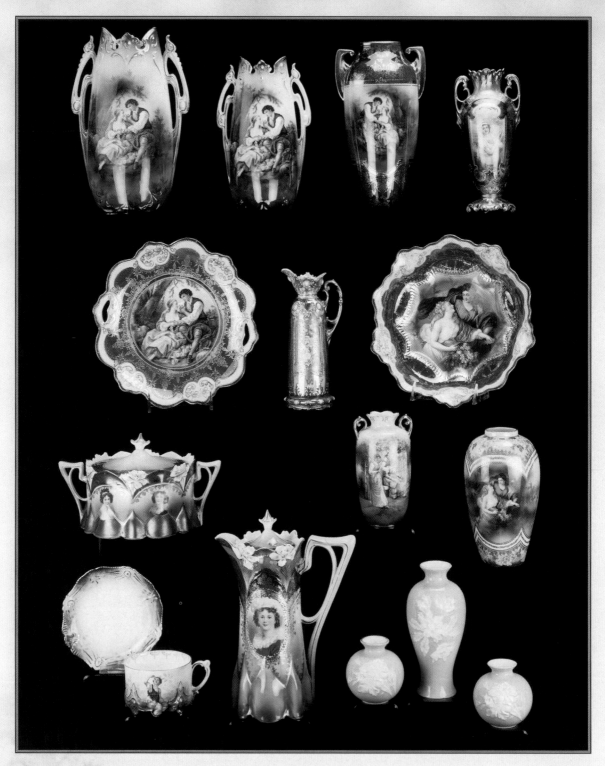

Row 1. Vase: The Cage, jeweled, ornate handles, 12"h., RSP (rm). $3,000.00 – 3,500.00. Vase: The Cage, jeweled, ornate handles, 10"h., RSP (rm). $2,000.00 – 2,500.00. Vase: The Cage, cobalt, gold handles, 11"h., (four marks), RSP (rm), beehive, Boucher, Madame LeBrun. $3,000.00 – 3,500.00. Vase: Winter season, red, pedestal, ornate gold, 9"h., RSP (rm). $1,200.00 – 1,600.00.
Row 2. Plate: The Cage, red, open-handled, 10"d., unmk. $1,000.00 – 1,400.00. Ewer: Floral, jeweled, green, 8¼"h., RSP (rm). $1,000.00 – 1,400.00. Bowl: Peace Bringing Plenty, red, 10"d., RSP (rm). $2,000.00 – 2,400.00.
Row 3. 1. Cracker jar/lid: Madame LeBrun, green tiffany, 5"h. x 6¼"w., unmk. $1,800.00 – 2,200.00. Vase: Women gathering grain, 6"h., RS Suhl. $600.00 – 800.00. Vase: Peace Bringing Plenty, floral, 7"h., signed LeBrun. $800.00 – 1,200.00.
Row 4. Cup: Melon Boy (melon eater), 2¼"h. x 3½"w., RSP (rm). $400.00 – 600.00. Saucer: Jeweled (with cup), 5½"d., unmk. $200.00 – 300.00. Chocolate pot/lid: Madame LeBrun, green, ornate flower and gold, 10"h., unmk. $1,500.00 – 2,000.00. Vase: Embossed flower, green, 3"h. (paté, clay paste used in making porcelain), 3"h. (steeple). $200.00 – 300.00. Vase: Embossed flower, green, 6½"h., paté (steeple), $200.00 – 300.00. Vase: Embossed flower, green, 3"h., paté (steeple). $200.00 – 300.00.

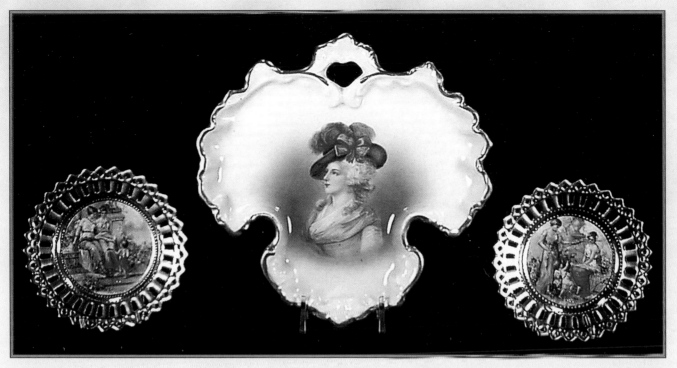

Butter pats, ladies and child, reticulated gold rim, 3¾"d (ESG). $100.00 – 150.00 each. Nappy, lady with black hat and red bow, open-handled, 7" x 6¾"l. (ESG). $100.00 – 150.00.

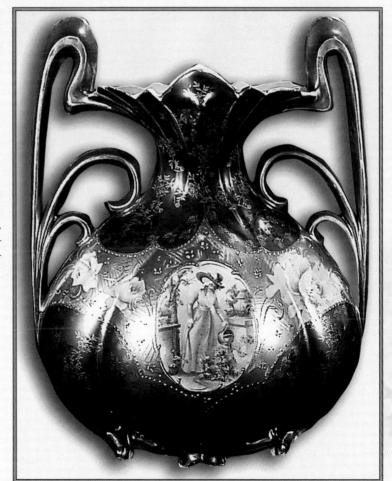

Vase, lady watering flowers, tiffany, gold trim, ornate handles, 8"h. (Royal Vienna, Germany). $1,400.00 – 1,600.00.

Plate: Diana the huntress, Victorian lady, and cherubs, cobalt and gold trim, 9¾"h. (RSP, RSG). $850.00 – 950.00. Chocolate pot: portrait of lady, reverse image, black/white, gold trim, 10"h. (RSP, RSG). $3,000.00+. Plate: Floral, cobalt, jewels, point and clover mold, 10"d. (RSG). $800.00 – 1,000.00. Mustard pot/lid: Floral, pedestal, gold trim, unmk. $200.00 – 350.00. Pin tray: Floral, red with gold trim, 5½"l. x 3¼"w. (RSG). $150.00 – 250.00.

Vase, portrait of lady (negative type), black/white, 9"h. (RS Suhl). $1,400.00 – 1,800.00.

Vase, portrait of lady, reverse side.

Desk set, horsemen scenes.
$500.00 – 700.00.

Desk set, floral, pink scroll. Pin holder/inkwell, 3½"h. x 6"w. Calendar holder, 4"h. x 2½"w. Stamp box/lid, 4"l x 1"w. Blotter, 4"l. x 3"w. Pad edges (four), 3½" x 3½". $800.00 – 1,000.00 set.

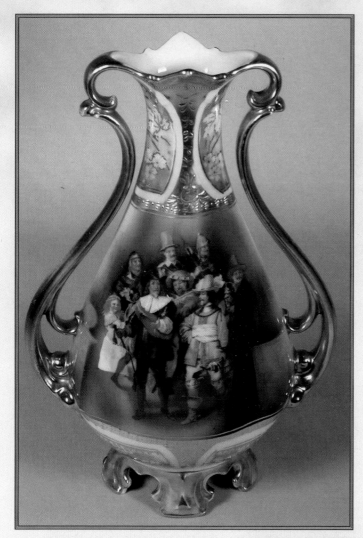

Vase, Nightwatch by Rembrandt, ftd., ornate gold handles and trim, 8¾"h. (RSG). $800.00 – 1,000.00.

Cup and saucer, The Cage, coffee cup, brown tones. Cup, 2¼"h. Saucer, 5½"d. $150.00 – 250.00.

Row 1. Bowl: Schooner, jeweled, brown tones, RSP (rm). $1,000.00 – 1,200.00. Bowl: Schooner, brown tones, RSP (rm). $800.00 – 1,000.00. Cup/saucer: Melon eaters, cup (3"h., RSP, rm), saucer (4½"d., unmk.). $300.00 – 500.00. Cup/saucer: Dice players, cup (3"h. RSP rm), saucer (4½"d., unmk). $300.00 – 500.00. Chocolate pot: Schooner, 10"h., RSP (rm). $1,200.00 – 1,600.00.
Row 2. Vase: Street scene, 8"h., RSP (rm). $600.00 – 800.00. Bowl: Castle scene, gold trim, 10½"d., RSP (rm). $800.00 – 1,000.00. Vase: Scenic, ornate handles, 12½"h., unmk. $800.00 – 1,200.00. Bowl: Scenic, sheepherder/cottage, RSG. $600.00 – 800.00.
Row 3. Urn: Bridge scene (house by stream), pedestal, 8"h., RS Poland. $600.00 – 1,000.00. Bowl: Sheepherder scene, 10½"d., RS Poland. $800.00 – 1,000.00. Hatpin holder: Windmill scene, 4½"h., RS Poland. $400.00 – 800.00. Covered box/lid: Scenic, unmk. $250.00 – 350.00. Vase: Cottage scene, handles, 12"h., RS Poland. $900.00 – 1,200.00.
Row 4. Child's set: Scenic. Cake plate (two), open-handled, 3½"d., unmk. Teapot, 5"h., unmk. Sugar/lid, 2¾"h., unmk. Creamer, 3"h., unmk. Cup (1½"h.). Saucer (2"d.), unmk. Set, $1,000.00 – 1,400.00.

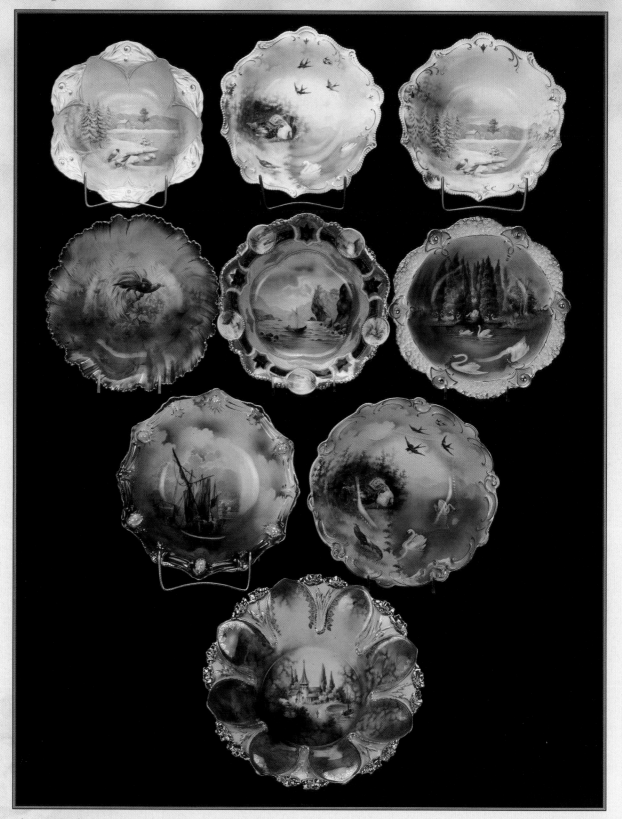

Row 1. Bowl: Snowbirds, satin, 10¾"d., RSP (rm). $1,800.00 – 2,200.00. Bowl: Barnyard (three scenes), 10¾"d., RSP (rm). $1,800.00 – 2,000.00. Bowl: Snowbirds, 10¾"d., RSP (rm). $1,800.00 – 2,000.00.
Row 2: Bowl: Bird of paradise, brown tones, 11"d., RSP (rm). $3,000.00 – 3,500.00. Bowl: Man on mountain, five medallions of sheepherder, snowbird, and cove, black trim, 11"d., RSP (rm). $4,000.00+. Bowl: Swans/pine trees, satin, 11"d., RSP (rm). $1,400.00 – 1,600.00.
Row 3. Bowl: Schooner, brown tones, jeweled, 11"d., RSP (rm). $1,000.00 – 1,400.00. Bowl: Barnyard (three scenes), 11"d., RSP (rm). $2,500.00 – 2,800.00.
Row 4. Bowl: Castle scene, eight petals, brown tones, gold trim, 11¾"d., RSP (rm). $1,400.00 – 1,600.00.

Row 1. Tankard: Barnyard scene, icicle mold, 14"h., RSP (rm). $3,200.00 – 3.500.00. Vase: Mill scene, cobalt trim, bulbous, 6"h., RSP (rm). $600.00 – 800.00. Tankard: Sheepherder, 11"h., RSP (rm). $3.800.00 – 4,200.00. Tankard: Dutch maidens, red trim, 13½"h., unmk. $1,600.00 – 2,000.00.
Row 2. Dresser tray: Black swan (on lake), open handle. $900.00 – 1,200.00. Plate: Shell or fan, open-handled, satin. $400.00 – 600.00. Plate: Black swans, open-handled, 9½"d. $800.00 – 1,200.00.
Row 3. Cup/saucer: Fishing (man, boy, and girl), cup (2¼"h.), saucer (4½"h.), R.S. Suhl, artist-signed. $250.00 – 350.00. Mustard/lid: Floral, 3"h., RSP (rm). $150.00 – 250.00. Toothpick holder: Man on mountain (cove), 2½"h., RSP (rm). $250.00 – 400.00. Mustard/lid: Winter season, iris mold, 3"h., RSP (rm). $1,700.00 – 2,000.00.
Row 4. Dresser set: Floral, long box, tall box, and small box. Set, $250.00   350.00. Bowl: Swans, reticulated, satin, 10"d., unmk. $500.00 – 800.00. Sugar/lid: Turkey, pedestal, 5½"h., Wheelock. $400.00 – 600.00. Creamer: Barnyard scene, pedestal, 5"h., Wheelock. $400.00 – 600.00.

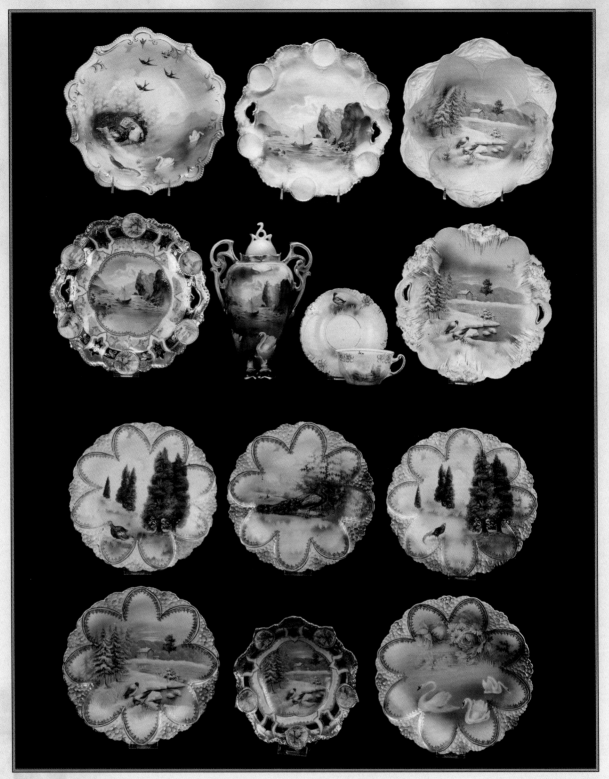

Row 1. Bowl: Three scenes (turkey, swans, and birds), 10½"d., RSP (rm). $1,800.00 – 2,000.00. Plate: Man on mountain (cove), open-handled, 10"d., RSP (rm). $800.00 – 1,000.00. Bowl: Snowbird, 10½"d., unmk. $1,200.00 – 1,600.00.
Row 2: Plate: Man on mountain (center), medallions (two snowbirds, two man on mountain, two cottage/pine trees), black trim, 9½"d., RSP (rm). $3,000.00 – 4,000.00. Urn/lid: Man on mountain, swan, lake, ornate handles, 9½"d., RSP (rm). $2,000.00 – 3,000.00. Cup/saucer: cup (man on mountain), saucer (duck), RSP (rm). $300.00 – 400.00. Plate: Snowbirds, icicle mold, open-handled, 9½"d., $1,200.00 – 1,400.00.
Row 3. Plate: Turkey/pine trees, 8½"d., RSP (rm). $600.00 – 800.00. Plate: Peacock, 8½"d., RSP (rm). $600.00 – 800.00. Plate: Chinese pheasant, 8½"d., RSP (rm). $600.00 – 800.00.
Row 4. Plate: Snowbirds, 8½"d., RSP (rm). $1,000.00 – 1,400.00. Bowl: Snowbirds, ftd. (three legs), medallions, black trim, 7"d., RSP (rm). $2,400.00 – 3.000.00. Plate: Swans/roses, 8½"d., RSP (rm). $600.00 – 800.00.

Row 1. Bowl: Swans/gazebo, satin, 10¾"d., RSP (rm). $500.00 – 800.00. Bowl: Swans, satin, 10"d., RSP (rm). $700.00 – 1,000.00. Bowl: Swans/pine trees, 10¾"d., unmk. $500.00 – 800.00.

Row 2. Bowl: Floral, green/gold, black trim, 10½"d., RSP (rm). $800.00 – 1,200.00. Bowl: Poinsettia, iris mold, satin, 10"d., Wheelock. $350.00 – 450.00. Bowl: Floral, satin, 10¾"d., RSP (rm). $300.00 – 500.00.

Row 3. Bowl: Barnyard scene, icicle mold, satin, 10¾"d., RSP (rm). $1,000.00 – 1,500.00. Bowl: Turkey/pine trees, 10½"d., RSP (rm). $600.00 – 900.00.

Row 4. Celery: Swans, open-handled, satin, 12"l., RSP (rm). $500.00 – 800.00.

Plates, Melon Boys: dice players and melon eaters, 10¼"d., green/gold, medallions, jewels, RSP (rm). $3,000.00 – 3,500.00 each.

Vases, Melon Boys, dice players and melon eaters, ftd., ornate gold handles and trim, 32 jewels, green tones, one boy on reverse side, 11"h. x 10"w., RSP (rm). $4,000.00 – 5,000.00 each. Tankard, Melon Boys, dice players, 14"h., RSP (rm). $7,000.00 – 8,500.00.

Melon Boys (Melon Eaters)

Row 1. Plate: Cobalt, open-handled, green/gold trim, blue jewels, 11½"d., RSP (rm). $4,500.00 – 5,200.00. Chocolate pot: Cobalt, gold trim, blue jewels, 10"h., RSP (rm). $5,000.00 – 5,500.00. Urn/lid: Pedestal, satin, red trim, jeweled, handled, 12"h., RSP (rm). $2,200.00 – 2,400.00.
Row 2. Sugar: Jeweled, 5"h., RSP (rm). $600.00 – 800.00. Creamer: Jeweled, 4"h., RSP (rm). $600.00 – 800.00. Plate: Open-handled, gold, 9¾"d., RSP (rm). $1,400.00 – 1,800.00.
Row 3. Plate: Jeweled, gold, 8½"d., RSP (rm). $1,200.00 – 1,400.00. Sugar: Jeweled, gold, 4½"d., RSP (rm). $600.00 – 800.00. Creamer: Jeweled, gold, 4"h., RSP (rm). $600.00 – 800.00. Teapot: Jeweled, gold, 5"h., RSP (rm). $900.00 – 1,200.00.
Row 4. Vase: Red, handled, 8"h., RSP (rm). $800.00 – 1,200.00. Vase: Jeweled, ftd., ornate, 7"h., RSP (rm). $2,500.00 – 3,000.00. Vase: Jeweled, ftd., 9"h., RSP (rm). $1,400.00 – 1,800.00.

Melon Boys (Dice Players)

Row 1. Plate: Cobalt, open-handled cake plate, blue jewels, 10¼"d., RSP (rm). $4,500.00 – 5,200.00. Vase: Red trim, jeweled, 10½"d., unmk. $2,000.00 – 2,500.00. Plate: Red, open-handled, 11"d., RSP. $2,000.00 – 2,500.00.

Row 2. Ewer: Jeweled. 9¼"h., RSP (rm). $1,800.00 – 2,200.00. Vase: Jeweled, red, pedestal, handles, 8"h., unmk. $1,500.00 – 1,800.00. Vase: Jeweled, pedestal, handles, 8"h., RSP (rm). $1,200.00 – 1,500.00. Vase: Jeweled, pedestal, ornate handles, gold ribbon, 8"h., RSP (rm). $2,000.00 – 2,500.00.

Row 3. Cracker jar/lid: 7"h., RSP (rm). $2,500.00 – 3,000.00. Vase: Jeweled, gold trim, handles, 6"h., RSP (rm). $1,000.00 – 1,200.00. Vase: Jeweled, red trim, handles, 7"h., RSP (rm). $1,200.00 – 1,400.00.

Row 4. Plate: Cobalt, jeweled, 7½"d., RSP (rm). $2,500.00 – 3,000.00. Vase: Red, jeweled, ornate handles, 13½"h., RSP (rm). $3,000.00 – 3,500.00. Plate: Jeweled, floral with gold trim, 8½"d., RSP (rm). $1,400.00 – 1,600.00.

182

Melon Boys (Melon Eaters)

Row 1. Vase: Jeweled, red trim, 10¼"h., unmk. $2,000.00 – 2,500.00. Vase: Jeweled, 11½"h., RSP (rm). $1,600.00 – 1,800.00. Vase: Jeweled, gold drape trim, 8"h., unmk. $2,000.00 – 2,500.00. Vase: Jeweled, red trim, 13½"h., unmk. $3,000.00 – 3,500.00.

Row 2. Demitasse pot/lid: Jeweled, 9"h., RSP (rm). $2,400.00 – 2,800.00. Bowl: Jeweled, gold trim, 9¼"d., unmk. $1,200.00 – 1,400.00. Chocolate pot/lid: Jeweled, 9"h., RSP (rm). $1,800.00 – 2,000.00.

Row 3. Plate: Jeweled, gold drape trim, 6"d., RSP (rm). $400.00 – 500.00. Cracker jar/lid: Jeweled, gold drape trim, 4"h. x 6½"w., RSP (rm). $2,400.00 – 2,800.00. Plate: Jeweled, red trim, 6"d., RSP (rm). $600.00 – 800.00.

Row 4. Plate: Jeweled, green, 9"d., RSP (rm). $1,400.00 – 1,800.00. Vase: Jeweled, pedestal, red, 7¾"h., unmk. $1,400.00 – 1,800.00. Plate: Jeweled, green, 9"d., RSP (rm). $1,400.00 – 1,800.00.

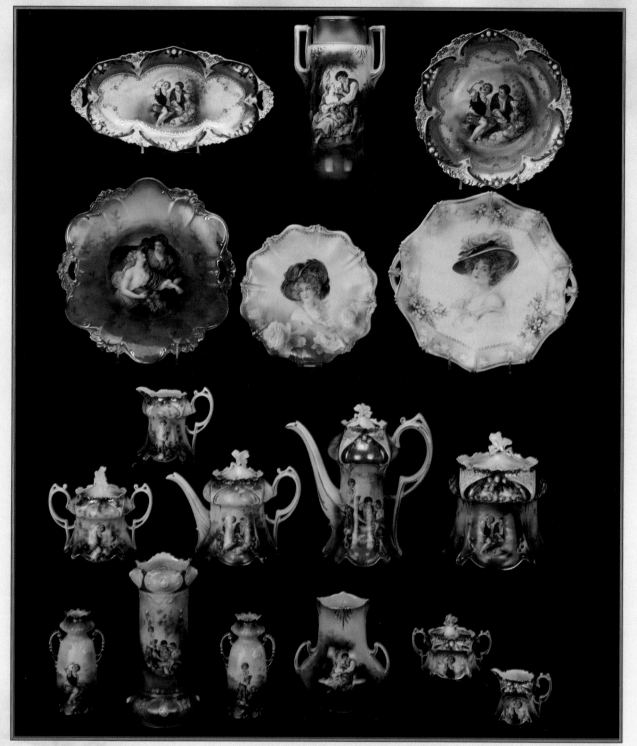

Row 1. Celery: Melon Boys (melon eaters), open-handled, green trim, jeweled, 13½"l., RSP (rm). $1,200.00 – 1,500.00. Vase: The Cage, handled, 9½"h., RSP (rm), RS Suhl, beehive, and Boucher (artist-signed). $1,200.00 – 1,500.00. Bowl: Melon Boys (melon eaters), green trim, jeweled, 10½"d., RSP (rm). $2,500.00 – 3,000.00.

Row 2. Plate: Peace Bringing Plenty open-handled, 11"d., RSP (rm), Madame LeBrun (artist-signed). $1,200.00 – 1,600.00. Plate: Gibson Girl (Gina), 9"d., RSP (rm). $800.00 – 1,200.00. Plate: Gibson Girl (Mary), 11"d., RSP (rm). $1,800.00 – 2,000.00.

Row 3. Sugar/lid: Melon Boys (melon eaters), 5½"h., RSP (rm). $600.00 – 800.00. Creamer: Melon Boys (dice players), 4"h., RSP (rm). $600.00 – 800.00. Teapot/lid: Melon Boys (melon eaters), 6½"h., RSP (rm). $900.00 – 1,200.00. Demi-coffeepot/lid: Melon Boys (dice players), 9½"h., RSP (rm). $2,500.00 – 3,000.00. Cracker jar/lid: Melon Boys (melon eaters), 8"h., RSP (rm). $2,500.00 – 3,000.00.

Row 4. Vase: Melon Boys (melon eaters), gold handles, 6"h., RSP (green). $900.00 – 1,200.00. Vase: Melon Boys (dice players/melon eaters on back), red trim, jeweled, satin, 9¼"h., RSP (rm). $1,400.00 – 1,800.00. Vase: Melon Boys (dice players), gold handles, 6"h., RSP (green). $900.00 – 1,200.00. Vase: The Cage, handles, 6"h., artist-signed, Boucher. $600.00 – 800.00. Sugar/lid: Melon Boys (melon eaters), miniature, green trim, jeweled, 3½"h., RSP (rm). $500.00 – 600.00. Creamer: Melon Boys (melon eaters), miniature, green trim, jeweled, 2½"h., RSP (rm). $500.00 – 600.00.

Melon Boys (Dice Players)

Row 1. Bowl: Red, 10¼"d., RSP (rm). $2,500.00 – 3,000.00. Bowl: Gold trim, 9"d., RSP (rm). $1,200.00 – 1,400.00. Bowl: Red, jeweled, gold drape trim, 10"d., RSP (rm). $3,000.00 – 3,500.00.

Row 2. Plate: Gold trim, 8½"d., RSP (rm). $800.00 – 1,000.00. Plate: Cobalt, gold trim, jeweled, open-handled, 11"d., RSP (rm). $4,500.00 – 5,000.00. Plate: Red, gold trim, jeweled, 8½"d., RSP (rm). $1,200.00 – 1,600.00.

Row 3. Creamer: Jeweled, gold trim, 3"h., RSP (rm). $400.00 – 600.00. Sugar/lid: Jeweled, gold trim, 2½"h., RSP (rm). $500.00 – 700.00. Saucer: Jeweled, gold trim, 4½"d., unmk. $175.00 – 275.00. Cup: Jeweled, gold trim, 3"h., RSP (rm). $175.00 – 275.00. Vase: Jeweled red/purple, gold handles, 8"h., RSP (rm). $1,500.00 – 1,800.00.

Row 4. Cup/saucer: Jeweled gold trim, cup (3"h.), saucer (4½"d.), RSP (rm). $300.00 – 500.00. Chocolate pot: Jeweled, gold trim, 10½"h., RSP (rm). Vase: Red, stick spout, 7¼"h., unmk. $400.00 – 600.00. Vase: Pedestal, handles, 9½"h., unmk. $800.00 – 1,200.00.

Melon Boys

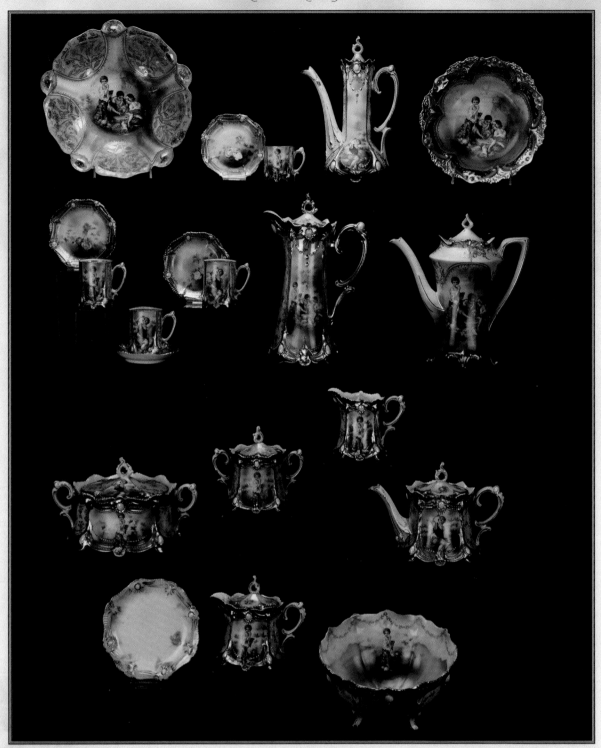

Row 1. Bowl: Dice players, gold panels, 10½"d., RSP (rm). $1,500.00 – 1,800.00. Cup/saucer: Dice players, jeweled, cup (3"h.), saucer (4½"d.). $350.00 – 450.00. Demitasse pot/lid: Melon eaters, jeweled, 9½"h., RSP (rm). $2,400.00 – 2,800.00. Bowl: Dice players, cobalt and gold trim, 8¼"d., RSP (rm). $2,500.00 – 3,500.00.

Row 2. Cups/saucers (three): Cup (one dice player) 3"h., saucer (two melon eaterss), 4½"d., jeweled, RSP (rm). $350.00 – 450.00 each. Chocolate pot/lid: Dice players, jeweled, gold trim, 10½"h., RSP (rm). $4,500.00 – 5,500.00. Coffeepot/lid: Dice players, 9"h., RSP (rm). $2,500.00 – $3,000.00.

Row 3. Cracker jar: Dice players, jeweled, 5"h., RSP (rm). $2,400.00 – 2,800.00. Sugar/lid: Dice players, jeweled, 5"h., RSP (rm). $600.00 – 800.00. Creamer: Dice players, jeweled, 4"h., RSP (rm). $600.00 – 800.00. Teapot/lid: Melon eaters, jeweled, 5½"h., RSP (rm). $900.00 – 1,200.00.

Row 4. Underplate (for syrup): Jeweled, 5½"h., RSP (rm). $1,000.00 – 1,500.00. Syrup/lid: Dice players, jeweled, 5"h., RSP (rm). $1,000.00 – 1,500.00. Bowl: Dice players outside and inside, jeweled, RSP (rm). $1,800.00 – 2,000.00.

Row 1 Bowl: Lady with fan, corduroy mold, 11"d., RSP (rm). $1,500.00 – 2,000.00. Bowl: Lady with dog, corduroy mold, 11"d., RSP (rm). $1,500.00 – 2,000.00. Bowl: Lady feeding chickens, corduroy mold, 11"d., RSP (rm). $1,500.00 – 2,000.00.
Row 2. Plate: Melon Boys (dice players), red trim, open-handled, 10"d. $1,400.00 – 1,800.00. Bowl: Lady watering flowers, corduroy mold, 11"d., RSP (rm). $1,500.00 – 2,000.00. Bowl: Melon Boys (melon eaters), red trim, 10¼"d. $1,400.00 – 1,800.00.
Row 3. Berry Set: Melon Boys (melon eaters). Lg – 10¼"d., RSP (rm). $1,400.00 – 1,800.00. Sm. – 5¼"d., RSP (rm). $500.00 – 800.00. $7,000.00 – 8,000.00 set.
Row 4. Bowl: Melon Boys (dice players), green/gold, 10½"d., RSP (rm). $1,400.00 – 1,800.00. Bowl: Melon Boys (melon eaters), green/gold, 10½"d., RSP (rm). $1,400.00 – 1,800.00.

Row 1. Vase: Allegorical scene, handled, 17"h., unmk. $4,000.00 – 4,500.00. Vase: Women with sheep, handles, 11"h., R. S. Suhl. $1,200.00 – 1,600.00. Vase: Women spinning yarn, handled, 17"h., unmk. $4,000.00 – 4,500.00.
Row 2. Vase: Women gathering grain (wheat), 17"h., R. S. Suhl. $4,000.00 – 4,500.00. Vase: House in forest/sheepherder and sheep, R. S. Suhl. $400.00 – 600.00. Vase: House in forest/sheepherder and sheep, R. S. Suhl. $400.00 – 600.00. Bowl: House in forest/sheepherder and sheep, R. S. Suhl. $500.00 – 600.00.

Row 1. Vase: Crown cranes, parrots on back, ring handles, 14"h., R. S. Suhl. $4,500.00 – 5,500.00. Vase: Parrots, crown crane on back, ring handles, 14"h., R. S. Suhl. $4,500.00 – 5,500.00.
Row 2. Vase: Floral, handles, 14½"h., R. S. Suhl. $1,200.00 – 1,600.00. Vase: Allegorical scene, 9"h., R. S. Poland. $1,400.00 – 1,800.00. Vase: Allegorical scene, 9"h., R. S. Poland. $1,400.00 – 1,800.00. Vase: "Night Watch," handles, 14½"h., unmk. $1,200.00 – 1,600.00.
Row 3. Vase: Floral, handles, 12"h., R. S. Suhl. $1,000.00 – 1,400.00. Vase: Floral, handles, 14"h., R. S. Tillowitz. $1,200.00 – 1,600.00.

Chocolate set, swans, icicle mold. Pot, 10½"h. Cups, 3"d. Saucers, 4½"d. RSP (rm). $3,000.00 – 3,500.00 set.

Mug, swans, icicle mold, 3½"h., RSP (rm). Cup/saucer, swans, icicle mold. Cup, 3½"d. Saucer, 5½"d. Shaving mug, icicle mold, 3½"h., unmk. Cup/saucer, $400.00 – 450.00. Mug, $700.00 – 900.00.

Demitasse set or child's set, swans, icicle mold. Pot, 6¼"h., RSP (rm). Cup, 2"h., RSP (rm). Saucer, 4½"d., unmk. $3,200.00 – 3,600.00 set.

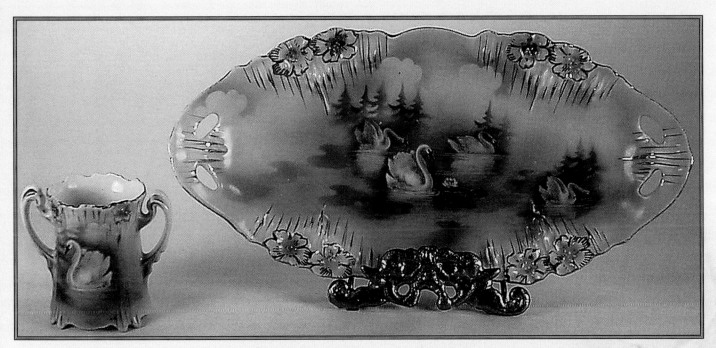

Toothpick holder, swan, icicle mold, handles, 2¼"h., unmk. $500.00 – 700.00. Relish tray, swans, icicle mold, open-handled, 9½"l. x 4½"w., RSP (rm). $300.00 – 400.00.

Berry set, swans, icicle mold. Large bowl, 10½"d. Desserts, 5½"d., RSP (rm). $2,000.00 – 2,200.00 set.

Bun tray, swans, icicle mold, 4"h., RSP (rm). $700.00 – 900.00.

192

Sugar/lid, swan, icicle mold, 4½"h., RSP (rm). Creamer, swan, icicle mold, 4"h., RSP (rm). $900.00 – 1,200.00 set.

Cracker jar/lid, swan, icicle mold, handles, 5"h. x 6"d., RSP (rm). $900.00 – 1,100.00.

Hair receiver/lid, swan, icicle mold, 4"h., RSP (rm). $300.00 – 400.00. Dresser tray, swans, icicle mold, open-handled, 11½"l. x 7¼"w., RSP (rm). $800.00 – 1,000.00. Pin tray, swans, icicle mold, 5½"l. x 3¼"w., RSP (rm). $400.00 – 600.00.

Tankard, swans, icicle mold, 14"h., unmk. $3,200.00 – 3,500.00. Tankard, swans, icicle mold, 11½"h., unmk. $2,200.00 – 2,500.00.

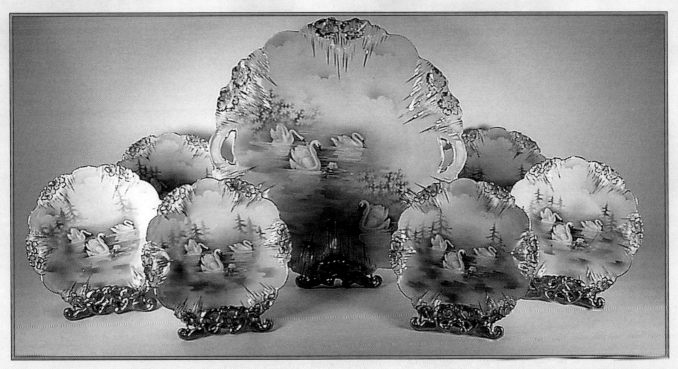

Cake set, swans, icicle mold. Cake plate, open-handled, 11"d., RSP (rm). Plates (small), icicle mold, 5¾"d., RSP (rm). $2,500.00 – 3,000.00 set.

Syrup/underplate, swan, icicle mold. Syrup, 4½"h. x 5"w., RSP (rm). Underplate, 6"d., RSP (rm). Syrup, $500.00 – 600.00. Underplate, $250.00 – 300.00. Set, $800.00 – 1,000.00.

Mustard/lid, floral, hidden image, 3½"h. x 3"w., unmk. $350.00 – 400.00.

Mustard Pots

Row 1. Floral, 3½"h. $75.00 – 125.00. Swans, 3½"h. $200.00 – 250.00. Ostrich, 3½"h. $1,200.00 – 2,000.00. Floral, 3¼"h. $100.00 – 150.00. Swans, jeweled, 3¾"h. $200.00 – 250.00. Floral, jeweled, 3¾"h. $175.00 – 225.00.

Row 2. Floral, 3¼"h. $100.00 – 150.00. Floral, 3½"h. $100.00 – 150.00. Floral, 3½"h. $100.00 – 150.00. Floral, 3¼"h. $100.00 – 150.00. Floral, 3"h. $100.00 – 150.00. Floral, reticulated, 3"h., steeple mark. $150.00 – 200.00.

Row 3. Floral, 3½"h. $125.00 – 175.00. Madame LeBrun, 3½"h. $800.00 – 1,200.00. Countess Potocka, 3½"h. $800.00 – 1,200.00. Madame Recamier, 3½"h. $800.00 – 1,200.00. Floral, 3½"h. $75.00 – 150.00. Man/ mountain (cove), 3½"h. $250.00 – 300.00.

Row 4. Floral, 3½"h. $100.00 – 150.00. Floral, carnation mold, 3½"h. $300.00 – 350.00. Floral, 3½"h. $75.00 – 125.00. Floral, 3½"h. $100.00 – 150.00. Floral, 3½"h. $100.00 – 150.00.

Row 5. Rooster, 3½"h. $300.00 – 400.00. Floral, carnation mold, cobalt, 3½"h. $900.00 – 1,200.00. Floral, 3½"h. $100.00 – 150.00. Floral, iris mold, 3½"h. $150.00 – 250.00. Floral, ftd., 3½"h. $150.00 – 200.00.

Mustard Pots

Row 1. Man/mountain, jeweled, 3¾"h. $250.00 – 300.00. Floral, stippled, 3¾"h. $150.00 – 200.00. Floral, 3½"h. $100.00   150.00. Cottage scene, 3½"h. $250.00 – 300.00. Floral, 3¾"h. $150.00 – 200.00. Floral, jeweled, 3¾"h. $150.00 – 200.00.

Row 2. Mill scene, 3½"h. $250.00 – 300.00. Sheepherder, 3½"h. $275.00 – 325.00. Scenic, jeweled, 3¾"h. $225.00 – 275.00. Floral, cobalt, 3½"h. (steeple mark). $300.00 – 400.00. Floral, jeweled, 3½"h. $200.00 – 250.00. Three scenes (rare), 3½"h. $400.00 – 450.00.

Row 3. Man/mountain (cove), 3¾"h. $250.00 – 300.00. Floral, 3½"h. $100.00 – 150.00. Floral, 3½"h. $100.00 – 150.00. Floral, pedestal, 4"h. $200.00 – 250.00. Floral, 3½"h. $200.00 – 250.00. Floral, 3¾"h. $150.00 – 200.00.

Row 4. Floral, 2½"h. $100.00 – 150.00. Mill scene, 2½"h. $250.00 – 300.00. Floral, 2½"h., raised star. $100.00 – 150.00. Sheepherder, 2½"h. $250.00 – 300.00. Floral, 2½"h. $100.00 – 150.00. Floral, 2½"h. $100.00 – 150.00.

Row 5. Floral, feather, 3½"h. $150.00 – 200.00. Floral, feather, 3½"h. $150.00 – 200.00. Floral, 3½"h. $75.00 – 125.00. Floral, 3½"h. $100.00   150.00. Floral, 3"h. $100.00   150.00.

Mustard Pots

Row 1. Floral, sunflower, 3¼"h. $75.00 – 125.00. Floral, 3½"h. $50.00 – 100.00. Floral, 3¾"h. $125.00 – 175.00. Chicken, 3¾"h. $325.00 – 400.00. Floral, 3½"h. $100.00 – 150.00. Floral, sunflower, 3½"h. $300.00 – 400.00.

Row 2. Floral, 3½"h. $75.00 – 125.00. Floral, carnation mold, 3½"h. $275.00 – 375.00. Floral, 3½"h., raised star. $100.00 – 125.00. Floral, carnation mold, 3½"h. $275.00 – 375.00. Floral, 3"h. $100.00 – 150.00. Floral, 3½"h. $75.00 – 125.00.

Row 3. Floral, 3½"h. $100.00 – 150.00. Floral, 3½"h. $100.00 – 150.00. Hidden image, 3½"h., raised star. $350.00 – 400.00. Man/mountain, 3¾"h. $300.00 – 350.00. Floral, 3¾"h. (steeple mark). $125.00 – 175.00. Floral, iris mold, 3¾"h. $150.00 – 200.00.

Row 4. Bowtie, lid missing. $100.00 – 150.00. Floral, 3½"h. $125.00 – 175.00. Floral, 3½"h. $125.00 – 175.00. Floral, 3½"h. $100.00 – 150.00. Floral, 3½"h. $125.00 – 175.00.

Row 5. Floral, 3½"h. $125.00 – 175.00. Floral, 3½"h. $100.00 – 150.00. Hidden image, 3½"h., raised star. $350.00 – 400.00. Sheepherder, 3½"h. $250.00 – 300.00. Floral, 3"h. $150.00 – 200.00.

Mustard Pots

Row 1. R. S. Tillowitz set: Floral. Plate, toothpick holder, salt & pepper shaker. Mustard: 2½"h. $250.00 – 300.00. R.S. Germany set: Floral. plate (open-handled), salt & pepper shaker, mustard: (3"h.) $200.00 – 250.00. R. S. Germany set: Floral. Plate (open-handled), salt shaker, mustard: (3¼"h.) $200.00 – 250.00. R. S. Tillowitz set: Floral. Plate (open-handled), salt & pepper shaker, mustard: 3½"h. $200.00 – 250.00.
Row 2. R. S. Germany set: Floral. Plate (open-handled), toothpick holder, salt shaker, mustard: (3"h.) $250.00 – 300.00 set. Floral, swirl mold, 3½"h. $75.00 – 125.00. Floral, 3½"h. $75.00 – 125.00. Floral, 3½"h. $75.00 – 125.00. Floral, swirl mold, 3½"h. $75.00 – 125.00.
Row 3. Floral, 3¼"h. $75.00 – 125.00. Floral, 3"h. $75.00 – 125.00. Floral, 3½"h. $75.00 – 125.00. Floral, 3¾"h. $75.00 – 125.00. Floral, 3½"h. $75.00 – 125.00. Floral, 3½"h. $75.00 – 125.00.
Row 4. Floral, square mold, twig handle, 3¼"h. $150.00 – 200.00. Snowbird, 3½"h. $300.00 – 350.00. Floral, 3½"h. $75.00 – 125.00. Floral, square mold, twig handle, 3½"h. $150.00 – 200.00. Floral, 3"h. $75.00 – 125.00.
Row 5. Floral, jeweled, 3¾"h. $150.00 – 200.00. Floral, 3¾"h. $150.00 – 175.00. Floral, 3¾"h. $75.00 – 125.00. Floral, swag/tassel, tapestry, 3½"h. $100.00 – 150.00. Floral, 3¾"h. $200.00 – 275.00.

Child's Chamber Sets

Row 1. Set #1. Wash bowl: Pink floral, unmk. Chamber pot: Pink floral, unmk. Covered box: Pink floral, unmk. Pitcher: Pink floral, unmk. Covered box: Pink floral, unmk. $800.00 – 1,000.00 set.

Row 1. Set #2. Cup/saucer: Floral decor, cup (2"h.), saucer (4"d.), unmk. Sugar/lid: Duck, floral, 3½"h., unmk. Creamer: Duck, floral, 2¼"h., unmk. Teapot: Chinese pheasant, floral, 5¼"h., unmk. $1,000.00 – 1,400.00 set.

Row 2: Child's wash stand: $400.00 – 600.00. Set #3. Wash bowl: Floral, light tan, bronze highlights, 5"d., unmk. Pitcher: Floral, light tan, bronze highlights, 4½"h., unmk. Covered box/lid: Floral, light tan, bronze highlights, 3¼"h., unmk. Waste drain: Floral, light tan, bronze highlights, 3¼"h., unmk. Covered box/lid: Floral, light tan, bronze highlights, unmk. Covered box/lid: Floral, light tan, bronze highlights, 2"h., unmk. $800.00 – 1,000.00 set.

Row 3. Child's wash stand. $300.00 – 400.00. Tea set (swallows) in original box (Daisy). Wash bowl: Birds, pine trees, 7"d., unmk. Chamber pot: Birds, unmk. Covered box/lid: Birds, 2"w. x 4"l., unmk. Covered box/lid: Birds, 2½"l., unmk. Pitcher: Birds and trees, 5¾"h., unmk. $1,400.00 – 1,600.00 set.

Child's wash bowl set (in original box), floral strawflowers, unmk. Pitcher, 6"h. Bowl, 5¾"d. Chamber pot, 2⅜"h. Covered box/lid, 3¾"l. Soap box/lid, 2½"l. $1,200.00 – 1,500.00 set.

Child's wash bowl set, floral. Pitcher, 7"h. Bowl, 8"d. Toothbrush box/lid, 5"l. Soap dish/lid, 3"l. $800.00 – 1,000.00 set.

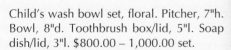

Child's tea set, doll miniatures, garlands. Teapot/lid, 2½"h. Sugar/lid, 1¾"h. Creamer, 1½"h. Cup, ⅞"h. Saucer, 2"d. $3,400.00 – 3,600.00 set.

Child's tea set, floral, pink roses. Pot/lid, 4½"h. Sugar/no lid, 2"h. Creamer, 2"h. Cup, 1½"h. Saucer, 3"d. $1,200.00 – 1,400.00 set.

Cups/saucers, miniatures, RSP (rm). $400.00 – 600.00 each.

Child's tea set, floral. Pot/lid, 4½"h. Sugar/lid, 2½"h. Creamer, 2"h. Cups, 2"h. Saucers, 3"d. Plates, 3½"d. $1,600.00 – 1,800.00 set.

Child's tea set, floral, large pink rose, blue border. Pot/lid, 5½"h. Sugar/lid, 3"h. Creamer, 2½"h. Cups, 2"h. Saucers, 3"d. $1,500.00 – 1,700.00 set.

Child's tea set, floral. Sugar, 2"h. Teapot, 3"h. Cup, 1½"h. Saucer, 2½"d. Creamer, 2"h. $1,800.00 – 2,000.00.

Child's tea set, floral, pink roses. Pot/lid, 3½"h. Sugar/lid, 2½"h. Creamer, 2"h. Cups, 2"h. Saucers, 3"d. $1,500.00 – 1,800.00 set.

Child's tea set, colonial people, no creamer. Pot/lid, 3½"h. Sugar/lid, 2½"h. Cups, 1½"h. Saucers, 3"d. $1,400.00 – 1,600.00 set

Child's tea set. Floral, gold trim. Pot/lid, 4½"h. Sugar/lid, 2½"h. Creamer, 3½"h. Cups, 2"h. Saucers, 3"d. Plates, 3½"d. Open-handled cake plates, 5½"d. $1,600.00 – 1,800.00 set.

Vase, cottage scene, brown tones, ornate handles, pedestal, 10"h., RSP (rm). $800.00 – 1,000.00.

Chocolate set, cottage scene, brown tones. Pot/lid, 9½"h. Cup, 3"h. Saucer, 4½"d., RSP (rm). $2,500.00 – 3,000.00 set.

Tankard, mill scene, brown tones, 13"h., RSP (rm). $1,600.00 – 2,000.00.

Sugar and creamer, cottage scene, brown tones, pedestal, ornate handles. Sugar, 4"h. Creamer, 4"h., RSP (rm). $500.00 – 700.00.

Tea set: castle, mill, and cottage scenes, brown tones. Pot/lid, ball feet, 3½"h. Creamer, ball feet, 3"h. Sugar/lid, 4"h. Cups, 1¾"h. Saucers, 4½"d., RSP (rm). Set with four cups and saucers, $2,000.00 – 2,200.00.

Chocolate set, mill scene, brown tones, ball feet. Pot/lid, 9½"h. Cups, 3"h. Saucers, 4½"d., RSP (rm). $2,500.00 – 3,000.00 set.

Cracker jar/lid, triple scene (castle, mill, cottage), brown tones, handles, ball feet, 5"h. x 9½"w., RSP (rm). Front and back views. $1,500.00 – 1,800.00.

Hatpin holder, mill scene, brown tones, 4½"h., RSP (rm). $600.00 – 900.00.

Candlestick, double scene (mill and castle), brown tones, 6"h., RSP (rm). Front and back views. $900.00 – 1,100.00.

Vase, cottage scene, brown tones, pedestal, ornate handle, 8"h., RSP (rm). $800.00 – 1,000.00.

Bowl, castle sunset scene, footed, brown tones, 6"d. x 5"h., RSP (rm). $400.00 – 600.00.

Bowl, castle scene, brown tones and purple highlights, 10"d., RSP (rm). $700.00 – 900.00.

Chocolate set, castle, mill, and cottage scenes, brown tones with purple highlights. Pot/lid, 9½"h. Cups, 3"h. Saucers, 4½"d., RSP (rm). $2,500.00 – 3,000.00 set.

Tankard, castle scene, brown tones, footed, 13"h., RSP (rm). $2,200.00 – 2,500.00.

Chocolate set, castle scene, brown tones. Pot/lid, 9½"h., RSP (rm). Cups, 3"h., RSP (rm). Saucers, 4½"d., RSP (rm). $2,500.00 – 3,000.00 set.

Tea set, castle scene, brown tones, teapot, creamer, and sugar, RSP (rm). $1,200.00 – 1,500.00 set.

Berry set, castle scene, brown tones, large bowl, oval, open-handled, 13"l. x 8"w., RSP (rm). Desserts, 5"d., RSP (rm). $1,600.00 – 2,000.00 set.

Bun tray, castle scene, brown tones, open-handled, 13"l. x 8"w., RSP (rm). $900.00 – 1,200.00.

Jam jar/underplate, castle scene, handles, brown tones. Jar, 5¼"h. x 4"w. Underplate, 6"d., RSP (rm). $700.00 – 900.00.

Creamer/sugar/lid, fruit décor, acorn mold. Creamer, 3½"h. Sugar, 4½"h., RSP (rm). $400.00 – 500.00 set.

Chocolate set, fruit décor. Pot/lid, 9"h. Cups, 3"h. Saucers, 4½"d., RSP (rm). $1,800.00 – 2,000.00 set.

Biscuit jar/lid, fruit décor, iris mold, RSP (rm). $800.00 – 1,000.00.

Tankard, fruit and floral décor, 13"h., RSP (rm). $800.00 – 1,200.00.

Chocolate set, fruit décor. Pot, 9"h. Cups, 3"h. Saucers, 4½"d., RSP (rm). Set with four cups and saucers, $1,500.00 – 1,800.00.

Berry set, fruit décor, grape mold. Large bowl, 10"d. Desserts, 5"d., RSP (rm). Seven-piece set (missing four dessert plates), $1,000.00 – 1,200.00.

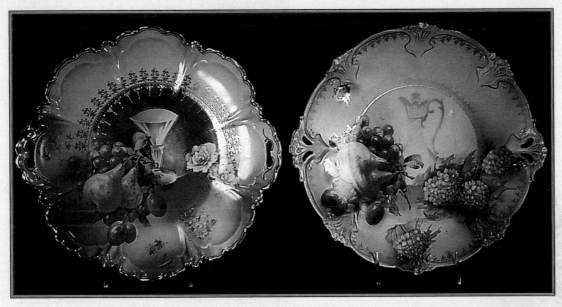

Cake plates, fruit décor, open-handled, RSP (rm). $250.00 – 350.00 each.

217

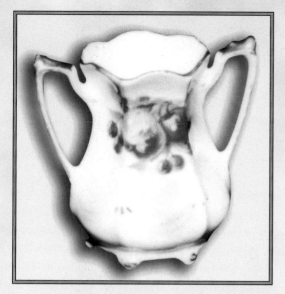

Toothpick holder, fruit décor, handles, 2½"h., RSP (rm). $200.00 – 300.00.

Plate, fruit décor/pitcher, silhouette, open-handled, 11"d., RSP (rm). $500.00 – 700.00.

Mustard pot/lid, fruit décor, spoon, 3½"h, RSP (rm). $300.00 – 400.00.

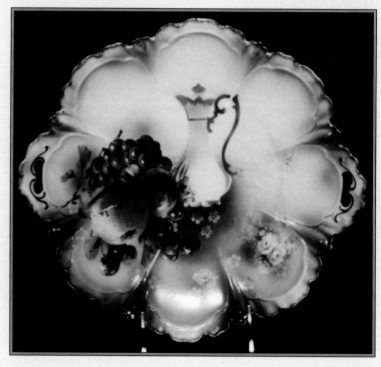

Plate, fruit décor/chocolate pot, silhouette, open-handled, 11"d, RSP (rm). $500.00 – 700.00.

Bowl, fruit décor, pitcher silhouette, 10"d., RSP (rm). $500.00 – 700.00.

Bowl, fruit décor, champagne glass, 10½"d., RSP (rm). $500.00 – 700.00.

Plate, fruit décor, iris mold, 9"d., RSP (rm). $250.00 – 350.00.

Bowl, fruit décor, iris mold, 10"d., RSP (rm). $600.00 – 800.00.

Bowl, fruit décor, five panels, 10"d., RSP (rm). $450.00 – 550.00.

Bowl, fruit décor, five panels, 10"d., RSP (rm). $450.00 – 550.00.

Bowl, fruit décor, five panels, 10"d., RSP (rm) $450.00 – 550.00.

Bowl, fruit décor, black with gold filigree, RSP (rm). $800.00 – 1,000.00.

Celery bowl, fruit décor, open-handled, iris mold, 12"l., RSP (rm). $350.00 – 450.00.

Plate, fruit décor (peeled orange), open-handled, 10"d., unmk. $350.00 – 500.00.

Bowl, fruit décor, bowl-in-bowl, 10"d., RSP (rm). $500.00 – 700.00.

Row 1. Plate: Floral, open-handled, gold petals, 9½"d., unmk. $300.00 – 500.00. Mug: Floral, rose panel, ball feet, 3½"h., RSP (rm). $200.00 – 400.00. Chocolate pot/lid: Floral, rose panel, ball feet, 9"h., RSP (rm). $700.00 – 1,000.00. Tankard: Floral, skirted, gold background, 15"h., unmk. $1,400.00 – 1,800.00. Tankard: Floral, rose panel, ball ft., 14½"h., RSP (rm). $1,000.00 – 1,500.00.

Row 2. Bowl: Floral, six gold petals, 9"d., unmk. $300.00 – 500.00. Chocolate pot/lid: Floral, skirted, gold background, 10½"h., unmk. $800.00 – 1,200.00. Sugar/lid: Floral, skirted, gold background, 4½"h., unmk. $300.00 – 500.00. Creamer: Floral, skirted, gold background, 3¼"h., unmk. $300.00 – 500.00. Coffeepot/lid: Floral, rose panel, ball feet, 9"h., unmk. $400.00 – 700.00.

Row 3. Perfume/ stopper: Floral, 5½"h., R. S. Poland. $300.00 – 500.00. Cups/saucers: (Four, go with teapot shown here), floral, rose panel, ball feet, cup (2"h.), saucer (4½"d.), RSP (rm). $75.00 – 150.00 each. Sugar/lid: Floral, rose panel, ball feet, 3½"h., RSP (rm). $300.00 – 500.00. Creamer: Floral, rose panel, ball feet, 3"h., RSP (rm). $300.00 – 500.00. Teapot: Floral, rose panel, ball feet, 4"h., RSP (rm). $400.00 – 600.00.

Row 1. Bowl: Floral, carnation mold, 12"d., RSP (rm). $700.00 – 1,000.00. Bowl: Floral, carnation mold, cobalt, 12"d., RSP (rm). $2,000.00 – 2,500.00.
Row 2. Bowl: Floral, carnation mold, 12"d., RSP (rm). $700.00 – 1,000.00.
Row 3. Bowl: Floral, carnation mold, 12"d., RSP (rm). $700.00 – 1,000.00. Bowl: Floral, gold carnation mold, 12"d., RSP (rm). $1,000.00 – 1,400.00.

Row 1. Lemonade pitcher: Floral, carnation mold, satin, 9"h., RSP (rm). $1,500.00 – 2,000.00. Lemonade pitcher: Floral, carnation mold, cobalt, 9"h., RSP (rm). $2,500.00 – 2,800.00. Lemonade pitcher: Floral, carnation mold, satin, 9"h., RSP (rm). $1,500.00 – 2,000.00.
Row 2. Sugar/lid: Floral, carnation mold, satin, 4½"h., RSP (rm). $200.00 – 400.00. Creamer: Floral, carnation mold, satin, 4"h., RSP (rm). $200.00 – 400.00. Lemonade pitcher: Floral, carnation mold, 9"h., RSP (rm). $1,500.00 – 2,000.00. Creamer: Floral, carnation mold, satin, 5½"h., RSP (rm). $200.00 – 400.00. Teapot: Floral, carnation mold, satin, 4½"h., RSP (rm). $500.00 – 700.00. Sugar/lid: Floral, carnation mold, satin, 4½"h., RSP (rm). $200.00 – 400.00.
Row 3. Cracker jar: Floral, carnation mold, satin, 5"h., RSP (rm). $600.00 – 900.00. Cracker jar: Floral, carnation mold, satin, 5"h., RSP (rm). $600.00 – 900.00. Cracker jar: Floral, carnation mold, satin, 5"h., RSP (rm). $600.00 – 900.00.
Row 4. Sugar/lid: Floral, carnation mold, cobalt, 4½"h., RSP (rm). $1,200.00 – 1,600.00. Creamer: Floral, carnation mold, cobalt, 4"h., RSP (rm). $1,200.00 – 1,600.00. Sugar/lid: Floral, carnation mold, satin, 4½"h., RSP (rm). $200.00 – 400.00. Creamer: Floral, carnation mold, satin, 4"h., RSP (rm). $200.00 – 400.00.

Row 1. Bowl: Floral, carnation mold, satin, 10"d., RSP (rm). $300.00 – 400.00. Plate: Floral, carnation mold, open-handled, satin, 11"d., RSP (rm). $400.00 – 600.00. Bowl: Floral, carnation mold, satin, 10½"d., RSP (rm). $400.00 – 500.00.
Row 2. Bowl: Floral, satin, 10½"d., RSP (rm). $300.00 – 400.00. Pitcher: Floral, miniature, ball feet, satin, 6"h., RSP (rm). $500.00 – 600.00. Bowl: Floral, carnation mold, satin, 10½"d., RSP (rm). $300.00 – 400.00.
Row 3. Vase: Floral, ornate gold handles, satin, 9"h., RSP (rm). $350.00 – 450.00. Mug: Floral, iris mold, satin, 3¾"h., RSP (rm). $250.00 – 350.00. Plate: Floral, open-handled, gold trim, satin, 12"d., RSP (rm). $250.00 – 450.00. Vase: Floral, gold handle, reticulated shirt, ftd., 10"h., RSP (rm). $700.00 – 1,000.00.
Row 4. Bowl: Floral, iris mold, satin, 10"d., RSP (rm). $400.00 – 500.00. Dresser tray: Carnation mold, open-handled, satin, 11½"l., RSP (rm). $400.00 – 500.00.

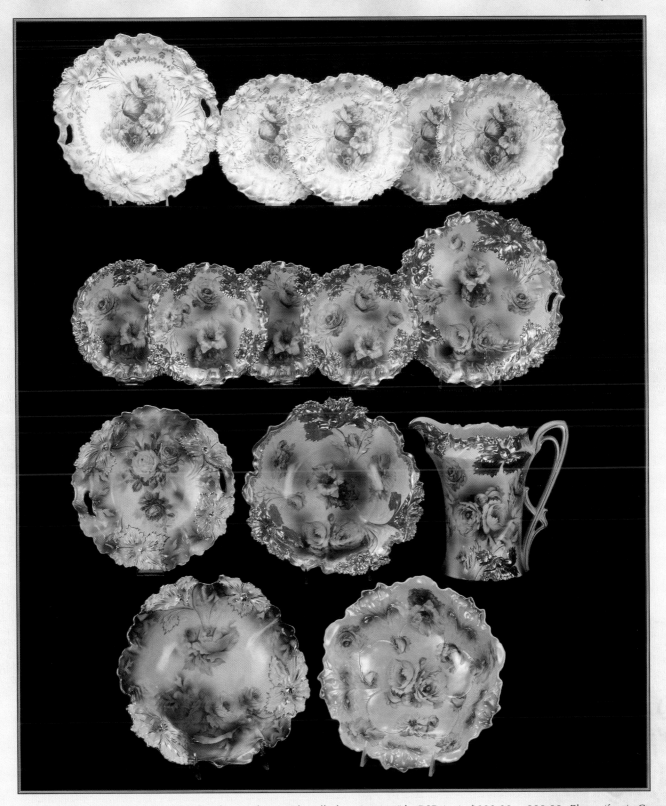

Row 1. Cake set. Plate: Carnation mold, floral, pastel, open-handled, satin, 10½"d., RSP (rm). $600.00 – 800.00. Plates (four): Carnation mold, floral, pastel, satin, 8"d., RSP (rm). $200.00 – 300.00 each. Set, $1,400.00 – 1,500.00.
Row 2. Cake set. Plates (four): "Watered Silk," carnation mold, pink floral, gold trim, satin, 7½"d., RSP (rm). $300.00 – 400.00 each. Plate: "Watered Silk," carnation mold, pink floral, gold trim, satin, 10"d., RSP (rm). $1,000.00 – 1,400.00. Set, $2,200.00 – 2,500.00.
Row 3. Plate: Carnation mold, floral, satin, 9½"d., RSP (rm). $250.00 – 500.00. Bowl: "Watered Silk," carnation mold, floral, gold trim, satin, 10½"d., RSP (rm). $1,000.00 – 1,400.00. Lemonade pitcher: "Watered Silk," carnation mold, floral, gold trim, satin, 9"h., RSP (rm). $1,200.00 – 1,500.00.
Row 4. Bowl: Carnation mold, floral, satin, 10½"d., RSP (rm). $300.00 – 500.00. Bowl: Iris mold, floral, satin, 10½"d., RSP (rm). $300.00 – 500.00.

Chocolate set, carnation mold, "Watered Silk," floral, ornate gold, RSP (rm). Pot/lid, 9¼"h. Cups, 3"h. Saucers, 4½"d. $2,400.00 – 2,800.00 set.

Cracker jar/lid, carnation mold, "Watered Silk," floral, ornate gold, 5½"h. x 9"w., RSP (rm). $800.00 – 1,200.00.

Bowl, carnation mold, "Watered Silk," floral, ornate gold, 12"d., RSP (rm). $1,200.00 – 1,400.00.

Row 1. Bowl: Pink carnation mold, "Watered Silk," gold trim, satin, 11½"d., RSP (rm). $1,200.00 – 1,400.00. Demi-cups: Pink carnation mold, "Watered Silk," gold trim, satin, 2¼"h., RSP (rm). $100.00 – 150.00 each. Demi-coffeepot/ lid: Pink carnation mold, "Watered Silk," gold trim, satin, 9"h., RSP (rm). $1,200.00 – 1,600.00. Tankard: Pink carnation mold, "Watered Silk," gold trim, satin, 13"h., RSP (rm). $1,500.00 – 2,000.00.

Row 2. Relish: Floral, jewels, satin, 8½"l. x 5"w., RSP (rm). $300.00 – 500.00. Sugar/lid: Floral, ornate handles, satin, 5"h., RSP (rm). $150.00 – 300.00. Creamer: Floral, ornate handles, satin, 4"h., RSP (rm). $150.00 – 300.00. Dessert: Pink carnation, "Watered Silk," gold trim, satin, 5½"d., RSP (rm). $150.00 – 250.00. Bowl: Pink carnation, "Watered Silk," gold trim, satin, 9½"d., RSP (rm). $800.00 – 1,200.00.

Row 3. Tankard: Floral, scattered flowers, skirted, satin, 11½"h., RSP (rm). $600.00 – 1,000.00. Bowl: Floral, scattered flowers, satin, 10½"d., RSP (rm). $500.00 – 800.00. Cup/saucer: Floral, scattered flowers, satin, cup (3"h.), saucer (4½"d.), unmk. $75.00 – 150.00. Chocolate pot/lid: Floral, scattered flowers, satin, 10"h., RSP (rm). $800.00 – 1,200.00.

Row 4. Cracker jar/lid: Floral, scattered flowers, satin, 9"d. x 5"w., RSP (rm). $600.00 – 900.00. Bowl: Floral, scattered flowers, three legs, satin, 7½"d., RSP (rm). $250.00 – 500.00. Dessert: Floral, scattered flowers, satin, 5"d., RSP (rm). $75.00 – 150.00.

Row 1. Bowl: Fruit (peeled orange), 10¼"d., RSP (rm). $350.00 – 500.00. Bowl: Fruit (apple, grapes, cherries), 10½"d., RSP (rm). $450.00 – 550.00. Bowl: Fruit (pitcher, pears, grapes), 10¼"d., RSP (rm). $450.00 – 550.00.

Row 2. Breakfast set: Bowl, satin, 6"d., RSP (rm). $125.00 – 175.00. Underplate (with first bowl): 7"d., $150.00 – 200.00. Vase: Allegorical scene, ring handles, ftd., 4¼"h., RSP (rm). $350.00 – 500.00. Bowl: Countess Potocka, 10½"d., unmk. $2,400.00 – 3,000.00. Shaving mug: Mirror, handle, 3¾"h., RSP (rm). $350.00 – 600.00. Basket: Floral, ruffled rim, handle, 5"l. x 3"w., unmk. $250.00 – 400.00.

Row 3. Desk set: unmk., $1,200.00 – 1,500.00 set. Pen holder, 4"l. x 3"h. $150.00 – 200.00. Inkwell, 1½"h. x 3"l. $150.00 – 200.00. Stamp wetter, 2¼"w. x 4". $100.00 – 150.00. Blotter, 4½"l. x 2¼"w. $150.00 – 200.00. Pen holder, 6½"l. $150.00 – 200.00. Stamp box/ lid, 3½"l. x 2"h. $150.00 – 200.00. Vase: "Night Watch," 3½"h., unmk. $300.00 – 500.00. Vase: Lady/flower, 3½"h., RSG. $400.00 – 600.00. Creamer: Gold leaf, 3¾"h., RSP (rm). $150.00 – 200.00. Sugar/lid: Gold leaf, 4"h., RSP (rm). $150.00 – 200.00.

Row 4. Child's tea set: Floral, unmk. $1,200.00 – 1,500.00 set. Coffeepot/ lid: 5"h. $150.00 – 200.00. Teapot/lid: 4"h. $125.00 – 150.00. Cake plate: 3½"d. $75.00 – 100.00. Cup: 1½"h. $50.00 – 75.00. Saucer: 2"d. $50.00 – 75.00. Sugar/lid: 2¾"h. $125.00 – 150.00. Creamer: 3"h., 100.00 – 125.00. Dresser tray: Floral, iris mold, open-handled (in silver holder), 11"l., unmk. $500.00 – 750.00.

Row 1. Bowl: Floral, 10½"d., RSP (rm). $200.00 – 350.00. Bowl: Floral, acorn mold, 10½"d., RSP (rm). $250.00 – 400.00. Bowl: Floral, tiffany border, 10¼"d., RSP (rm). $250.00 – 400.00.

Row 2. Bowl: Floral, sunflower mold, 9½"d., RSP (rm). $250.00 – 400.00. Plate: Floral, leaf mold, tiffany, 11"d., RSP (rm). $300.00 – 400.00. Bowl: Floral, bowl-in-bowl, 10½"d., RSP (rm). $300.00 – 400.00.

Row 3. Chocolate pot/lid: Floral, sunflower mold, satin, RSP (rm). $450.00 – 600.00. Cup: Floral, sunflower mold, satin. $75.00 – 150.00. Butter dish: Floral, sunflower mold, satin. $400.00 – 600.00. Sugar/lid: Floral, sunflower mold, satin. $150.00 – 250.00. Creamer: Floral, sunflower mold, satin. $150.00 – 250.00. Bowl: Floral, sunflower mold, satin, 10½"d., RSP (rm). $350.00 – 500.00.

Row 4. Cup/saucer: Floral, cup (2"h.), saucer (4½"d.), unmk. $75.00 – 150.00. Demitasse coffeepot/lid: Floral, 9"h., unmk. $350.00 – 500.00. Condiment set: Mustard/spoon (3"h.), salt/pepper shakers (1¾"h.). $400.00 – 600.00. Toothpick holder: 2¼"h. $125.00 – 200.00. Tea set: Cut-glass mold, sugar/ lid, creamer, teapot/ lid (5"h.). $600.00 – 800.00.

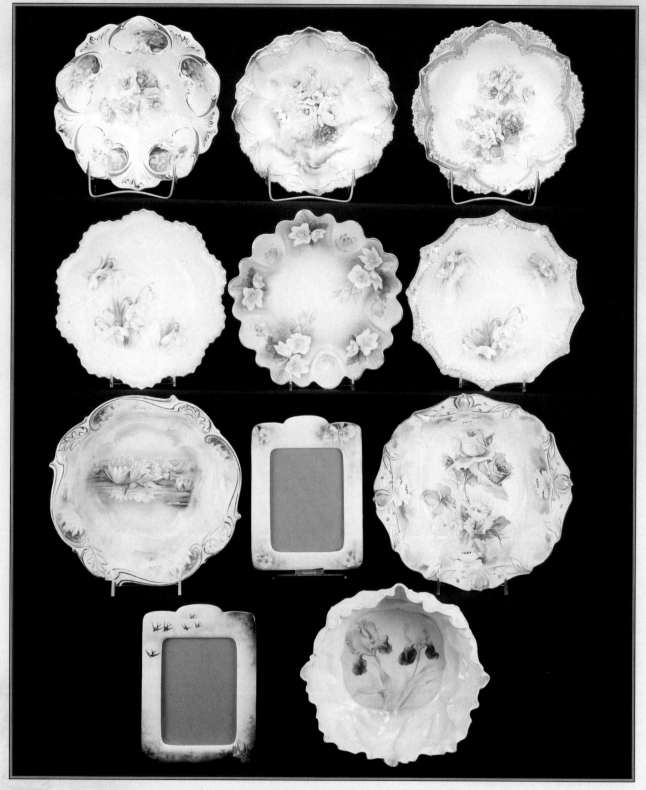

Row 1. Bowl: Floral, 10¾"d., RSP (rm). $200.00 – 350.00. Bowl: Floral, 10½"d., RSP (rm). $200.00 – 350.00. Bowl: Floral, satin, 10½"d., RSP (rm). $200.00 – 350.00.

Row 2. Bowl: Floral, satin, 10¼"d., RSP (rm). $200.00 – 350.00. Bowl: Floral (Christmas rose), 10½"d., RSP (rm). $250.00 – 400.00. Bowl: Floral, 10¼"d., RSP (rm). $200.00 – 350.00.

Row 3. Bowl: Floral, 10¾"d., RSP (rm). $250.00 – 400.00. Picture frame: Floral, 8½"l. x 6"w., $300.00 – 450.00. Bowl: Floral, square mold, 10½"d., RSP (rm). $200.00 – 350.00.

Row 4. Picture frame: Bluebirds/castle, 8½"l. x 6"w. $400.00 – 500.00. Bowl: Cabbage bowl, floral (iris), 9½"d., RSG. $250.00 – 400.00.

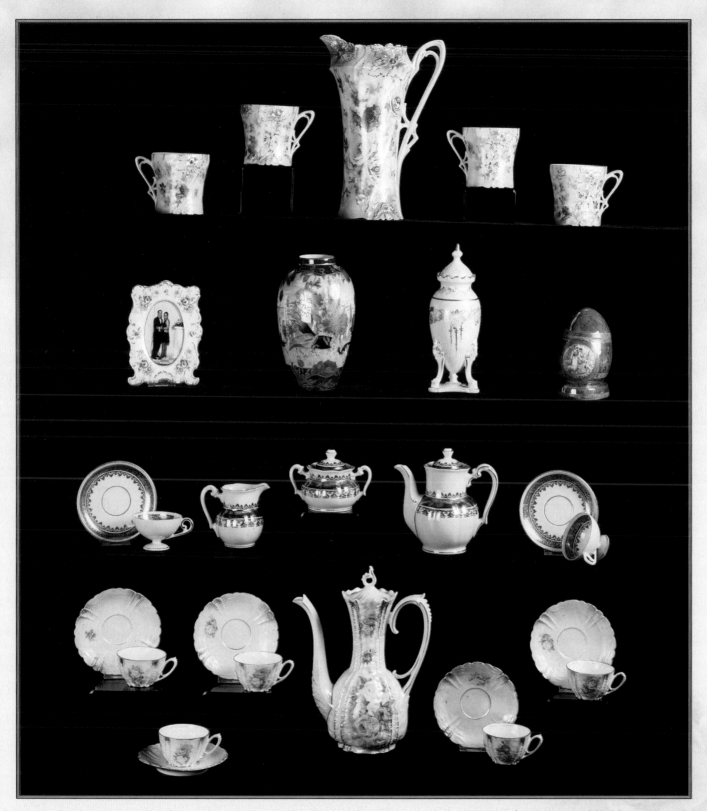

Row 1. Tankard & mug set: Floral, carnation mold, satin. Tankard, 11"h., Mugs (six), 3½"h., RSP (rm). $4,000.00 – 4,500.00 set.

Row 2. Picture frame: Floral, 6"l. x 4¼"w., unmk. $150.00 – 200.00. Vase: Peacock, 7½"h., beehive (dot). $250.00 – 300.00. Urn/lid: pedestal, ftd., 8½"h., Schlegelmilch, 1861, hand painted in gold. $300.00 – 350.00. Egg/ lid: Lady/sheep, 4¾"h., Suhl, 1861 crown. $450.00 – 500.00.

Row 3. Tea set. Cup/saucer: gold trim, cup (1¼"h.), saucer (4¼"d.), Oscar Schlegelmilch (OS). Creamer: gold trim, 3"h., O.S. Sugar/lid: gold trim, 3"h., O.S. Teapot/lid: gold trim, 5½"h., O.S. $700.00 – 900.00 set.

Row 4. Demitasse coffee set: Floral. Pot/ lid, 9"h., RSP (rm). Six cups & saucers, cups (2"h.), saucers (4¼"h.), RSP (rm). $800.00 – 1,200.00 set.

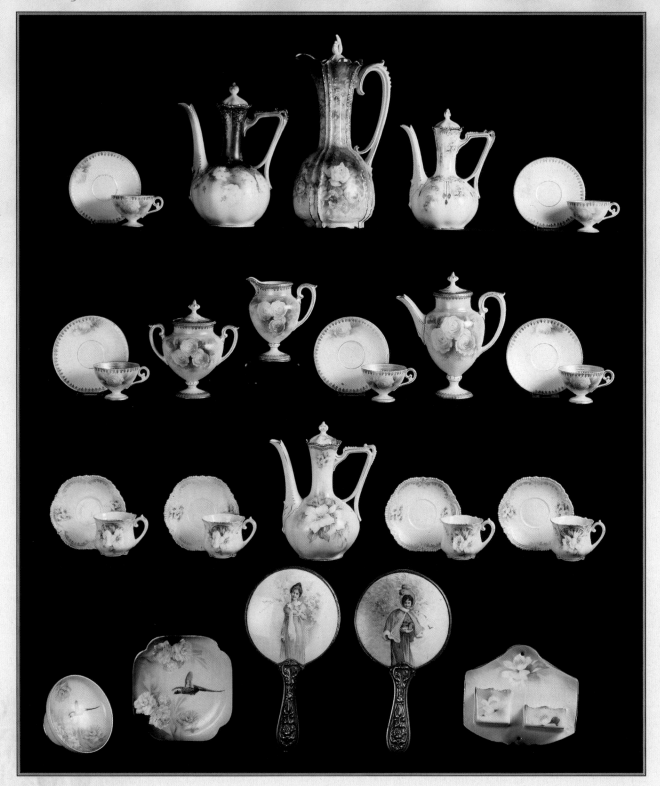

Row 1. Cup/saucer: (goes with Row 2 tea set). $100.00 – 150.00. Demitasse coffeepot/lid: Floral, 8"h., RSP (rm). $400.00 – 450.00. Chocolate pot/lid: Floral, 11"h., RSP (rm). $500.00 – 600.00. Demitasse coffeepot/lid: Floral, 7"h., RSP (rm). $350.00 – 400.00. Cup/saucer: (goes with Row 2 tea set). $100.00 – 150.00.

Row 2. Tea set: Floral, pedestal, satin, RSP (rm). Pot/lid: 7"h., Sugar/lid: 5½"h., Creamer: 4½"h., Cup: 2"h., Saucer: 4¼"d. $2,400.00 – 2,700.00 set.

Row 3. Demitassee coffee set: Floral, satin, RSP (rm). Pot/ lid: 7¼"h., Cup: 2"h., Saucer: 4¾"d. $800.00 – 1,200.00 set.

Row 4. Salt (?): Quail (bird in flight), 4"h., RS Poland (red). $250.00 – 300.00. Plate: Quail (bird in flight), 5½"d. $400.00 – 500.00. Mirror: Handle (back), Summer "Charmer," hand-painted. $500.00 – 600.00. Mirror: handle (back), Winter "Charmer," hand-painted. $500.00 – 600.00. Wall match holder (double): Floral, RSP (rm). $250.00 – 300.00.

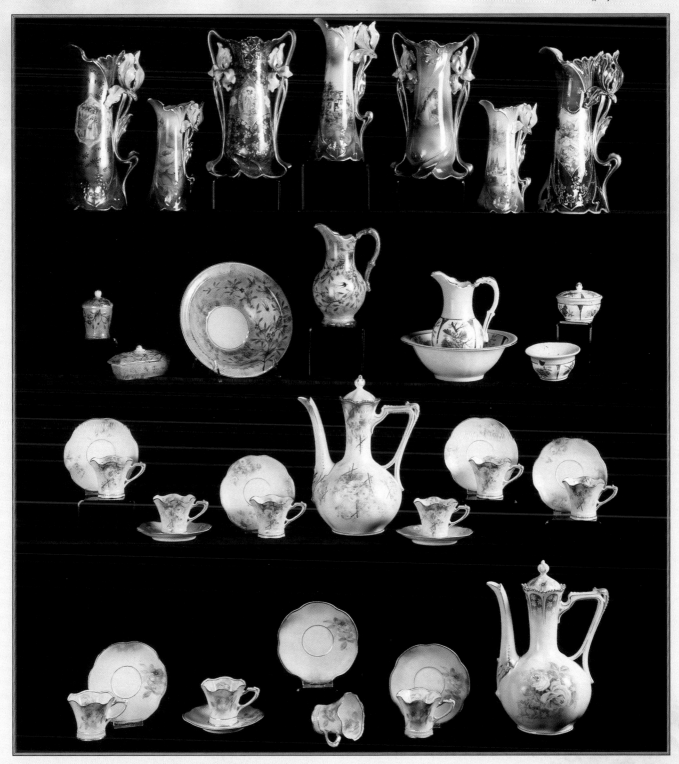

Row 1. Ewer: Iris handle (double scene), lady/ dog, and lady watering flowers, tiffany, gold trim, 10"h., Royal Vienna, Germany (red crown). $3,000.00 – 4,000.00. Ewer: Iris handle, Floral, 7"h., Royal Vienna Germany (red crown). $1,500.00 – 2,000.00. Vase: Double iris handle (double scene), lady/dog and lady watering flowers, tiffany, gold trim, 9¼"h., unmk. $2,000.00 – 2,500.00. Ewer: Iris handle, cottage scene, 8¾"h., Royal Vienna, Germany. $2,500.00 – 3,000.00. Vase: Double iris handle, flossie, 10"h., Royal Vienna, Germany. $2,000.00 – 2,500.00. Ewer: Iris handle, castle scene, 7"h., Germany, Royal, Frankfort (in gold). $1,500.00 – 2,000.00. Ewer: Iris handle, floral, cobalt, 10¼"h., Royal Vienna, Germany (red crown). $3,500.00 – 4,500.00.
Row 2. Wash stand set: Floral/ birds, miniature size, unmk. Jar/ lid (2½"h.), soap dish/ lid (3½"l. x 1½"w.), wash bowl (7"d.), pitcher (6"h.). $800.00 – 1,200.00 set. Wash stand set: Floral, miniature size, unmk. Wash bowl (7"d.), pitcher (6"d.), jar/ lid (2"h.), waste bowl with drain (2"h.). $700.00 – 1,000.00 set.
Row 3. Demi-coffee set: Floral, RSP (rm). Pot/ lid (8½"h.), cups (2"h.), saucers (4"d.). $1,000.00 – 1,400.00 set.
Row 4. Demi-coffee set: Floral, RSP (rm). Pot/lid (8½"h.), cups (2"h.), saucers (4"h.). $800.00 – 1,200.00 set.

Ewer, iris ornate gold handle, floral, 8½"h. x
4½"w., unmk. $1,500.00 – 2,000.00.

Ewer, iris ornate gold handle, floral, 10½"h., satin
finish, unmk. $2,200.00 – 2,500.00.

Tankard, floral, stippled, 13"h., RSP (rm). $800.00 – 1,000.00.

Tankard, floral, modified iris mold, very colorful, 11"h., unmk. $700.00 – 1,000.00.

Tankard, Countess Litta portrait, rosebud handle, 14"h., R.S. steeple mark. $900.00 – 1,100.00.

Chocolate pot/lid, floral, rosebud handle, 11½"h., unmk. $400.00 – 600.00.

Chocolate pot/lid, floral, pedestal, ornate lid, pink tints, 10½"h. x 7½"w., unmk. $400.00 – 600.00.

Coffeepot/lid, floral, satin, gold trim, 9¾"h., unmk. $300.00 – 500.00.

Tankard, floral, ornate gold with large yellow roses, 13"h., RSP (rm). $1,500.00 – 1,800.00.

Row 1. Tankard: Floral, cobalt strip, 13"h., RSP (rm). $4,000.00+. Tankard: Floral, carnation mold, satin, 11"h., RSP (rm). $800.00 – 1,200.00.

Row 2. Tankard: Floral, scattered flowers, satin, 14"h., RSP (rm). $1,800.00 – 2,200.00. Tankard: Floral, cobalt, jeweled, 14"h., RSP (rm). $4,000.00+.

Row 3. Tankard: Floral, cobalt and gold trim, 13"h., RSP (rm). $2,400.00 – 2,800.00. Tankard: Floral, carnation mold, satin, 13"h., RSP (rm). $1,400.00 – 1,800.00.

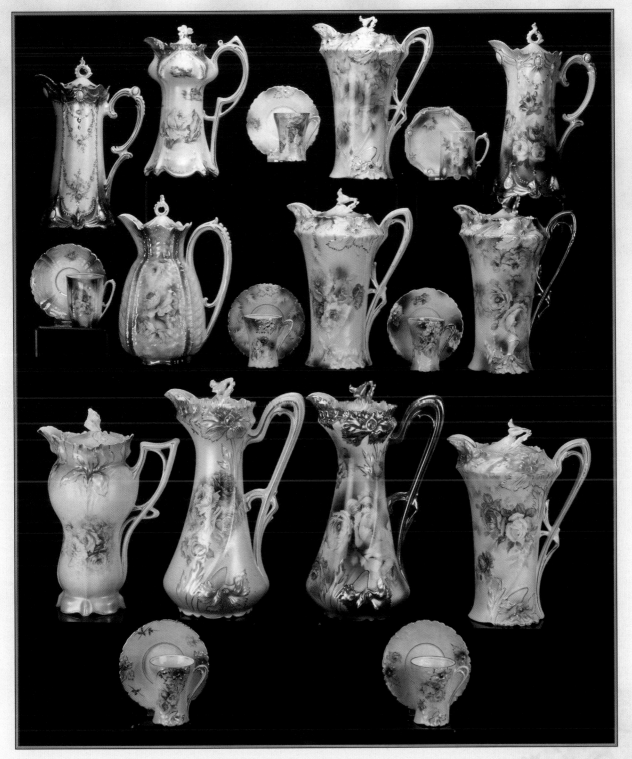

Row 1. Chocolate pot/lid: Floral, jeweled, red trim, satin, 10½"h., RSP (rm). $600.00 – 800.00. Chocolate pot/lid: Floral, 8¼"h., RSP (rm). $400.00 – 600.00. Cup/saucer: Floral, cup (3"h.), saucer (4½"d.). $150.00 – 200.00. Chocolate pot/lid: Floral, satin, 10½"h., RSP (rm). $600.00 – 800.00. Cup/saucer: Floral, cup (3"h.), saucer (4½"d.). $150.00 – 200.00. Chocolate pot/lid: Floral, jeweled, 10½"h., RSP (rm). $600.00 – 800.00.

Row 2. Cup/saucer: Floral, cup (3"h.), saucer (4½" d.). $150.00 – 200.00. Chocolate pot/lid: Floral, ribbed mold, 9¾"h., RSP (rm). $600.00 – 800.00. Cup/saucer: Floral, cup (3"h.), saucer (4½"d.). $150.00 – 200.00. Chocolate pot/lid: Floral, satin, 10½"h., RSP (rm). $600.00 – 800.00. Cup/saucer: Floral, cup (3"h.), saucer (4½"d.). $150.00 – 200.00. Chocolate pot/lid: Floral, satin, 10½"h., RSP (rm). $600.00 – 800.00.

Row 3. Chocolate pot/lid: Floral, iris mold, satin, 10½"h., RSP (rm), Gesetzilch, Geschutzet. $600.00 – 800.00. Chocolate pot/lid: Floral, carnation mold, satin, gold carnations and handle, 12"h., RSP (rm). $1,200.00 – 1,600.00. Chocolate pot/lid: Floral, carnation mold, satin, 12"h., RSP (rm). $900.00 – 1,200.00. Chocolate pot/lid: Floral, carnation. $800.00 – 1,200.00.

Row 4. Cups/saucers: (go with chocolate pot, Row 3, #2) Cups, 3"h. Saucers, 4½"d. $150.00 – 250.00 each set.

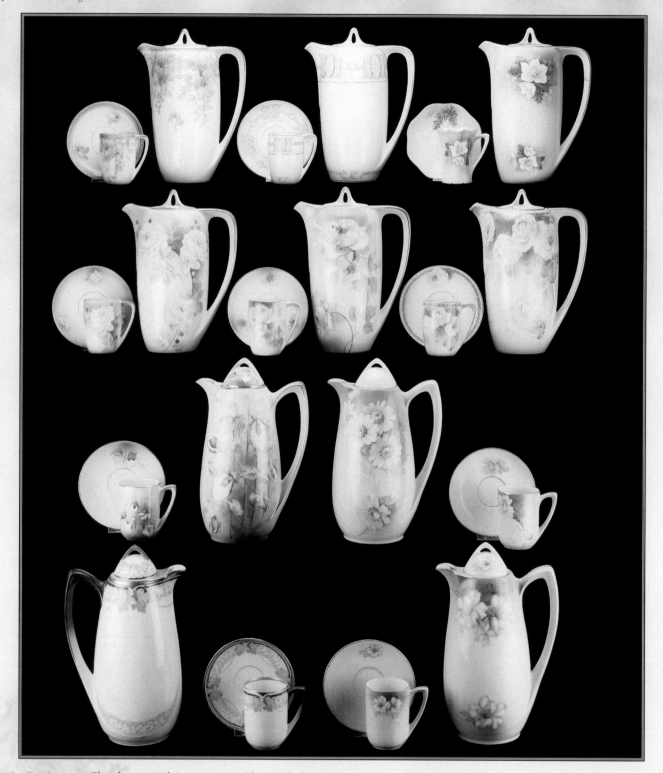

Row 1. Cup/saucer: Floral, cup (3"h.), saucer (4½"d.), RSG. $50.00 – 100.00. Chocolate pot: Floral, 8½"h., RSG. $200.00 – 250.00. Cup/saucer: Floral, cup (3"h.), saucer (4½"d.), RSG. $50.00 – 100.00. Chocolate pot: Floral, 8½"h., RSG. $200.00 – 250.00. Cup/saucer: Floral, cup (3"h.), saucer (4½"d.), RSG. $50.00 – 100.00. Chocolate pot: Floral, 8½"h., RSG. $250.00 – 300.00.
Row 2. Cup/saucer: Floral, cup (3"h.), saucer (4½"d.), RSG. $50.00 – 100.00. Chocolate pot: Floral, 8½"h., RSG. $250.00 – 300.00. Cup/saucer: Floral, cup (3"h.), saucer (4½"d.), RSG. $50.00 – 100.00. Chocolate pot: floral, 8½"h., RSG. $250.00 – 300.00. Cup/saucer: Floral, cup (3"h.), saucer (4½"d.), RSG. $50.00 – 100.00. Chocolate pot: Floral, 8½"h., RSG. $300.00 – 400.00.
Row 3. Cup/saucer: Floral, cotton plant, cup (3"h.), saucer (4½"d.), RSG. $150.00 – 200.00. Chocolate pot: Floral, cotton plant, 8½"h., RSG. $400.00 – 500.00. Chocolate pot: Floral, daisy, 8½"h., R. S. Tillowitz/Schlegelmilch (in script). $350.00 – 400.00. Cup/saucer: Floral, daisy, cup (3"h.), saucer (4½"d.), R. S. Tillowitz/Schlegelmilch (in script). $50.00 – 100.00.
Row 4. Chocolate pot: Floral, 8½"h., RSG. $250.00 – 350.00. Cup/saucer: Floral, cup (3"h.), saucer (4½"d.), RSG. $50.00 – 100.00. Cup/saucer: Floral, cup (3"h.), saucer (4½"d.), RSG. $50.00 – 100.00. Chocolate pot: Floral, 8½"h., RSG. $250.00 – 350.00.

Row 1. Chocolate pot/lid: Floral, 8¼"h., RSG. $200.00 – 250.00. Chocolate pot: Floral, 8¼"h., unmk. $400.00 – 500.00. Chocolate pot: Floral, ftd., red trim, 9"h., RSP (rm). $500.00 – 600.00. Chocolate pot: Floral, ftd., swan in medallion, 9"h., unmk. $400.00 – 500.00.

Row 2. Chocolate pot: Floral, 7½"h., RSP (rm). $250.00 – 350.00. Chocolate pot: Floral, 8¼"h., RSG (blue), Reinhold Schlegelmilch (in script). $250.00 – 350.00. Chocolate pot: Floral, 7¼"h., RSG, hand-painted. $150.00 – 250.00. Chocolate pot: Floral, 8¼"h., RSP (rm). $400.00 – 500.00.

Row 3. Chocolate pot: Chinese pheasant/pine trees, 8¼"h., RSP (rm). $500.00 – 600.00. Chocolate pot: Floral, cobalt trim, 9"h., unmk. $2,000.00 – 2,400.00. Chocolate pot: Floral, 8½"h., RSP (rm). $300.00 – 350.00.

Row 4. Chocolate pot: Floral, ftd., 9"h., RSP (rm). $400.00 – 500.00. Coffeepot: Floral, 7½"h., RSP (rm). $450.00 – 500.00. Chocolate pot: Floral, 8¾"h., RSP (rm). $700.00 – 800.00.

Row 1. Cup/saucer: Floral, cup (3"h.), saucer (4½"d.), RSG (green). $50.00 – 100.00. Chocolate pot: Floral, 8¼"h., RSG (green). $250.00 – 350.00. Cup/saucer: Floral, cup (3"h.), saucer (4½"d.), RSG (green). $50.00 – 100.00. Chocolate pot: Floral, 8¼"h., RSG (green). $250.00 – 350.00. Cup/saucer: Floral, cup (3"h.), saucer (4½"d.), RSG (green). $50.00 – 100.00. Chocolate pot: Floral, 8¼"h., RSG (green). $250.00 – 350.00.

Row 2. Cup/saucer: Floral, cup (3"h.), saucer (4½"d.), RSG (green). $50.00 – 100.00. Chocolate pot: Floral, 7½"h., RSG (green). $250.00 – 350.00. Cup/saucer: Floral, cup (3"h.), saucer (4½"d.), RS Tillowitz. $50.00 – 100.00. Chocolate pot: Floral, 8¼"h., RSP (rm). $450.00 – 550.00. Cup/saucer: Floral, cup (3"h.), saucer (4½"d.), RS Tillowitz. $50.00 – 100.00. Chocolate pot: Floral, 8¼"h., RS Tillowitz – Silesia (blue). $250.00 – 350.00.

Row 3. Cup/saucer: Floral (poppy), cup (3"h.), saucer (4½"d.), matches pot, RSG (blue). $50.00 – 100.00. Cup/saucer: White, gold band, cup (3"h.), saucer (4½"d.), RSG. $50.00 – 100.00. Chocolate pot: White, gold band, 7"h., unmk. $150.00 – 250.00. Cup/saucer: Floral, cup (3"h.), saucer (4½"d.), matches pot, RSG. $50.00 – 100.00. Cup/saucer: Floral, cup (3"h.), saucer (4½"d.), matches pot, RSG. $50.00 – 100.00.

Row 4. Chocolate pot: Floral (poppy), 8¼"h., RSG (green). $250.00 – 350.00. Cup: Floral, 3"h., RSP (rm). $100.00 – 150.00. Chocolate pot: Floral, 9"h., RSP (rm). $500.00 – 600.00. Chocolate pot: Floral, 8¼"h., RSG (green). $250.00 – 350.00.

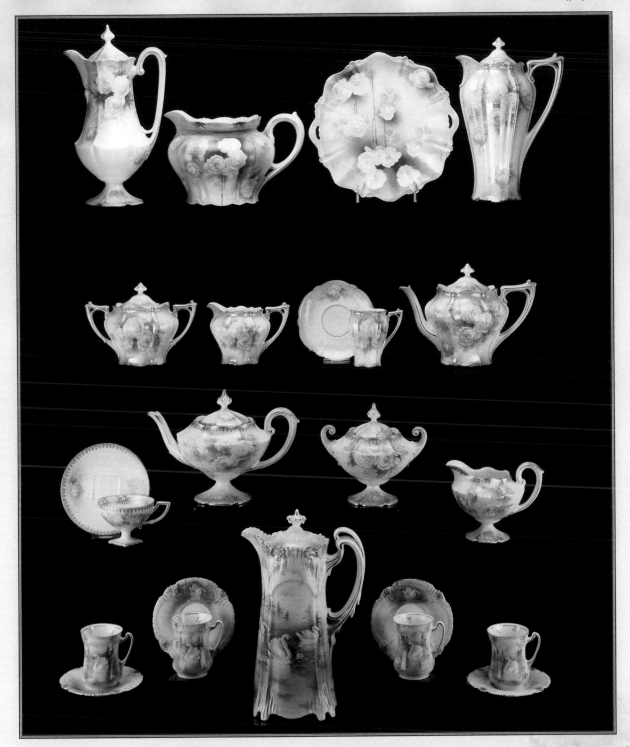

Row 1. Chocolate pot/lid: Cabbage rose, pedestal, satin, 9½"h., RSP (rm). $700.00 – 800.00. Cider pitcher: Cabbage rose, satin, 5¾"h., RSG. $500.00 – 600.00. Plate: Cabbage rose, open-handled cake plate, satin, 9½"d., RSP (rm). $300.00 – 350.00. Chocolate pot/lid: Cabbage rose, satin, 9¼"h., RSP (rm). $400.00 – 500.00.
Row 2. Sugar: Cabbage rose, satin, 4"h., RSP (rm). $150.00 – 200.00. Creamer: Cabbage rose, satin, 3½"h., RSP (rm). $125.00 – 175.00. Cup/saucer: Cabbage rose, satin, cup (3½"h.), RSP (rm); saucer (4"d.), unmk. $100.00 – 150.00. Teapot/lid: Cabbage rose, satin, 4½"h., RSP (rm). $400.00 – 500.00.
Row 3. Cup/saucer: Cabbage rose, pedestal, satin, cup (3"h.), saucer (4½"d.), RSP (rm). $150.00 – 200.00. Teapot/lid: Cabbage rose, pedestal, satin, 4½"h., RSP (rm). $600.00 – 700.00. Sugar/lid: Cabbage rose, pedestal, satin, 3½"h., RSP (rm). $250.00 – 300.00. Creamer: Cabbage rose, pedestal, satin, 4"h., RSP (rm). $250.00 – 300.00.
Row 4. Cup/saucer: Swan, icicle mold, cup (3"h.), saucer (4½"d.), unmk. $250.00 – 300.00. Cup/saucer: Swan, icicle mold, cup (3"h.), saucer (4½"d.), unmk. $250.00 – 300.00. Chocolate pot/lid: Swans, icicle mold, 9½"h., unmk. $1,200.00 – 1,600.00. Cup/saucer: Swan, icicle mold, cup (3"h.), saucer (4½"d.), unmk. $250.00 – 300.00. Cup/saucer: Swan, icicle mold, cup (3"h.), saucer (4½"d.), unmk. $250.00 – 300.00.

California Poppy

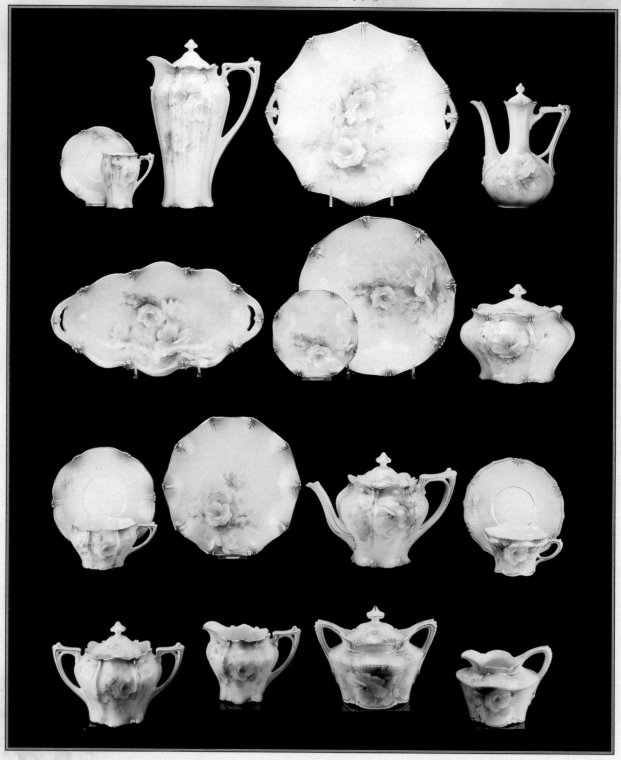

Row 1. Cup/saucer: Cup, 3¼"h., RSP (rm); saucer, 4½"d., unmk. $75.00 – 125.00. Chocolate pot/lid: 9"h., RSP (rm). $600.00 – 700.00. Plate: Open-handled, 11"d., RSP (rm), $350.00 – 400.00. Demitasse pot/lid: 6"h., RSP (rm). $500.00 – 600.00.
Row 2. Celery: Open-handled, 11"l., RSP (rm). $300.00 – 375.00. Dessert bowl: 5"d., RSP (rm). $75.00 – 125.00. Bowl (master fruit): 9"d., RSP (rm). $350.00 – 400.00. Cracker jar/lid: 4"h., RSP (rm). $300.00 – 400.00.
Row 3. Cup/saucer: Cup (2½"h.), saucer (5½"d.), RSP (rm), Royal Berlin. $100.00 – 150.00. Plate: (goes with Row 1, #3) 8"d., RSP (rm). $150.00 – 250.00. Teapot/lid: 4"h., RSP (rm). $450.00 – 500.00. Cup/saucer: Cup (2½"h.), saucer (5½"d.), RSP (rm). $100.00 – 150.00.
Row 4. Sugar/lid: 3½"h., RSP (rm). $125.00 – 175.00. Creamer: 3½"h., RSP (rm). $100.00 – 150.00. Sugar/lid: 4"h., RSP (rm). $125.00 – 175.00. Creamer: 3"h., RSP (rm). $100.00 – 150.00.

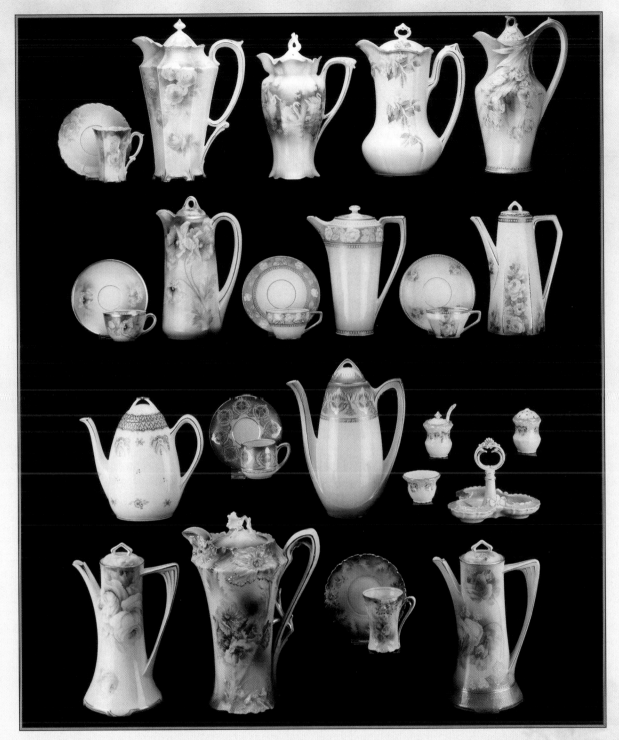

Row 1. Cup/saucer: Cabbage rose, cup, 3"h., RSP (rm); saucer (4½"d.). $75.00 – 125.00. Chocolate pot/lid: Floral, 9"h., RSP (rm). $700.00 – 800.00. Chocolate pot/lid: Floral, 8"h., unmk. $250.00 – 300.00. Chocolate pot/lid: Floral, 8¼"h., RSP (rm). $600.00 – 700.00. Chocolate pot/lid: Floral, 8¾"h., RSP (rm). $250.00 – 350.00.

Row 2. Cup/saucer: Poppy, cup (1½"h.), saucer (4½"d.), RSG (green). $75.00 – 125.00. Chocolate pot/lid: Poppy, 8"h., RSG (green). $150.00 – 200.00. Cup/saucer: Floral, gold roses border, 7¾"h., warranted 18K gold. $75.00 – 125.00. Chocolate pot/lid: Floral (roses border), 7¾"h., warranted 18K gold. $250.00 – 300.00. Cup/saucer: Floral (rose column), cup (1½"h.), saucer (4½"d.), RSG (green). $75.00 – 125.00. Chocolate pot/lid: Floral (rose column), gold trim, 7"h., unmk. $250.00 – 300.00.

Row 3. Demitasse coffeepot/lid: blue/white, 5½"h., RSG. $150.00 – 200.00. Cup/saucer: Geometric design, cup (1¾"h.), saucer (4½"d.), RSG. $75.00 – 125.00. Coffeepot/lid: Geometric design, 7¾"h., RSG (green). $200.00 – 250.00. Condiment set (miniature): Mustard/lid, sugar shaker (2"h.), toothpick holder (1¼"h.), unmk; caddy (4¼"h.), RSP. $500.00 – 600.00.

Row 4. Demitasse coffeepot/lid: Floral, 8"h., RSG (green). $200.00 – 300.00. Chocolate pot/lid: Floral, carnation mold, satin, 9½"h., RSP (rm). $800.00 – 1,200.00. Cup/saucer: Floral, carnation mold, satin, cup (2¾"h., RSP), saucer (4½"d., unmk.). $150.00 – 200.00. Demitasse coffeepot/lid: Floral, 8"h., RSG (green). $200.00 – 250.00.

Row 1. Chocolate pot/lid: Hanging basket, floral, icicle mold, 9"h., RSP (rm). $1,000.00 – 1,400.00. Cup/saucer: Hanging basket, cup (3"h.), saucer (4½"d.), unmk. $150.00 – 200.00. Plate: Floral, open-handle cake plate, satin, 10½"d, RSP (rm). $250.00 – 300.00. Cup/saucer: Floral, satin, cup (3"h., RSP rm), saucer (4¼"d.), unmk. $75.00 – 125.00. Chocolate pot/lid: Floral, satin, 9½"h., RSP (rm). $650.00 – 750.00.

Row 2. Cup/saucer: Floral, satin, cup (3¾"h.), saucer (4½"d.), RSP (rm). $75.00 – 125.00. Chocolate pot/lid: Floral, satin, 9½"h., RSP (rm). $650.00 – 750.00. Tureen/lid: Floral, satin, pedestal, 6½"h., RSP (rm). $700.00 – 800.00. Teapot/lid: Floral, (goes with Row 4, sugar & creamer), satin, 4½"h., unmk. $350.00 – 450.00.

Row 3. Cup/saucer: Floral (lily), cup, 3"h., RSG (blue), saucer (4½"d.), Reinhold, Schlegelmilch, Tillowitz, Germany (in red). $75.00 – 125.00. Chocolate pot/lid: Floral, satin, lily, 8¼"h., RSG. $250.00 – 300.00. Cracker jar/lid: Floral, satin, 5¾"h., RSP (rm). $500.00 – 600.00. Cup/saucer: Floral, satin, cup (3"h., RSP rm), saucer (4½"d., unmk.). $75.00 – 125.00. Chocolate pot/lid: Floral, satin, 9"h., unmk. $500.00 – 600.00.

Row 4. Sugar shaker: Floral, ftd., satin, 4½"h., RSP (rm). $150.00 – 250.00. Salt and pepper shakers: Floral, satin, 2½"h., RSP (rm). $100.00 – 150.00 each. Sugar/lid: Floral, satin, 3½"h., RSP (rm). $150.00 – 200.00. Creamer: Floral, satin, 4¼"h., RSP (rm). $100.00 – 150.00. Cracker jar/lid: Floral, satin, 4¼"h., unmk. $500.00 – 600.00.

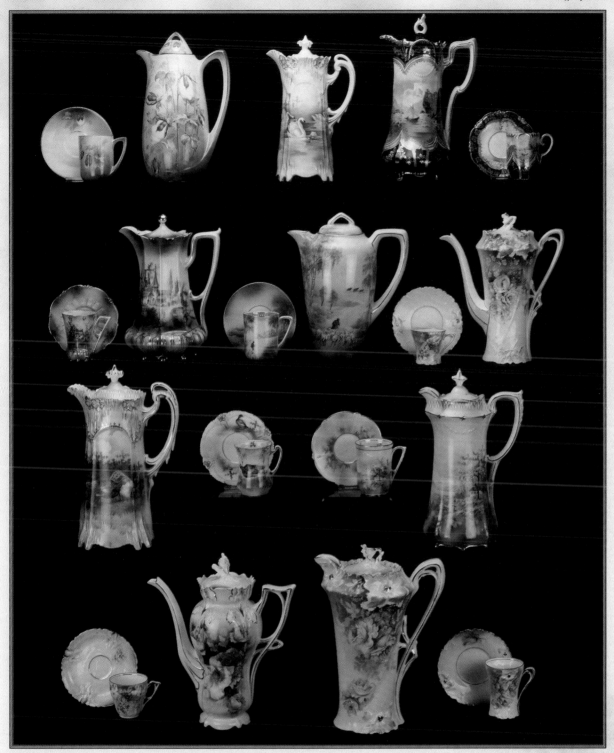

Row 1. Cup/saucer: Cotton plant, cup (3"h.), saucer (5"d.), R.S. Germany. $150.00 – 200.00. Chocolate pot/lid: Cotton plant, 9¾"h., R. S. Germany. $400.00 – 500.00. Chocolate pot/lid: Swan, icicle mold, 9½"h., R. S. Germany. $1,200.00 – 1,600.00. Chocolate pot/lid: Man on mountain (cove), black trim, RSP (rm). $3,000.00 – 3,500.00. Cup/saucer: Man on mountain, black trim, cup (3"h.), saucer (4½"d.) $300.00 – 500.00.
Row 2. Cup/saucer: Cottage scene, cup (3"h.), saucer (4½"d.), RSP (rm). $150.00 – 200.00. Chocolate pot/lid: Castle scene, 9½"h., RSP (rm). $1,000.00 – 1,200.00. Cup/saucer: Sheepherder scene, cup (3"h.), saucer (4½"d.). $175.00 – 295.00. Chocolate pot/lid: Sheepherder scene, 10"h., R. S. Germany. $600.00 – 800.00. Cup/saucer: Floral, cup (3"h.), saucer (4½"d.), RSP (rm). $100.00 – 150.00. Coffeepot/lid: Carnation, 10"h., RSP (rm). $600.00 – 800.00.
Row 3. Chocolate pot/lid: Barnyard scene, icicle mold, RSP (rm). $1,800.00 – 2,000.00. Cup/saucer: Barnyard scene, cup (3"h., turkey), saucer (4½"d., duck) $200.00 – 300.00. Cup/saucer: Sheepherder scene, cup (3"h.,) saucer (4½"d.). $175.00 – 250.00. Chocolate pot/lid: Sheepherder scene, 11"h., RSP (rm). $1,200.00 – 1,600.00.
Row 4. Cup/saucer: Floral, cup (2¼"h.), saucer (4½"d.). $100.00 – 150.00. Coffeepot/lid: Floral, iris mold, 9"h., RSP (rm). $300.00 – 500.00. Chocolate pot/lid: Floral, carnation mold, 10"h., RSP (rm). $500.00 – 700.00. Cup/saucer: Floral, carnation mold, cup (3"h.), saucer (4½"d.), RSP (rm). $100.00 – 150.00.

Row 1. Plate: Floral, blue ribbon, 10½"d., RSP (rm). $300.00 – 500.00. Cracker jar/lid: Pink, gold ribbon, 6½"h., unmk. $500.00 – 700.00. Chocolate pot/lid: Floral, gold ribbon, 9"h., unmk. $600.00 – 800.00. Plate: Floral, white ribbon, 10½"d., unmk. $300.00 – 500.00.
Row 2. Mug: Floral, blue ribbon, 3¼"h., RSP (rm). $300.00 – 400.00. Salt/pepper shakers: Floral, 3"h., unmk. $200.00 – 300.00. Lemonade pitcher: Floral, white ribbon, gold trim, 6"h., unmk. $700.00 – 1,000.00. Chocolate pot/lid: Pink, gold bow, 6"h., unmk. $600.00 – 800.00. Pitcher (milk): Floral, blue ribbon, 5"h., unmk. $500.00 – 800.00. Sugar/lid: Pink, gold bow, 4½"h., unmk. $200.00 – 300.00. Creamer: Pink, gold bow, 3¼"h., unmk. $200.00 – 300.00.
Row 3. Bun bowl: Pink, gold ribbon, 12½"l. x 8"w., unmk. $400.00 – 600.00. Berry bowl & dessert: Pink, gold ribbon, (lg. bowl – 10¼"d., $300.00 – 500.00), (dessert – 5"d., $200.00 – 400.00). Salt/pepper shakers: Floral, gold ribbon, 3"h., unmk. $100.00 – 200.00 each. Syrup & underplate: Blue, gold ribbon & handle (syrup – 2½"h.), (underplate – 6"l. x 5"w.), unmk. $400.00 – 600.00. Toothpick holder: Floral, gold ribbon, 2¼"h., unmk. $400.00 – 600.00.
Row 4. Celery: Floral, blue ribbon, 12"l. x 6"w., unmk. $300.00 – 500.00. Plate: Pink, gold ribbon, 6"d., unmk. $200.00 – 400.00. Bun bowl: Floral, blue ribbon 12½"l. x 8"w., unmk. $400.00 – 600.00.

Berry set, bowtie, blue and gold ties. Large bowl, 9"d. Desserts, 5"d., unmk. Large, $300.00 – 500.00. Small, $200.00 – 400.00.

Syrup, bowtie, pink and gold ties, 4"h. x 4"w., unmk. $300.00 – 500.00.

Sugar/lid, bowtie, blue with gold ties, 2½"h. x 5"w., unmk. $200.00 – 300.00. Creamer, bowtie, blue with gold ties, 3"h. x 4½"w., unmk. $200.00 – 300.00.

Lemonade pitcher, floral, gold trim, satin, 6½"h. x 9½"w., RSP (rm). $300.00 – 500.00.

Chocolate set, floral, rose column, ornate handle, gold trim, RSP (rm). Pot, pedestal, 9½"h. Cups, pedestal, 3"h. Saucers, 4½"d. $1,500.00 – 1,800.00 set.

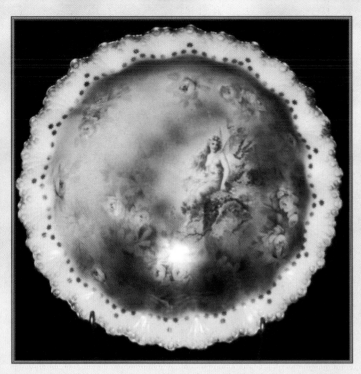

Bowl, lady (wings), on cliff, gold trim, 10"d., RSP (rm). $1,400.00 – 1,800.00.

Bowl, swans, unusual scene, 10"d., RSP (rm). $1,400.00 – 1,800.00.

Tea set, wreath of roses, satin, RSP (rm). Pot, 6½"h. Creamer, 4½"h. Sugar/lid, 5"h. $1,200.00 – 1,500.00. Cup/saucer, $100.00 – 150.00.

Hatpin holder, floral, ornate handles, gold trim, satin, 5"h. x 4"w., RSP (rm). $400.00 – 600.00.

Lemonade pitcher, floral, hanging green jewels, satin, 5¼"h. x 8"w., RSP (rm). $300.00 – 500.00.

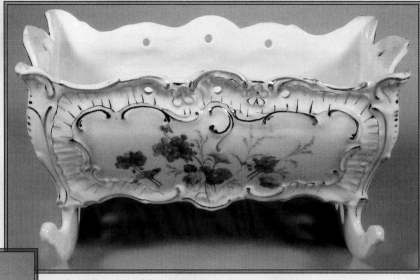

Basket, floral, gold trim, cradle legs, 9"l., E.S. Prussia. $300.00 – 500.00.

Dresser tray, floral, open-handled, gold trim, satin, 12½"l. x 8½"w. (Royal Vienna). $400.00 – 600.00. Candlestick holders, floral, gold trim, satin, pedestal, 6"h. (Royal Vienna). $400.00 – 600.00 pair. Covered piece/lid, floral, gold trim, satin, 3½"h. x 4"w. (Royal Vienna). $200.00 – 400.00.

Salad bowl, 5"h. x 10½"d., RSP (rm). $400.00 – 600.00. Underplate, floral, 10½"d. (Germany indented). $300.00 – 500.00.

Plate, Spring "Charmer," keyhole, floral, tiffany border, 8¼"d., RSP (rm). $3,000.00 – 3,500.00. Ewer, Fall season, pedestal, ornate gold handle, satin, 10½"h., RSP (rm). $3,600.00 – 4,000.00. Plate, cherub and harp, satin, 8½"d., RSP (rm). $3,500.00 – 4,500.00. Mustard pot/lid, Winter season, satin, iris mold, 3¼"h., RSP (rm). $1,000.00 – 1,400.00. Covered box/lid, floral, satin, 6½"l. x 6"w., RSP (rm). $300.00 – 450.00. Cup/saucer, floral, satin, gold trim. Cup, 2⅛"h. Saucer, gold trim, RSP (rm). $150.00 – 200.00.

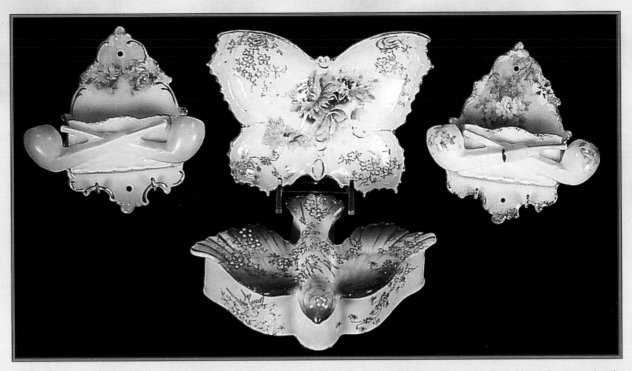

Hanging match holder, floral, applied pipes, 4¾"l. x 4½"w., unmk. $400.00 – 500.00 each. Pin tray, butterfly shaped, 4"h. x 5½"w., unmk. $300.00 – 450.00. Covered box/lid, floral, bird shaped, 5½"l. x 3½"w., unmk. $600.00 – 800.00.

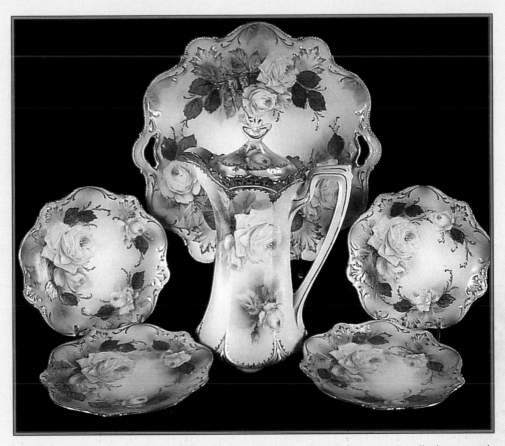

Cake set. Plate, open-handled, peach roses, gold trim, 10¾"d., RSP (rm). Small plates, 6¼"d., RSP (rm). Five-piece cake set, $600.00 – 800.00. Chocolate pot/lid, peach roses, gold trim, 9"h. (green RSG steeple). $600.00 – 800.00.

Tea set, floral, morning glory mold, ornate handles. Pot/lid, 7"h. $400.00 – 600.00. Sugar/lid, 5"h. x 5"w. $200.00 – 300.00. Creamer, 4½"h. $200.00 – 400.00.

Child's tea set, colonial people, tiffany trim. Pot/lid, 4"h. x 4"w. $400.00 – 600.00. Cups, 1¼"h. x 1¼"d. Saucers, 3"d. $150.00 – 200.00.

Chocolate set, floral, cut glass. Pot/lid, 10"h. $700.00 – 900.00. Cups, 2¼"h. x 2¾"d. Saucers, 5"d. $200.00 – 300.00. Set, $1,500.00 – 1,800.00.

Chocolate set, cotton plant, gold trim (RSG). Pot/lid, 9½"h. x 6½"w. $400.00 – 500.00. Cups, 2¼"d. Saucers, 4½"d. $150.00 – 200.00 each. Set, $1,200.00 – 1,400.00.

Tea set, floral, gold trim, RSP (rm). Pot/lid, 8"h. x 6"w. Sugar/lid, 5½"h. x 5"w. Creamer, 5"h. x 4"w. $600.00 – 800.00.

Tea set, hexagonal, floral, gold trim. Pot/lid, 7½"h. x 7"w. Sugar/lid, 5"h. x 5¼"w. Creamer, 4"h. x 4¼"w. $600.00 – 800.00.

Sugar/lid, floral, morning glory mold, ornate handles, 5"h. x 5"w. $150.00 – 250.00. Creamer, floral, morning glory mold, ornate handle, 4½"h. $150.00 – 200.00. Spooner, floral, morning glory mold, 4½"h. $200.00 – 300.00. Butter dish/lid, 4½"h. x 7½"d. $250.00 – 400.00.

Sugar/lid, sunflower, footed, gold trim, purple tint, 4½"h. x 5½"w. (RSP). $200.00 – 350.00. Cracker jar/lid, sunflower, footed, gold trim, purple tint, 6½"h. x 6½"w. (RSP). $800.00 – 1,200.00. Creamer, sunflower, footed, gold trim, purple tint, 3½"h. x 4½". (RSP). $200.00 – 350.00. Mustard, sunflower, footed, gold trim, purple tint, 3¼"h. x 3"w. (RSP). $300.00 – 400.00.

Coffee set, carnation mold, floral, satin, RSP (rm). Pot/lid, 9"h. $600.00 – 800.00. Cups, 2¼"d. x 2"h.
Saucers, 4¼"d. $100.00 – 150.00.

Plate, Madame LeBrun, Greek Key, red, gold trim, 8"d., unmk.
$1,000.00.

Plate, Madame LeBrun, red, gold trim, 10½"d., unmk. $1,200.00.

Plate, Countess Potocka, Greek Key, red, gold trim, 8"d., unmk. $1,000.00.

Plate, scattered flowers, point and clover mold, 9"d., RSP (rm). $350.00.

Plaque, two scenes (mill & swans), red and blue flower border, 11"d., unmk., rare. $2,400.00 – 2,800.00.

Plaque, snowbirds, red with blue flower border, 11"d., unmk., rare.
$2,800.00 – 3,200.00.

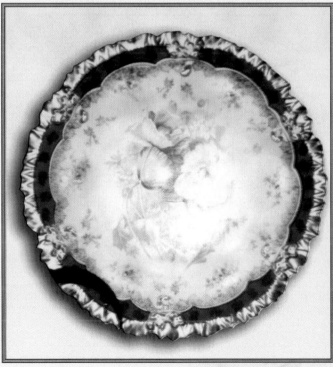

Plate, scattered flowers, red and gold border, 9"d., RSP (rm). $350.00.

Plate, floral, satin, red and gold trim, 9"d., RSP (rm). $250.00.

Plate, rosebud mold, red panels, 8½"d., unmk. $400.00 – 600.00.

Bowl-in-bowl, floral, wheat mold, 10"d., unmk. $400.00 – 600.00.

Tankard, floral, stippled, red, 13"h. RSP (rm). $800.00 – 1,000.00.

Cracker jar/lid, floral, ball feet, red, gold trim, 5"h. x 9"w., RSP (rm). $550.00 – 650.00.

Sugar/lid, Countess Potocka portrait, red, gold trim, 4½"h. Creamer, 3½"h., unmk. $800.00 – 1,000.00 set.

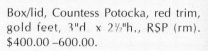

Box/lid, Countess Potocka, red trim, gold feet, 3"d. x 2½"h., RSP (rm). $400.00 –600.00.

Syrup/lid, Madame LeBrun, ornate, red trim, 4½"h., unmk. Underplate, Madame LeBrun, ornate, red trim, 5¼"d., unmk. $800.00 – 1,000.00.

Cup/saucer, Madame LeBrun, red trim. Cup, pedestal, 2½"h. (RSG steeple). Saucer, 4½"d. $300.00 – 500.00 set.

Vase, The Painter, red, gold trim, 8½"h. (RS Suhl). $600.00 – 800.00.

Relish, four medallions, castle and cottage scene, floral, open-handled, red medallions and trim. $500.00 – 700.00.

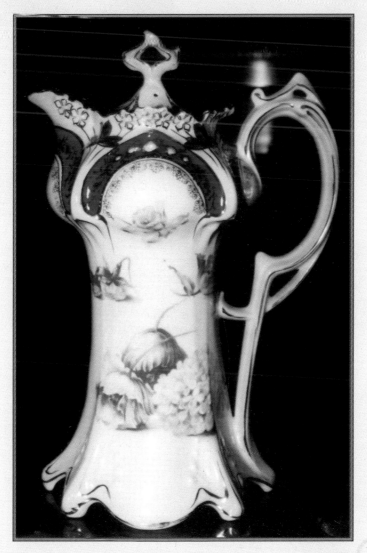

Chocolate pot, scattered flowers, red trim, ornate handle, 11"h., RSP (rm). $650.00.

Bowl, floral, footed, point and clover, red, gold trim, 2½"h. x 7"d. (RSP). $200.00 – 300.00.

Bun tray, floral, open-handled, point and clover, red, gold trim, 13"l., RSP (rm). $400.00 – 600.00.

Plate, floral, open-handled, point and clover, red, gold trim, 11"d., RSP (rm).
$450.00 – 500.00.

Celery, floral, open-handled, point and clover, red, gold trim, 15"l. x 5½"w., RSP (rm). $400.00 – 600.00.

271

Plates (two), floral (chrysanthemum), open-handled, red, 11"d., unmk. $300.00 – 500.00 each. Sugar/lid, floral (chyrsanthemum), red, 4½"h., unmk. $150.00 – 200.00. Vase, floral (chrysanthemum), red, 5½"h., unmk. $200.00 – 300.00. Creamer, floral (chyrsanthemum), red, 3½"h., unmk. $150.00 – 200.00.

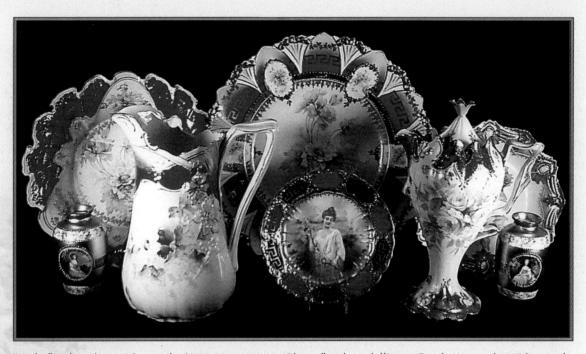

Bowl, floral, red, 10¾"d., unmk. $350.00 – 400.00. Plate, floral medallions, Greek Key, red, 12"d., unmk. $500.00 – 700.00. Plate, floral, jewels, red, 8½"d., RSP (rm). $300.00 – 400.00. Vases (two matching), colonial ladies in medallions, heavy gold. $400.00 – 500.00 pair. Pitcher, floral, red, 9½"h., unmk. $500.00 – 700.00. Plate, Spring season, Greek Key, red/green. $600.00 – 800.00. Chocolate pot, floral, red, gold trim, pedestal, ornate, 10"h. $800.00 – 1,000.00.

Plate, Madame LeBrun, red, gold trim, 7¾"d. $800.00 – 1,000.00. Ewer, colonial people, red, ornate gold handle and trim, 6"h. $500.00 – 650.00. Vase, Madame LeBrun, red/green with ornate gold handles and trim, 5"h. (Royal Vienna, gold). $500.00 – 600.00. Vase, Madame LeBrun, white hat, red, gold trim, 6¼"h. $600.00 – 700.00. Plate, Madame Recaimer, red, gold trim, 7¾"d. $800.00 – 1,000.00.

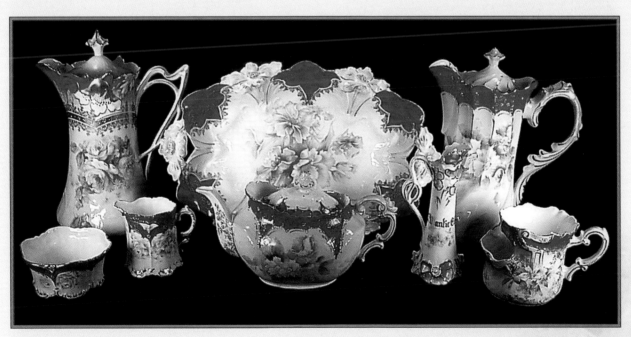

Chocolate pot/lid, floral, red, gold trim, 9¾"h, unmk. $400.00 – 500.00. Bowl, floral, open-handled, red, gold trim, 13"l. x 8"w., unmk. $500.00 – 600.00. Chocolate pot/lid, floral, fold-over handle, red, gold trim, 9½"h., unmk. $400.00 – 500.00. Creamer, 2¾"h. $200.00 – 300.00. Sugar, 1¾"h. x 3¾"d., unmk. $200.00 – 300.00. Teapot/lid, floral, red grim, 5"h. x 8"w. unmk. $200.00 – 300.00. Ewer, floral, ornate handle, red trim, "Atlantic City" souvenir, 5¾"h., unmk. $200.00 – 250.00. Mug, $400.00 – 500.00.

Plate, floral, open-handled, red trim, 10"d., unmk. $100.00 – 200.00. Chocolate pot/lid, Madame LeBrun in gold tapestry medallion on front and back, floral, red, 10½"h. $1,000.00 – 1,500.00. Cup, 3"h. Saucer, 4½"d., RSP (rm). Cup/saucer $100.00 – 200.00. Plate, Summer season, six floral medallions, red, 10½"d., RSP (rm). $1,600.00 – 2,000.00. Vase, Queen Louise portrait, red trim, 5"h., unmk. $200.00 – 300.00.

Plate, floral, 12 red petals, gold trim, 12"d., unmk. $450.00 – 550.00. Cracker jar/lid, floral, pedestal base, handles, red, gold trim, 5"h. x 9½"w., unmk. $400.00 – 600.00. Demitasse pot/lid, floral, ornate pedestal base and handle, red, gold trim, 9"h., unmk. $400.00 – 600.00. Nappy, floral, strap handle, red, gold trim, 8", unmk. $200.00 – 400.00. Syrup/lid, floral, pedestal base, red, gold trim, 4½"h., unmk. $250.00 – 500.00. Relish, floral, open-handled, red, gold trim, 9½"l., unmk. $200.00 – 300.00.

Cup/saucer, floral, daisy outline transfer, red trim, unmk. Cup, 2½"h. Saucer, 5¾"d. Cup/saucer, $75.00 – 125.00. Milk pitcher, 6½"h. $200.00 – 300.00. Relish, open-handled, 6¾"l. x 5"w. $100.00 – 150.00. Butter pats (six), 3"d. $30.00 – 50.00 each. Mustard/lid, 3"h. $100.00 – 150.00. Bell, 3½". $250.00 – 300.00.

Plate, floral, red, gold trim, satin, 8"d., unmk. $200.00 – 300.00. Plate, floral, red, satin, 11"d., RSP (rm). $500.00 – 600.00. Plate, floral, scattered flowers, red, satin, 8½"d., RSP (rm). $400.00 – 500.00. Mustard/lid, floral, red, gold trim, satin, 3¼"h., RSP (rm). $100.00 – 150.00. Demitasse pot/lid, floral, red, gold trim, 9"h., unmk. $400.00 – 600.00. Syrup/lid, floral, scattered flowers, ftd., red, 5"h., RSP (rm). $250.00 – 500.00.

Scroll mold: Plate, floral, red, 8½"d., unmk. $75.00 – 150.00. Tray, floral, open-handled, red, 11½"l. x 8"w., unmk. $250.00 – 350.00. Bowl, floral (scroll), red, 10½"d, unmk. $150.00 – 250.00. Cup/saucer, floral, red. Cup, 2¾"h. Saucer, 4"h. Cup/saucer, $150.00 – 250.00. Calendar holder, floral, red, 3½"h., unmk. $300.00 – 400.00. Letter holder, floral, red, 5"h., unmk. $300.00 – 400.00. Basket, floral, gold handle, red, 4"h. x 5½"l., unmk. $250.00 – 350.00. Cup/saucer, floral, demitasse, red. Cup, 2½"h. Saucer, 4"h., unmk. Cup/saucer, $75.00 – 150.00. Box/lid, floral, heart-shaped, red, 4½"l. x 4"w., unmk. $250.00 – 300.00. Hair receiver/lid, floral, red, 4½"d., unmk. $100.00 – 200.00. Relish, floral, open-handled, red, 6"l. x 4½"w., unmk. $175.00 – 275.00.

Pair of 11" iris variant cake plates. $400.00 – 500.00 each. Red fernery, $500.00 – 600.00. Shaving mug, $100.00 – 200.00. Mustard with spoon, $400.00 – 500.00.

Woodland & House in the Forest Tea set, medieval scenes, gold trim. Pot, 4"h. Sugar/lid, 3½"h. x 6"w. Creamer, 3½"h. $500.00 – 700.00.

Plate, sheepherder, 10-sided, reticulated, 10"d. (RSG). $600.00 – 800.00.

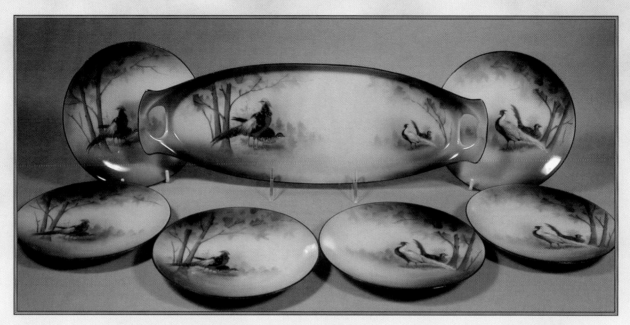

Tray set, pheasants. Large open-handled tray, 15½"l. x 5¼"w. Small plates (six), 6½"d. $800.00 – 1,000.00.

Berry set, house/lake scene, octagonal-shaped, gold trim (RSG). Large bowl, 8½" x 8½". Desserts (six), 4½" x 4½". $800.00 – 1,000.00.

Candlestick holder, sheepherder scene, handle, 3½"h. x 4½"w. (RSG). $400.00 – 600.00.

Cracker jar/lid, woman/oxen, gold trim, 5¼"h. x 8"w. (RSG). $600.00 – 800.00.

Row 1. Relish tray: Man/cart, 12¾"l. x 6⅝"w., unmk. $150.00 – 200.00. Dresser tray: Golden pheasant, woodland scene, open-handled, 11¾"l. x 7"w., RS Germany hand painted in gold. $250.00 – 300.00. Relish: Cottage, woodland scene, 9"l. x 4"w., RSG (green), RS Germany, hand painted in gold, artist-signed, "Klett." $100.00 – 150.00.

Row 2. Chocolate set: Woodland scene. Pot/lid: man/cart, 9¼"h., RSG, artist-signed, "Kolb." $600.00–800.00. Cups/saucers: Woodland scene, duck/sheepherder, cups (3"h.), saucers (4½"d.), artist-signed, "Rein" or "Kolb," RSG (green), RSG hand painted in gold. $200.00 – 300.00 each. Sugar/lid: Man/cart, RSG (green), artist-signed, "Kolb." $100.00 – 150.00. Creamer: Sheepherder, artist signed "Kolb," RSG hand painted in gold. $100.00 – 150.00. Salt shaker: Man on horse, woodland scene, 2¾"h., RSG (green). $100.00 – 150.00. Pepper shaker: Man on horse, woodland scene, 2¾"h., RSG (green). $100.00 – 150.00.

Row 3. Plate/cup (snack set): Woodland scene, pheasants, 8¼"d., RSG (in blue). $150.00 – 200.00. Tray (top): Diana the huntress, miniature, reticulated, 6"l. x 3"w., RSG (green). $150.00 – 200.00. Tray (top): "Flora," miniature, reticulated, 6"l. x 3"w., RSG (green). $150.00 – 200.00. Tray: Lady and fan, open-handled, miniature, 4¾"l. x 2⅞"w., RSG (green). $150.00 – 200.00. Tray: Lady and dog, open-handled, miniature, 4¾"l. x 2⅞"w., RSG (green). $150.00 – 200.00. Tray: Lady feeding chickens, open-handled, miniature, 4¾"l. x 2⅞"w. (green). $150.00 – 200.00. Plate: Lady/oxen, woodland house, 8¼"d., RSG (green). $100.00 – 150.00.

Row 4. Sugar/lid: Sheepherder, RSG. $100.00 – 150.00. Creamer: Sheepherder, RSG. $100.00 – 150.00. Cracker jar/lid: Man/woman on horses, house, 5¼"h., RSG (green). $500.00 – 600.00. Sugar/lid: Gristmill, 3½"h., RSG (green). $100.00 – 150.00. Creamer: Sheepherder, 3"h., RSG (green). $100.00 – 150.00. Creamer: Pheasants, RSG (green). $100.00 – 150.00. Sugar/lid: Pheasants. $100.00 – 150.00. Card holder: Floral, RSG (green). $75.00 – 125.00.

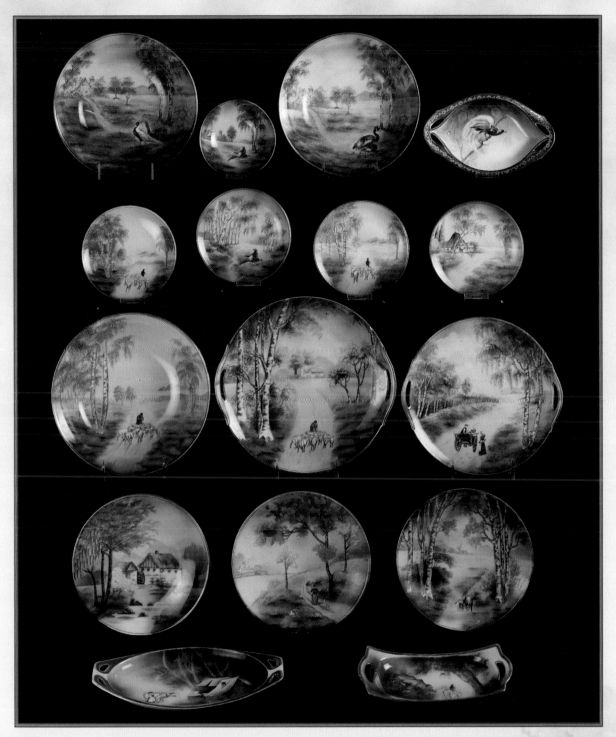

Row 1. Bowl: Pheasants, woodland scene/cottage, 10"d., RSG, artist-signed, "Kolb," hand painted in gold. $350.00 – 400.00. Plate: Pheasants, 6"d., artist-signed, "Schon," Germany hand painted in gold. $100.00 – 150.00. Bowl: Crown crane, woodland scene/cottage, artist-signed, "Klett," RS Germany hand painted in gold. $600.00 – 700.00. Relish tray: Bird of paradise, gold trim, 9¼"l., RS Tillowitz (in green). $250.00 – 300.00.
Row 2. Plates (four): go with plate #2 in row 3, sheepherder scenes, RSG. $100.00 – 150.00 each.
Row 3. Bowl: Sheepherder, 10"d., RSG (in green), RS Germany hand painted in gold. $300.00 – 350.00. Plate: Sheepherder, open-handled, RSG. $250.00 – 300.00. Plate: Man/cart, 10"d., RS Germany (green), RS Germany hand painted in gold. $300.00 – 350.00.
Row 4. Plate: Gristmill/stream, J.R. Company, 8¼"d., RSG. $75.00 – 125.00. Plate: Women/child picking flowers, 8¼"d., RS Germany (green), hand painted in gold, J.R. Germany. $75.00 – 125.00. Plate: Cows/stream, 8¼"d., artist-signed, "Krell," RS Germany hand painted in gold, JR Germany (green). $75.00 – 125.00.
Row 5. Tray: Woman/cows/cottage, open-handled, browns, gold trim, 10¼"l. x 6¼"w., RSG. $125.00 – 175.00. Relish tray: Sheepherder, open-handled, 8¾"l. x 4"w., RSG (green). $125.00 – 175.00.

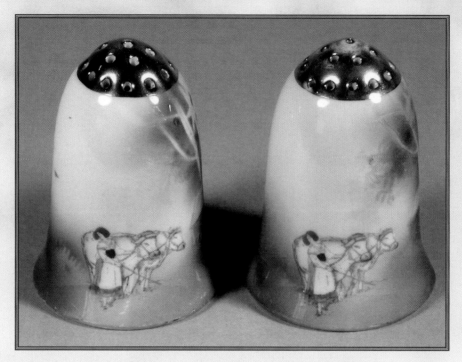

Salt and pepper shakers, woman/oxen, gold trim, 2¾"h. x 2"d. (base), RSG. $150.00 – 300.00.

Salt and pepper shakers, parrot, yellow, 2½"h. x 1½"d. (base), ES. $150.00 – 300.00.

Vase, lady with doves, handles, turquoise bead work on gold background, 6"h., ES. $500.00 – 700.00.

Bowl, floral, turquoise beads and gold trim, 10½"d. x 3"h., ES. $300.00 – 500.00.

Vase/lid, lady with peacock, turquoise bead work on gold background, 4½"h., ES. $600.00 – 800.00.

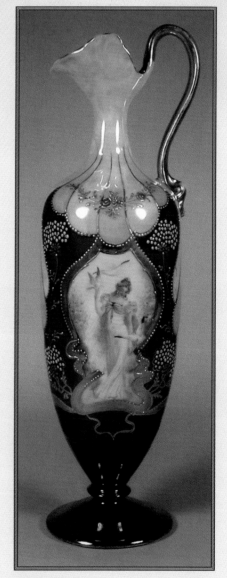

Ewer, lady with doves, pedestal base, red/blue, gold trim, 13½"h., ES. $600.00 – 800.00.

Vase, goddess of fire, ornate handles, red, blue trim, 13½"h., ES. $800.00 – 1,000.00.

Vase, woman holding flower, ornate gold handles, floral, red trim, 13¼"h., ES. $800.00 – 1,000.00.

Vase, lady with swallows, ornate gold handles, red, gold trim, 13½"h., ES. $800.00 – 1,000.00.

Vase, The Singer, ornate gold handles and trim, 11½"h., ES. $1,000.00 – 1,200.00.

Vase, The Artist, pink roses and gold trim, 8¾"h., ES. $450.00 – 600.00.

Bowl, Victorian scene, reticulated, green and gold trim, 11"l. x 10"w., unmk. $200.00 – 400.00.

Vase, maidens, floral, tapestry, ornate gold handles and trim, 7"h., ES. $500.00 – 700.00.

Stickpin holder (lid), button box (bottom), red, gold trim, 3"h. x 3½"d. (Beehive, St. Killian). $1,500.00. Plate, Procession of Bauhaus, gold and red, 9"d., OS. $800.00 – 1,200.00.

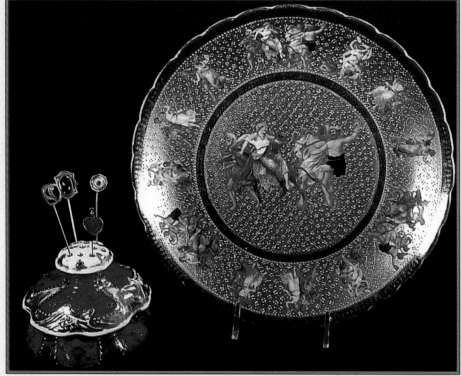

Relish, lady with doves, open-handled, two medallions, red, turquoise beads on heavy gold trim, 8¾"l. x 4⅞"w., FS. $400.00 – 600.00.

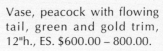

Vase, peacock with flowing tail, green and gold trim, 12"h., ES. $600.00 – 800.00.

289

Friedrich II child photo.

Entry to Friedrich II's castle in Pottsdam, Germany.

Friedrich II's castle (ville) in Pottsdam, Germany.

Friedrich II's castle gardens, Pottsdam, Germany.

Friedrich II's burial marker in Pottsdam, Germany.

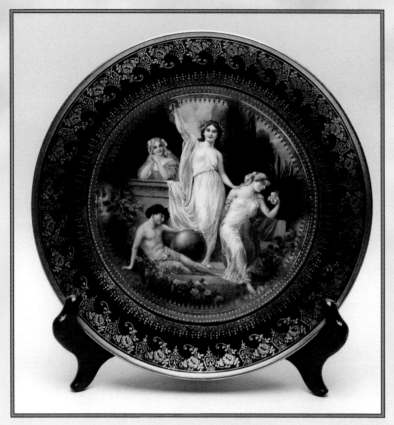

Wall plaque, maidens, cobalt, gold trim, 10"d. (Friedrich II – R.S. Suhl). $2,000.00 – 2,400.00.

Vase, Nightwatch, 11"h. (Friedrich II). $1,000.00 – 1,200.00.

Vase, maidens, cobalt, gold trim (Friedrich II). $2,500.00 – 3,000.00.

Vase, lady feeding chickens, cobalt, gold trim, 6⅜"h. (Friedrich II – R.S. Suhl). $900.00 – 1,200.00.

Vase, maidens (four), cobalt, gold trim, 13½"h.
(Friedrich II – R.S. Suhl). $3,500.00+.

Friedrich II – R.S. Suhl mark (double mark).

Vase, floral, poppies, gold handles and trim, 8"h.
(Friedrich II – R.S. Suhl, green mark). Double mark,
$600.00 – 800.00.

Vase, roses, handles, gold trim, 9¾"h. (Friedrich II – R.S. Suhl). $300.00 – 500.00.

Vases, floral, poppies, gold handles and trim, 17½"h. (Friedrich II). $4,000.00 – 5,000.00 pr.

Vase, floral, handles, gold trim, 8¼"h. (Friedrich II – R.S. Suhl). $400.00 – 600.00.

Vase, floral, gold trim, 8¼"h. (Friedrich II – R.S. Suhl). $400.00 – 600.00.

Friedrich II, crown mark.

Vase, floral, gold handles and trim, 5¾"h. (Friedrich II – R.S. Suhl). $200.00 – 300.00.

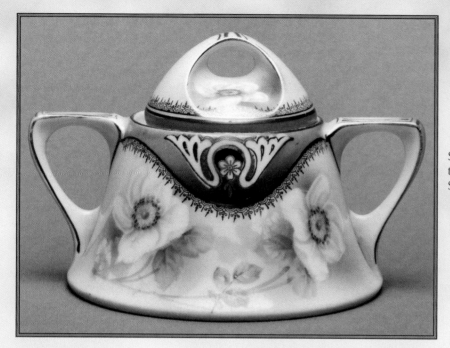

Sugar/lid, floral, green and gold trim, handles (Friedrich II – R.S. Suhl). $100.00 – 200.00.

Vase, floral, roses and garland, gold trim, 6½"h. (R.S. Poland – Made in (German) Poland. $300.00 – 400.00.

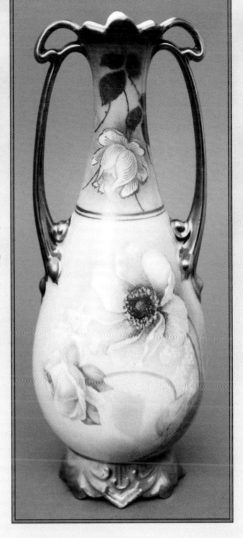

Vase, floral, ornate gold handles, foot, and trim, 9"h. (R.S. Poland – Made in (German) Poland. $500.00 – 600.00.

Vase, floral, gold trim, 6½"h. R.S. Poland – Made in (German) Poland. $300.00 – 400.00.

Vase, floral, large rose, 7⅜"h., R.S. Poland – Made in (German) Poland. $300.00 – 400.00.

Cracker jar/lid, floral, pedestal base, handles, gold trim, R.S. Poland – Made in (German) Poland. $400.00 – 600.00.

Bowl, floral, tiffany trim, 11"d. Poland China – Made in (German) Poland. $400.00 – 600.00.

Vases. Floral (clematis), gold handles, 10"h., R.S. Poland – Made in (German) Poland. $300.00 – 400.00 each.

Vase, peasant women, 4"h., R.S. Poland – Made in (German) Poland. $250.00 – 300.00.

Vases, floral, roses and garlands, gold handles, 8¼"h., R.S. Poland – Made in (German) Poland. $300.00 – 400.00 each.

Vase, floral, cobalt, gold handles and trim, 9¾"h., R.S. Poland – Made in (German) Poland. $700.00 – 900.00.

Cup/saucer, demitasse, jeweled, pedestal bases, R.S. Poland – Made in (German) Poland. $150.00 – 200.00.

Tea set: teapot, sugar/lid, creamer, pedestal bases, R.S. Poland — Made in (German) Poland. $400.00 – 600.00.

R.S. Poland mark.

Vase, fruit, handles, 5½"h. (R.S. Poland). $200.00 – 250.00.

Bird in Flight compote (pedestal base), plate, cup/saucer (R.S. Poland). Compote, $100.00 – 150.00. Plate, $100.00 – 150.00. Cup/saucer, $150.00 – 200.00.

Vase, floral (clematis), 4½"h. (R.S. Poland). $250.00 – 350.00.

Vase, floral, 9½"h., ftd., ornate handles (R.S. Poland). $600.00 – 800.00.

Bowls, hummingbirds, desserts, 5½"d. $900.00 – 1,200.00 each.

Vases, ostriches, handles, 5¾"h, (R.S. Poland), $1,200.00 – 1,400.00.

Single ostrich, miniature, green background, 3¾"h., unmk. $800.00 – 1,000.00.

Vase, tiger, miniature, 2⅜" (RS Poland). $1,500.00 – 1,800.00.

Vase, golden pheasant, ornate handles, 12"h. (R.S. Poland).
$1,200.00 – 1,400.00.

Vase, floral, miniature, 2⅜"h. (Friedrich II). $400.00 – 500.00.

Vase, lady sheepherders, 9"h. x 3½"d. (R.S. Suhl).
$300.00 – 400.00.

Vase, Melon Boys, dice players, 6"h. (R.S. Suhl).
$300.00 – 400.00.

Vase, women and cherubs, red, 8¼"h. (R.S. Suhl). $900.00 – 1,200.00.
Vase, Napoleon, red, 7½"h. (Friedrich II). $900.00 – 1,200.00.

Join in the Fun!

For several years, many collectors thought a club was needed for interested collectors that were willing to share and enjoy our hobby. In 1984, Bob and I planned and hosted a three-day mini-convention in Indianapolis, Indiana. An ad in Antique Trader attracted 20 families from various states to attend. In 1985 they decided to form a club: The International Association of R.S. Prussia Collectors, Inc. This year (2005) will mark the club's 20th anniversary. There are now over 500 family memberships in the U.S., Canada, Germany, and New Zealand.

The purposes of the organization are to:

Interest and educate others in collecting.

Recruit new members.

Increase knowledge through research.

Most importantly, promote the fellowship that creates many lasting friendships.

All members receive a quarterly newspaper. Each year, the club sponsors an annual convention, the highlight of the year. Members have the privilege of viewing 150 – 200 rooms of beautiful Schlegelmilch porcelain pieces, which are for sale, trade, or show. You may find that piece you have been searching for in the RSP Auction that is usually held on Friday evening. Several events are designed to entertain and educate the attending members. A banquet, with entertainment, will be the final event. Convention sites are held in different locations in the United States to provide equal opportunities for members to attend. In the past, they have been held in Indianapolis, Indiana (4), St. Louis, Missouri (2), Columbus, Ohio (3), Omaha, Nebraska (2), Cedar Rapids Iowa (1), Mt. Vernon, Illinois (2), Novi, Michigan (1), Lexington, Kentucky (1), Peoria, Illinois (1), Dayton, Ohio (1), and Kansas City, Missouri (1). This year (2006), it will be held in Michigan.

If you are interested in becoming a member, please contact me and I will see that you get an application so you can "join in the fun."

Mary I. McCaslin
6887 Black Oak Ct. E.
Avon, Indiana 46123–8013
e-mail: maryjack@indy.rr.com

Bibliography

"Antiques and Collectibles Price Guide." Antique Trader. F & W Publications.

"Antique Collectibles Price Guide 2005." Antique Trader. F & W Publications.

Barlock, Eileen. The Treasures of R.S. Prussia. 1976.

Brown Auction Co. (Kansas)

Capers, Ron. Capers' Notes on the Marks of Prussia. El Paso, Illinois: Alphabet Printing, 1996.

Cels, Nancy. "Further Thoughts of D.C. Ware." International Association of R.S. Prussia Collectors, Inc. newsletter, Issue #53, 2001.

———. "A Memorable Visit." International Association of R.S. Prussia Collectors, Inc. newsletter, Issue #64, 2004.

Chumley, Hayden C. Why R.S. Prussia? 1970.

Corban, Assid and Miriam. "Dating R.S.Poland — A New Perspective." International Association of R.S. Prussia Collectors, Inc. newsletter, Issue #47, 2000.

———. "The Origin of R.S. Poland Mark, Why Made in (German) Poland?" International Association of R.S. Prussia Collectors, Inc. newsletter, Issue #53, 2001.

———. "New Reinhold Bird Decoration Found In New Zealand." International Association of R.S. Prussia Collectors, Inc. newsletter, Issue #61, 2003.

———. " Solving the Mysteries of Prussian Marks." International Association of R.S. Prussia Collectors, Inc. newsletter, Issue #64, 2004.

Coy, Terry. "Juliette Recamier,1777 – 1849." International Association of R.S. Prussia Collectors, Inc. newsletter, Issue #58, 2002.

Encyclopedia Britannica (online). Various articles on artist, LeBrun, and other paintings.

Gaston, Mary Frank. "A Visit to Tillowitz, Poland. A Lot of Surprises." R.S. Prussia Club Newsletter, 1992.

———. The Collector's Encyclopedia of R.S. Prussia, Second Series. Collector Books, Paducah, Kentucky, 1986.

———. The Collector's Encyclopedia of R.S. Prussia, Third Series. Collector Books, Paducah, Kentucky, 1994.

———. The Collector's Encyclopedia of R.S. Prussia, Fourth Series. Collector Books, Paducah, Kentucky, 1995.

———. The Encyclopedia of R.S. Prussia. Collector Books, Paducah, Kentucky. 1982.

———. R.S. Prussia, Popular Lines. Collector Books, Paducah, Kentucky, 1999.

———. "R.S. Prussia." West Coast Peddler cover story, 1995.

———. "R.S. Prussia Club Restores Schlegelmilch Grave Site." Antiqueweek. Knightstown, Indiana, July 1992.

———. "R.S. Prussia Pilgrimage to Suhl, Germany. " Antiqueweek, Knightstown, Indiana, July 1992.

Grider, Rose. "Identification of Unmarked Pieces." Presentation at the International R.S. Prussia convention, 1991.

Hartwich, Bernd. Die Geschichte der Suhler Porzellanfabriken, 1861–1937. Fachschulabschlusearbeit (English translation: The History of the Suhl Porcelain Factories, 1861–1937) Herr Hartwich, a technical school student, wrote this for his final term paper. Transcribed by Ron Capers and prepared for the International R.S. Prussia Collectors Club and made available to its members.

Howard, David and Marlene. "Potocka." International Association of R.S. Prussia Collectors, Inc. newsletter, Issue #64, 2004.

———. "Collecting Children's Dishes." International Association of R.S. Prussia Collectors, Inc. newsletter, Issue #61, 2003.

Jim Wroda Auction Co. (Ohio)

Kempster, Jim. "R.S.P. Bargain Offerings." Butler Bros. Wholesale Catalogue. 1908.

Kindig, Ralph. "Rare Prussia Treasure Found in Virginia." Kerosene Lamp. Issue #45, 1999.

Krick, Wanda Faye. "Madame Vigee LeBrun and Child." International Association of R.S. Prussia Collectors, Inc. newsletter, Issue #55, 2002.

———. "An On-going Affair with the Melon Eaters." International Association of R.S. Prussia Collectors, Inc. newsletter, Issue #64, 2004.

Loomis, Donald. "E.S. Seasons?" International Association of R.S. Prussia Collectors, Inc. newsletter, Issue #62, 2003.

Marcus, Allen. "Many more afterwards... Mary Louise Elsabeth Vigee LeBrun."International Association of R.S. Prussia Collectors, Inc. newsletter, Issue #56, 2002.

———. "New Discovery of E.S. Related Marks Reported." International Association of R.S. Prussia Collectors, Inc. newsletter.

———. "Prussia Points." International Association of R.S. Prussia Collectors, Inc. newsletter, Issue #63, 2004.

Marple, Lee and Carol. "R.S.P. Box Lots." International Association of R.S. Prussia Collectors, Inc. newsletter, Issue #46, 1999.

———. "Another Visit with the Ding-a-Lings (Bells)." International Association of R.S. Prussia Collectors, Inc. newsletter, Issue #55, 2002.

———. "Reinhold's Picks (Toothpicks)." International Association of R.S. Prussia Collectors, Inc. newsletter, Issue #58, 2002.

———. "Strike Anywhere (Match holders)." International Association of R.S. Prussia Collectors, Inc. newsletter, Issue #64, 2004.

———. "War Breaks Out." International Association of R.S. Prussia Collectors, Inc. newsletter, Issue #54, 2001.

Matheson, Dorothy, and Oscar & Louise Freidrich. "There is Always Hope." International Association of R.S. Prussia Collectors, Inc. newsletter, Issue #44, 1999.

McCaslin, Bob. "Answers from the Past." International Association of R.S. Prussia Collectors, Inc., July 1992.

McCaslin, Bob and Mary. "Back to Suhl." International Association of R.S. Prussia Collectors, Inc. newsletter, Issue #16, 1992.

Schlegelmilch, Clifford J., and Oscar Schlegelmilch. R.S. Prussia Handbook of Erdmann and Reinhold Schlegelmilch. Prussia, Germany, 1970.

Sorenson, Don C. My Collection. R.S. Prussia, 1979.

Stuart, M.W. "The Wonderful Wearisome Mystery of R.S. Poland." International Association of R.S. Prussia Collectors, Inc. newsletter, Issue #47, 2000.

Terrell, George W. Collecting R.S. Prussia, 1980.

Tindell, Dianna. "Airbrush Applications in the Art of Restoration." International Association of R.S. Prussia Collectors, Inc. newsletter, Issue #50, 2000.

———. "Things to Consider When Cleaning a Collectible." International Association of R.S. Prussia Collectors, Inc. newsletter, Issue #49, 2002.

Van Patten, Joan. "Fake Prussia, Designed to Deceive." Presented at the 1988 International R.S. Prussia Convention.

Woody Auction Co. (Kansas)

Index
By series/theme

COLLECTOR BOOKS
informing today's collector

www.collectorbooks.com

For over two decades we have been keeping collectors informed on trends and values in all fields of antiques and collectibles.

DOLLS, FIGURES & TEDDY BEARS

6315	**American Character Dolls**, Izen	$24.95
6317	**Arranbee Dolls**, The Dolls that Sell on Sight, DeMillar/Brevik	$24.95
2079	**Barbie Doll** Fashion, Volume I, Eames	$24.95
4846	**Barbie Doll** Fashion, Volume II, Eames	$24.95
6546	Collector's Ency. of **Barbie Doll** Exclusives & More, 3rd Ed., Augustyniak	$29.95
6451	Collector's Encyclopedia of **Composition Dolls**, Volume II, Mertz	$29.95
6636	Collector's Encyclopedia of **Madame Alexander Dolls**, Crowsey	$24.95
5904	Collector's Guide to **Celebrity Dolls**, Spurgeon	$24.95
5599	Collector's Guide to **Dolls of the 1960s and 1970s**, Sabulis	$24.95
6030	Collector's Guide to **Horsman Dolls**, Jensen	$29.95
6455	**Doll Values**, Antique to Modern, 8th Edition, DeFeo/Stover	$14.95
5689	**Nippon Dolls** & Playthings, Van Patten/Lau	$29.95
6467	**Paper Dolls** of the 1960s, 1970s, and 1980s, Nichols	$24.95
5365	**Peanuts Collectibles**, Podley/Bang	$24.95
6336	Official **Precious Moments** Collector's Guide to Company **Dolls**, Bomm	$19.95
6026	**Small Dolls of the 40s & 50s**, Stover	$29.95
5253	Story of **Barbie**, 2nd Ed., Westenhouser	$24.95
5277	**Talking Toys** of the 20th Century, Lewis	$15.95
2084	**Teddy Bears, Annalee's & Steiff** Animals, 3rd Series, Mandel	$19.95
4880	World of **Raggedy Ann** Collectibles, Avery	$24.95

TOYS & MARBLES

2333	Antique & Collectible **Marbles**, 3rd Edition, Grist	$9.95
6649	Big Book of **Toy Airplanes**, Miller	$24.95
5150	**Cartoon Toys & Collectibles**, Longest	$19.95
6471	Collector's Guide to **Tootsietoys**, 3rd Edition, Richter	$24.95
6633	**Hot Wheels**, The Ultimate Redline Guide, 2nd Ed., Clark/Wicker	$29.95
6466	**Matchbox Toys**, 1947 to 2003, 4th Edition, Johnson	$24.95
5830	**McDonald's** Collectibles, 2nd Edition, Henriques/DuVall	$24.95
6840	**Schroeder's Collectible Toys**, Antique to Modern Price Guide, 10th Ed.	$17.95
6638	The Other **Matchbox Toys**, 1947 to 2004, Johnson	$19.95
6650	**Toy Car** Collector's Guide, 2nd Edition, Johnson	$24.95
6642	20th Century **Paper Dolls**, Young	$19.95

FURNITURE

3716	American **Oak** Furniture, Book II, McNerney	$12.95
1118	Antique **Oak** Furniture, Hill	$7.95
6474	Collector's Guide to **Wallace Nutting** Furniture, Ivankovich	$19.95
3906	**Heywood-Wakefield** Modern Furniture, Rouland	$18.95
6338	**Roycroft** Furniture & Collectibles, Koon	$24.95
6343	**Stickley Brothers** Furniture, Koon	$24.95
1885	**Victorian** Furniture, Our American Heritage, McNerney	$9.95

JEWELRY, HATPINS, WATCHES & PURSES

4704	Antique & Collectible **Buttons**, Wisniewski	$19.95
6323	**Christmas Pins**, Past & Present, 2nd Edition, Gallina	$19.95
4850	Collectible **Costume Jewelry**, Simonds	$24.95
5675	Collectible **Silver Jewelry**, Rezazadeh	$24.95
6468	Collector's Ency. of Pocket & Pendant **Watches**, 1500 – 1950, Bell	$24.95
6554	**Coro Jewelry**, Brown	$29.95
6453	**Costume Jewelry 101**, Carroll	$24.95
4940	**Costume Jewelry**, A Practical Handbook & Value Guide, Rezazadeh	$24.95
5812	Fifty Years of Collectible **Fashion Jewelry**, 1925 – 1975, Baker	$24.95

6330	**Handkerchiefs**: A Collector's Guide, Guarnaccia/Guggenheim	$24.95
6464	Inside the **Jewelry Box**, Pitman	$24.95
5695	**Ladies' Vintage Accessories**, Johnson	$24.95
1181	100 Years of Collectible **Jewelry**, 1850 – 1950, Baker	$9.95
6645	100 Years of **Purses**, 1880s to 1980s, Aikins	$24.95
6337	**Purse Masterpieces**, Schwartz	$29.95
4729	**Sewing Tools** & Trinkets, Thompson	$24.95
6038	**Sewing Tools** & Trinkets, Volume 2, Thompson	$24.95
6039	Signed Beauties of **Costume Jewelry**, Brown	$24.95
6341	Signed Beauties of **Costume Jewelry**, Volume II, Brown	$24.95
6555	20th Century **Costume Jewelry**, Aikins	$24.95
5620	Unsigned Beauties of **Costume Jewelry**, Brown	$24.95
4878	Vintage & Contemporary **Purse Accessories**, Gerson	$24.95
5923	**Vintage Jewelry** for Investment & Casual Wear, Edeen	$24.95

ARTIFACTS, GUNS, KNIVES, TOOLS, PRIMITIVES

6021	**Arrowheads** of the Central Great Plains, Fox	$19.95
1868	Antique **Tools**, Our American Heritage, McNerney	$9.95
6469	Big Book of **Pocket Knives**, 2nd Edition, Stewart/Ritchie	$19.95
4943	Field Gde. to Flint **Arrowheads & Knives** of the N. American Indian, Tully	$9.95
3885	**Indian Artifacts** of the Midwest, Book II, Hothem	$16.95
4870	**Indian Artifacts** of the Midwest, Book III, Hothem	$18.95
5685	**Indian Artifacts** of the Midwest, Book IV, Hothem	$19.95
6565	**Modern Guns**, Identification & Values, 15th Ed., Quertermous	$16.95
2164	**Primitives**, Our American Heritage, McNerney	$9.95
6031	Standard **Knife** Collector's Guide, 4th Ed., Ritchie & Stewart	$14.95

PAPER COLLECTIBLES & BOOKS

5902	**Boys' & Girls' Book** Series, Jones	$19.95
6623	Collecting **American Paintings**, James	$29.95
5153	Collector's Guide to **Children's Books**, 1850 to 1950, Volume II, Jones	$19.95
6553	Collector's Guide to **Cookbooks**, Daniels	$24.95
1441	Collector's Guide to **Post Cards**, Wood	$9.95
6627	Early 20th Century **Hand-Painted Photography**, Ivankovich	$24.95
3973	**Sheet Music** Reference & Price Guide, 2nd Ed., Pafik/Guiheen	$19.95

GLASSWARE

5602	Anchor Hocking's **Fire-King** & More, 2nd Ed., Florence	$24.95
6321	**Carnival Glass**, The Best of the Best, Edwards/Carwile	$29.95
5823	Collectible **Glass Shoes**, 2nd Edition, Wheatley	$24.95
6821	Coll. **Glassware** from the 40s, 50s & 60s, 8th Edition, Florence	$19.95
6626	Collector's Companion to **Carnival Glass**, 2nd Ed., Edwards/Carwile	$14.95
1810	Collector's Encyclopedia of **American Art Glass**, Shuman	$29.95
6830	Collector's Encyclopedia of **Depression Glass**, 17th Ed., Florence	$19.95
1664	Collector's Encyclopedia of **Heisey Glass**, 1925 – 1938, Bredehoft	$24.95
3905	Collector's Encyclopedia of **Milk Glass**, Newbound	$24.95
5820	Collector's Guide to **Glass Banks**, Reynolds	$24.95
6454	**Crackle Glass** From Around the World, Weitman	$24.95
6559	**Elegant Glassware** of the Depression Era, 11th Edition, Florence	$24.95
6334	Encyclopedia of **Paden City Glass**, Domitz	$24.95
3981	Evers' Standard **Cut Glass** Value Guide	$12.95
6126	**Fenton Art Glass**, 1907 – 1939, 2nd Ed., Whitmyer	$29.95
6628	**Fenton Glass** Made for Other Companies, Domitz	$29.95
6462	Florences' **Glass Kitchen Shakers**, 1930 – 1950s	$19.95

5042	Florences' **Glassware Pattern Identification** Guide, Vol. I	$18.95
5615	Florences' **Glassware Pattern Identification** Guide, Vol. II	$19.95
6142	Florences' **Glassware Pattern Identification** Guide, Vol. III	$19.95
6643	Florences' **Glassware Pattern Identification** Guide, Vol. IV	$19.95
6641	Florences' **Ovenware** from the 1920s to the Present	$24.95
6226	**Fostoria** Value Guide, Long/Seate	$19.95
5899	**Glass & Ceramic Baskets**, White	$19.95
6460	**Glass Animals**, 2nd Edition, Spencer	$24.95
6127	The **Glass Candlestick** Book, Volume 1, Akro Agate to Fenton, Felt/Stoer	$24.95
6228	The **Glass Candlestick** Book, Volume 2, Fostoria to Jefferson, Felt/Stoer	$24.95
6461	The **Glass Candlestick** Book, Volume 3, Kanawha to Wright, Felt/Stoer	$29.95
6648	Glass **Toothpick Holders**, 2nd Edition, Bredehoft/Sanford	$29.95
6329	**Glass Tumblers**, 1860s to 1920s, Bredehoft	$29.95
5827	**Kitchen Glassware** of the Depression Years, 6th Edition, Florence	$24.95
6133	**Mt. Washington Art Glass**, Sisk	$49.95
6556	Pocket Guide to **Depression Glass** & More, 14th Edition, Florence	$12.95
6925	Standard Encyclopedia of **Carnival Glass**, 10th Ed., Edwards/Carwile	$29.95
6926	Standard **Carnival Glass** Price Guide, 15th Ed., Edwards/Carwile	$9.95
6566	Standard Encyclopedia of **Opalescent Glass**, 5th Ed., Edwards/Carwile	$24.95
6644	Standard Encyclopedia of **Pressed Glass**, 4th Ed., Edwards/Carwile	$29.95
6241	Treasures of **Very Rare Depression Glass**, Florence	$39.95
6476	**Westmoreland Glass**, The Popular Years, 1940 – 1985, Kovar	$29.95

POTTERY

6922	**American Art Pottery**, 2nd Edition, Sigafoose	$24.95
4851	Collectible **Cups & Saucers**, Harran	$18.95
6326	Collectible **Cups & Saucers**, Book III, Harran	$24.95
6344	Collectible **Vernon Kilns**, 2nd Edition, Nelson	$29.95
6331	Collecting **Head Vases**, Barron	$24.95
6621	Collector's Encyclopedia of **American Dinnerware**, 2nd Ed., Cunningham	$29.95
5034	Collector's Encyclopedia of **California Pottery**, 2nd Ed., Chipman	$24.95
6629	Collector's Encyclopedia of **Fiesta**, 10th Ed., Huxford	$24.95
3431	Collector's Encyclopedia of **Homer Laughlin China**, Jasper	$24.95
1276	Collector's Encyclopedia of **Hull Pottery**, Roberts	$19.95
5609	Collector's Encyclopedia of **Limoges Porcelain**, 3rd Ed., Gaston	$29.95
6637	Collector's Encyclopedia of **Made in Japan Ceramics**, First Ed., White	$24.95
2334	Collector's Encyclopedia of **Majolica Pottery**, Katz-Marks	$19.95
5677	Collector's Encyclopedia of **Niloak**, 2nd Edition, Gifford	$29.95
5679	Collector's Encyclopedia of **Red Wing Art Pottery**, Dollen	$24.95
5841	Collector's Encyclopedia of **Roseville Pottery**, Vol. 1, Huxford/Nickel	$24.95
5842	Collector's Encyclopedia of **Roseville Pottery**, Vol. 2, Huxford/Nickel	$24.95
5917	Collector's Encyclopedia of **Russel Wright**, 3rd Edition, Kerr	$29.95
6646	Collector's Ency. of **Stangl Artware, Lamps, and Birds**, 2nd Ed., Runge	$29.95
3314	Collector's Encyclopedia of **Van Briggle Art Pottery**, Sasicki	$24.95
5680	Collector's Guide to **Feather Edge Ware**, McAllister	$19.95
6124	Collector's Guide to **Made in Japan Ceramics**, Book IV, White	$24.95
6634	Collector's Ultimate Ency. of **Hull Pottery**, Volume 1, Roberts	$29.95
6829	The Complete Guide to **Corning Ware & Visions Cookware**, Coroneos	$19.95
1425	**Cookie Jars**, Westfall	$9.95
6316	Decorative **American Pottery & Whiteware**, Wilby	$29.95
5909	**Dresden Porcelain** Studios, Harran	$29.95
5918	Florences' Big Book of **Salt & Pepper Shakers**	$24.95
6320	Gaston's **Blue Willow**, 3rd Edition	$19.95
6630	Gaston's **Flow Blue China**, The Comprehensive Guide	$29.95

2379	**Lehner's Ency. of U.S. Marks** on Pottery, Porcelain & China	$24.95
4722	**McCoy Pottery**, Collector's Reference & Value Guide, Hanson/Nissen	$19.95
5913	**McCoy Pottery**, Volume III, Hanson & Nissen	$24.95
6333	**McCoy Pottery Wall Pockets** & Decorations, Nissen	$24.95
6135	**North Carolina Art Pottery**, 1900 – 1960, James/Leftwich	$24.95
5834	**Occupied Japan Collectibles**, Florence	$24.95
6335	Pictorial Guide to **Pottery & Porcelain Marks**, Lage	$29.95
5691	**Post86 Fiesta**, Identification & Value Guide, Racheter	$19.95
1440	**Red Wing Stoneware**, DePasquale/Peck/Peterson	$9.95
6037	**Rookwood Pottery**, Nicholson/Thomas	$24.95
6838	**R.S. Prussia** & More, McCaslin	$29.95
3443	**Salt & Pepper Shakers** IV, Guarnaccia	$18.95
3738	**Shawnee Pottery**, Mangus	$24.95
6828	The Ultimate Collector's Encyclopedia of **Cookie Jars**, Roerig	$29.95
6640	Van Patten's ABC's of Collecting **Nippon Porcelain**	$29.95
5924	**Zanesville Stoneware** Company, Rans/Ralston/Russell	$24.95

OTHER COLLECTIBLES

5838	Advertising **Thermometers**, Merritt	$16.95
5898	Antique & Contemporary **Advertising Memorabilia**, Summers	$24.95
5814	Antique **Brass & Copper**, Gaston	$24.95
1880	Antique **Iron**, McNerney	$9.95
6622	The Art of American **Game Calls**, Lewis	$24.95
6472	The A-Z Guide to Collecting **Trivets**, Rosack	$24.95
1128	**Bottle** Pricing Guide, 3rd Ed., Cleveland	$7.95
6345	**Business & Tax Guide** for Antiques & Collectibles, Kelly	$14.95
3718	Collectible **Aluminum**, Grist	$16.95
6342	Collectible **Soda Pop** Memorabilia, Summers	$24.95
5060	Collectible **Souvenir Spoons**, Bednersh	$19.95
5676	Collectible **Souvenir Spoons**, Book II, Bednersh	$29.95
5666	Collector's Encyclopedia of **Granite Ware**, Book 2, Greguire	$29.95
5836	Collector's Guide to **Antique Radios**, 5th Edition, Bunis	$19.95
6558	The Encyclopedia of Early American **Sewing Machines**, 2nd Ed., Bays	$29.95
6561	Field Guide to **Fishing Lures**, Lewis	$16.95
5683	**Fishing Lure** Collectibles, Volume 1, Murphy/Edmisten	$29.95
6328	**Flea Market Trader**, 14th Edition, Huxford	$12.95
6458	**Fountain Pens**, Past & Present, 2nd Edition, Erano	$24.95
6631	**Garage Sale** & Flea Market Annual, 13th Edition, Huxford	$19.95
4945	**G-Men and FBI Toys** and Collectibles, Whitworth	$18.95
2216	**Kitchen Antiques**, 1790–1940, McNerney	$14.95
6639	**McDonald's Drinkware**, Kelly	$24.95
6028	Modern **Fishing Lure** Collectibles, Volume 1, Lewis	$24.95
6131	Modern **Fishing Lure** Collectibles, Volume 2, Lewis	$24.95
6322	Pictorial Guide to **Christmas Ornaments** & Collectibles, Johnson	$29.95
6839	**Schroeder's Antiques** Price Guide, 24th Edition	$14.95
5007	**Silverplated Flatware**, Revised 4th Edition, Hagan	$18.95
6647	**Star Wars** Super Collector's Wish Book, 3rd Edition, Carlton	$29.95
6552	Summers' Guide to **Coca-Cola**, 5th Edition	$24.95
6827	Summers' Pocket Guide to **Coca-Cola**, 5th Edition	$12.95
4935	The W.F. Cody **Buffalo Bill** Collector's Guide, Wojtowicz	$24.95
6632	Value Guide to **Gas Station Memorabilia**, 2nd Ed., Summers & Priddy	$29.95
6841	Vintage **Fabrics**, Gridley/Kiplinger/McClure	$19.95
6036	Vintage **Quilts**, Aug/Newman/Roy	$24.95

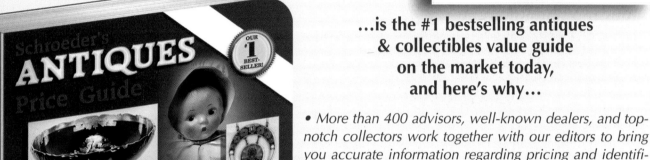